modern constructive bidding

marshall miles

master point press - toronto, canada

Master Point Press
331 Douglas Ave.
Toronto, Ontario, Canada
M5M 1H2
(416) 781-0351
Website: http://www.masterpointpress.com
Email: info@masterpointpress.com

Library and Archives Canada Cataloguing in Publication

Miles, Marshall, 1926-
      Modern constructive bidding / by Marshall Miles.

ISBN 1-894154-99-1

      1. Contract bridge--Bidding. I. Title.

GV1282.4.M546 2005   795.41'52   C2005-902499-2

Editor	Ray Lee
Cover and interior design	Olena S. Sullivan/New Mediatrix
Interior format	Luise Lee
Copy editing	Suzanne Hocking

Printed in Canada by Webcom Ltd.

1 2 3 4 5 6 7   09 08 07 06 05

table of contents

modern

constructive

bidding

introduction

Constructive, uncontested auctions, on the rare occasions in the modern bridge world that your opponents allow you the luxury, are the cornerstone of your bidding system. You and your partner want to bid accurately, giving yourselves the maximum chance of making a good decision as to the final contract. This is harder than it sounds, but what it comes down to is this: the secret of accurate bidding is always to bid all hands of a certain type in the same way.

Some bidding sequences will have specific meanings like, 'My high cards are concentrated in two suits with very little in the others,' or 'I have (or do not have) a singleton in the unbid suit,' or, 'I have exceptionally good trump support, but not much else.' Such bids are usually made when you know that partner will be the declarer and your hand will be exposed. Occasionally this will help an opponent on opening lead; more frequently it will help partner choose the best contract. When you don't have a hand justifying a special message, or when your previous bids have fully described your hand, there should be certain bids that say, in effect, 'I have nothing more to say. I am only bidding because you forced me to, perhaps because you have something more to say.'

Consistency of style is also critical. Each member of a regular partnership should know what the other is likely to do in various situations. Then it is possible to draw inferences, not only from what partner does, but also from what he doesn't do. If someone asked you what your regular partner would do with a certain hand, could you answer with confidence, or does his bidding vary with his mood?

Of course, I realize that most bridge players have several partners. If you play with only one person, you can discuss and agree upon the meanings of many sequences, but it is difficult to persuade several partners to play exactly the same conventions and treatments. Nevertheless, I think you should have agreements with all of your partners on such basic issues as whether to play 'Fast Arrival' or 'Picture Bidding.'

In this book I'm going to discuss some of the auctions in which serious partners ought to have agreements and frequently don't. I'm also going to suggest a number of modern expert treatments and conventions that I think are useful in addressing certain problem areas in constructive bidding. Let me start by posing a series of 'skill-testing questions' to see just how good your current agreements are.

In the sequence

Opener	Responder
1♠	2♣
2♠	4♠

is 4♠ a signoff, or does it show where your values are?

How do you play this auction:

Opener	Responder
1♣	1♡
2NT	4♡

How does it differ from

Opener	Responder
1♣	1♡
2NT	3♡

Is a two-over-one response by a non-passed hand unconditionally forcing to game in your methods? If not, what are the exceptions? Does a two-over-one response by a passed hand guarantee a rebid?

When you have the equivalent of an opening bid and a fit opposite partner's opening bid, you will not let the bidding die short of game. Most of the time it doesn't matter how you get to game, but occasionally it does. It is a nice bonus when you get a good result merely because you have a convention or treatment that routinely permits you to bid a slam that other players miss — or to stop at a safe level on a badly breaking hand. This is where you need some understandings about suit quality as well as high-card strength for your two-over-one auctions. Suppose partner opens the bidding with one of a major and you have 13 to 15 points. Do you usually make a two-over-one response just to let him know about your strength? If partner opens with 1♠, do either of these hands qualify for a 2♣ response in your methods:

♠ A J x ♡ K J x x ◇ K J x ♣ J x x

♠ A J ♡ K x x x ◇ A Q x ♣ 10 x x x

At the other end of the scale, would you and your regular partner get to an excellent slam on these cards:

♠ A Q 10 x x x	♠ K x x
♡ x	♡ J x
◇ A x x	◇ J x
♣ Q x x	♣ A K 10 9 x x

You should (at least, when the hand with a six-card spade suit is the opener)!

Can you quickly diagnose a potentially fatal weakness and get out while it is still safe? For example, would you get higher than 4♡ with these hands:

♠ A K J x x	♠ Q
♡ K x x	♡ A J 10 x x x
◇ J x	◇ A K Q x
♣ Q x x	♣ x x

You won't if you follow my suggestions!

Even simple Stayman auctions contain undiscussed minefields. What do the following sequences mean to you?

Opener	Responder
1NT	2♣
2♡	4◇

Opener	Responder
1NT	2♣
2♡	3♠

The earlier the partners discover their approximate combined strength, the easier it is to bid accurately. If they know they are in the possible slam zone, they will try to describe their hands in detail to show whether they have extra values and, if so, where they are located. If slam is unlikely, they will look for the safest game (at IMPs) or the best-scoring game (at match-points) while trying to provide no more information to the opponents than necessary. If the strength is almost evenly divided, there are two concerns — find the best contract and make it difficult for the opponents to find theirs. When it is obvious that the opponents have the balance of power, the question is whether it is better to keep quiet, so as not to risk a large penalty or help declarer when he plays the hand, or to try, at some risk, to interfere with the opponents' bidding.

In any system, notrump openings have a fairly narrow range of high card points, and responder can often tell immediately who can make what. Similarly, in strong club systems, like Precision, when opener starts with one of a suit other than clubs, showing roughly 11 to 15 points, his partner again knows approximately how high the partnership should be. If the opening bid was a major suit, showing five or more, and responder has adequate support and enough strength to bid game, but not enough for a slam, he can jump immediately to game in the major. This bid provides no information to the opponents except that responder is willing to play that contract. The opponents don't know whether his bid was a preempt or whether he expects his partner to make it. If the latter, they don't know whether his bidding was based on high card strength or distribution. That makes the opponents' decision whether or not to compete very difficult.

However, after a 'standard' opening suit bid, which may show almost any distribution and roughly 10 to 21 points, it is usually impossible to tell immediately which side the hand belongs to. Consequently, it is dangerous for responder to overbid, unless he is making an unambiguous preempt, for fear that opener, with a strong hand, will drive to a losing slam. You don't have that particular concern when playing Precision.

As an aside, suppose you are playing Precision and partner opens 1 ♡. Next hand passes and you hold

♠ x x   ♡ K 10 x x x   ◇ J x x x   ♣ x x

What do you think of your prospects? My estimate is that partner can take eight tricks in hearts, and the opponents can take ten or eleven tricks in spades. What can you do about it? (See Chapter 5 for my answer.)

While it usually takes a little longer for Standard bidders to discover their combined strength, they do have ways to limit their hands. I recommend an expanded use of a forcing notrump response to one of a major, both as a means for responder to limit his hand and as a way to give a more precise meaning to two-over-one responses. No more two-over-one responses with 'suits' like ♣10xxx or ♣Jxx, just to show game-forcing values. (See Chapter 2 for this discussion.)

Do you ever play step responses to show how much you like your hand? If so, when? Do you always look for an eight-card major fit when it is possible that you might have one? Unless you have played bridge for a long time with the right people, you may not be familiar with some of the conventions and treatments mentioned in Chapter 4.

When your agreed suit is a minor, do you have a way to ask for aces or keycards other than using 4NT? What is your priority in cuebidding: First-round controls up the line? First- or second-round controls up the line? Length first? What do you bid when you have two crucial controls but only room to show one of them without forcing the bidding to slam? I am pretty sure that you will find new ideas to consider in Chapter 6.

Playing so-called Standard bidding means different things to different people. I am going to suggest solutions to all of the problems I have just raised. Probably 75% of these answers are 'standard' in that they are accepted by a majority of top players, and most of my non-standard recommendations are identified as such: feel free to adopt them if they appeal to you and ignore them if they don't. Many of these ideas were suggested by others and adopted by me because I thought they were both logical and useful; some of them are my own ideas. However, frequently when I came up with a great new way to handle a problem, I later discovered that someone else had thought of it many years ago.

Finally, a word about my style of writing: I don't see any point in being wishy-washy. If I believe something, I say what I believe, without qualifications.

But when I say you *should* make a certain bid, it doesn't mean that no good player could possibly disagree (take a look at the Bidding Panel in any bridge magazine — experts frequently disagree!). However, I never tell you that you should bid a certain way just because I say so; I always give my reasons. You may not be convinced, because you may think the advantages I mention are illusory or are outweighed by other factors. But even if you disagree with me, you should find it useful to consider the pros and cons so that you can either develop your own treatment or continue to play the way you have been playing with even greater confidence.

CHAPTER 1

Opening the bidding

WHAT CONSTITUTES AN OPENING BID?

What do you need for an opening bid? The current vogue is to open all 12-point hands, but my tendency is *not* to open balanced 12-point hands unless they include some favorable feature. This could be good spot cards, or having the points mostly concentrated in aces and kings. I also like having 4432 distribution including four spades and a four-card minor: there can't be a serious rebid problem when, over partner's one of a suit response, you can rebid 1♠. With 5332 distribution, 12 points are usually enough unless the five-card suit is very weak or you have queens and jacks unsupported by higher honors.

Most people would open a 5431 12-count automatically, but it should not be so automatic in my view. Not everyone would agree, but I think it is a mistake to open the bidding with

♠ K   ♡ A J 8 x x   ◇ J x x x   ♣ K x x

Your suit is weak, and you have to count both the singleton king and the unsupported ◇J, both of which are of very dubious value, to get your 12 points. In a recent bidding panel, four out of five experts favored a pass with this hand. However, AKxxx of a suit with a side ace is a clear-cut opening bid: this is because your points are concentrated in your long suit. Something like Axxxx with an ace-king on the side is not quite as good. You probably need a suit like A109xx to go with your ace-king to justify opening with 5332 distribution, although with 5431 distribution I can't imagine passing with three quick tricks (referred to as honor tricks in the old days).

Whenever you have a close decision, you should tend to open when your long suit is a major and pass if it is a minor. You can even open with as few as 11 points and 5422 distribution if the five-card suit is a major *and* the honors are in the long suits. So you should pass with

♠ Q x   ♡ K x x x x   ◇ J x   ♣ A J x x

but should open the bidding with

♠ x x   ♡ K Q 9 8 x   ◇ x x   ♣ A Q 10 x

Don't get hung up on counting points, though: even 9 points may be enough with long suits and at least two quick tricks:

a) ♠ A J x x x x x ♡ x x ◇ x ♣ A x x
b) ♠ A x x x x x ♡ K Q x x x ◇ x ♣ x
c) ♠ x x ♡ x x x ◇ A K Q x x x x ♣ x

Both hands (a) and (b) qualify as 1♠ openers for me. If you hold the same high cards as in hand (b), but five spades and six hearts, it is better to pass originally and plan to come in with a Michaels Cuebid (or use Unusual 2NT if the opponents bid both minors). The hand is not strong enough to reverse, and if you open 1♡ you may never be able to show your spades at a reasonable level.

Hand (c) may make 3NT opposite as little as two aces, and one way to handle it is to open 3NT to show a solid (you hope) seven- or eight-card minor and no side ace or king. But if you are not playing Gambling 3NT (probably because you are playing Namyats and need 3NT to show a minor-suit preempt at the four-level), the best way to describe it is to open 1◇ and rebid a minimum number of diamonds at each opportunity until (you hope) partner bids notrump. (Opening three of a minor should deny a solid suit.)

While these are my recommendations, you will probably continue to open the hands you have been opening in the past, and who can say that you are wrong? Here, as ever, experts disagree. The Granovetters prefer stronger 'Roth-Stone'-type opening bids. Marty Bergen advocates opening at least one point lighter than I do on balanced hands, and he likes opening 1♡ on

♠ J x x ♡ K Q 10 x x x ◇ K x x x ♣ —

(9 points without two quick tricks). Meckstroth and Rodwell, hereafter referred to as Meckwell, open almost all 11-point hands and sometimes balanced 10-counts (although they do play a strong club system). What's right depends upon your bidding style (on later rounds) and what your partner has been led to expect.

It is possible to take this kind of aggressive bidding to extremes, as in the system California expert Tom Wood has developed, called Blue Jay. Playing Blue Jay, an opening one-bid in a major has a range of 8 to 21 points with at least a five-card suit, and the forcing club and 1NT bids start at 10 points. The responses and rebids are designed primarily to show distribution, and only secondarily to discover the combined strength of the hands. Wood's theory is that if the opponents can set you several tricks at a low level after you have found an eight- or nine-card fit, they could probably do just as well or better in a contract of their own. Over a 1♣ opening, which can be made on as few as 10 points, responder responds in the suit below his four-card suit, no matter how weak his hand is. With a minimum club bid and four of responder's suit, opener jumps to the two-level:

Opener	Responder
1♣	1◇[1]
2♡	

1. Showing hearts

— an auction where the hands could be 10 points opposite zero! With a good hand and four or more hearts opener rebids only one heart, which allows more room for each partner to describe his hand.

The downside, of course, is that no matter what you do, when you have such extremely wide ranges for your bids you lose accuracy in your constructive bidding. On the other hand, it is very hard to compete against such wide-range bids, and the opponents may let you bid unopposed to the two-level and play there, down one or two tricks undoubled, when they are cold for a vulnerable game. I won't try to explain the system in detail, but the success of systems like this one and the bidding style used by Bergen and Meckwell makes me wonder whether old-time, accurate constructive bidding is really the best way to go. But that is the way I still (attempt to) play and it is what I describe in this book.

SELECTING THE SUIT

Now we turn from the strength of the opening hand to the issue of selecting the actual opening bid. First let's dispose of notrump openings: everyone opens 1NT when the hand is within the agreed range and completely balanced. Whether you should open 1NT with five-card majors, weak doubletons (especially with 5422 distribution) or singleton kings are issues that will be discussed in the chapter on notrump bidding.

A long-time subject of debate amongst Standard bidders has been whether to open 1♣ or 1♠ with a 5-5 hand in the black suits. Most modern experts open 1♠ except with weak spades or very strong hands. The reason for choosing spades with most hands is that you may not be able to bid clubs then spades and then spades again without getting too high, and if you can't anticipate making three bids, it is more important to show your five-card major. If you do open 1♣ and fail to bid spades twice, partner will assume that you have only a four-card spade suit. However, with a hand as good as

$$♠ A Q 10 9 x \quad ♡ A x \quad ◇ x \quad ♣ A K J x x$$

it is better to open 1♣ since someone (perhaps even an opponent) is more likely to keep the bidding open than if you had opened 1♠. Not only could you miss a game by being passed out in 1♠ when partner holds

$$♠ x \quad ♡ K x x x x \quad ◇ x x x \quad ♣ Q x x x$$

but if partner has a little more and responds 1NT (which he will most of the time), you will have a hard time convincing him that your clubs are this good without going past 3NT. Opening 1♣ and jumping to 2♠ over a response of 1◊ or 1♡, followed by bidding 3♠ on the next round, shows your key features: at least five good clubs, at least five good spades, and a very strong hand. You should also open 1♣ with

$$♠ J x x x x ~~ ♡ A x ~~ ◊ x ~~ ♣ A K x x x$$

planning to rebid 1♠ just as though you had a four-card spade suit, since with such a weak suit it is unlikely that you belong in 4♠ opposite three-card support. Strengthen your hand to

$$♠ A 10 x x x ~~ ♡ A x ~~ ◊ x ~~ ♣ A K x x x$$

and I think it is best to open 1♣, hoping to bid and rebid spades — without a jump shift, since both your spade suit and your hand are too weak. With

$$♠ A K J x x ~~ ♡ x x ~~ ◊ x ~~ ♣ A K J x x$$

I would also open 1♣, and rebid 1♠, gambling on not being passed out there, but if partner then rebid his suit or bid 1NT, I would bid 3♠ since I can hardly expect partner to keep bidding without a lot of encouragement when he holds two black queens and little else.

With 6-5 distribution, you have similar factors to consider. Suppose you hold

$$♠ — ~~ ♡ A Q 10 x x ~~ ◊ x x ~~ ♣ A J 10 9 x x$$

Your suits are good, and you have a lot of playing strength. It is definitely right to open 1♣ and hope to bid and rebid hearts later. Change your hand to

$$♠ — ~~ ♡ A Q J x x ~~ ◊ x x ~~ ♣ K x x x x x$$

and you can no longer count on bidding three times, especially in competition. So my recommendation is to open 1♡: if you can't show everything, it is more important to show a good five-card major than to show a weak six-card minor. Change the jack of hearts to a low heart, and it is better to pass and show a two-suiter later via a cuebid or Unusual Notrump.

Another suit selection issue arises on hands with both minors and 4432 distribution: some players always bid clubs, others always bid diamonds. Unless the strength is very concentrated, as here:

$$♠ x x ~~ ♡ x x x ~~ ◊ A K x x ~~ ♣ A Q J x$$

you don't usually plan to bid both suits, but if you are planning to bid both suits you should, of course, open 1◊. Opening 1◊ also prepares you for competition. If you open 1♣ with

♠ J x ♡ J x x ◇ K J x x ♣ A Q J x

you will have a distasteful choice of rebids after a 1♠ or 2♠ overcall and a negative double by partner. With stoppers in both majors

♠ Q x x ♡ K x ◇ K x x x ♣ A J 10 x

where you plan to rebid 1NT over either major, I think you should open your better minor for at least two reasons: (a) if the opponents play the hand, you want partner to lead your better suit and (b) if partner has a close decision later in the hand, like whether to bid or try for slam, he will assume your high cards are more likely to be in the suit you bid than in an unbid suit. Some people are slavish about which minor they open holding both, and will even open four small rather than AKJx, but I have never discovered why. A few players like a 1◇ bid to guarantee four (or more), so they will open 1♣ with

♠ A Q x x ♡ Q x x x ◇ A Q x ♣ x x

I prefer to have a club bid guarantee at least three, so I would open 1◇. However, I still expect partner to play me for four or more diamonds — even though I may not have four diamonds when I hold both majors, as here.

REBID PROBLEMS

Now let's talk about a common rebid situation. If you open the bidding and partner bids a suit at the one-level, are you willing to rebid notrump with a singleton in his suit? Here's a typical example:

♠ x ♡ A Q x ◇ Q 10 x x ♣ A x x x x

You	Partner
1♣	1♠
?	

At this point you have two choices. Rebidding 2♣ is undesirable since that should imply a six-card suit instead of a weak five-card suit; that leaves rebidding 1NT as your better option. Alternatively you can open these hands 1◇ in the first place, and then rebid 2♣, something Eric Kokish strongly advocates. I favor the 1♣ followed by 1NT route. Opening 1◇ with four diamonds and five clubs may be your best choice when the diamonds are good and the hand does not fit into your 1NT or 2NT rebid ranges, but there is always the danger of playing in the wrong minor suit when responder has equal length in both minors. In fact, if he holds

♠ A J x x x   ♡ J x x   ◇ Q x   ♣ J x x

then after

You	Partner
1◇	1♠
2♣	

he should take a false preference to 2◇ to give you another chance to bid in case you have a good hand. This would not work out well if you had to pass with four diamonds, five clubs and a minimum hand. When rebidding one notrump with a singleton in partner's suit does not distort your message of overall strength, it seems to me like the least of evils.

It's different if one of your suits is a major. Although my agreement with partner is that we play five-card majors, I occasionally open 1♡ (admittedly with mixed results!) when holding something like

♠ A x x   ♡ A K J 9   ◇ J x x x x   ♣ x

since I hate to miss a 4-4 major fit when I hold an unbalanced hand. Should I open 1◇ and pass partner's 1NT response? I'd rather open 1♡ and rebid 2◇ if I have to. Of course I hope that it won't be necessary — that the opponents will play the hand and partner will get off to a heart lead, or that partner will raise hearts or even bid 1♠, which I will gladly raise to 2♠. If it goes

Me	Partner
1♡	1NT
2◇	2♡

the opponents may reopen the bidding. Otherwise I'll get good practice in playing 4-2 trump fits.

With 1-4-4-4 distribution, when the hearts are fairly weak and the minors are strong many players think you should open 1◇ and rebid 2♣ over a spade response. This sequence makes it very doubtful that you will discover a 4-4 heart fit. One reason is that partner will think it unlikely that you have four hearts after you have bid both minors (which normally shows at least nine minor-suit cards). Another reason is that a 2♡ rebid by him would be artificial and forcing at least one round (perhaps even to game depending upon your agreements) so partner could not afford to bid it with

♠ Q J x x   ♡ K 10 x x   ◇ x x   ♣ J x

He will probably pass or bid 2◇, getting you to a 4-2 trump fit in either case, while if you had rebid 1NT, he could have bid 2♡, non-forcing and non-invitational.

Similarly, if you had

♠ x   ♡ A Q x   ◇ K 10 x   ♣ A K J x x x

you could (and, in my opinion, should) open 1♣ and rebid 2NT over partner's 1♠ response. Rebidding 3♣ implies that you do not have stoppers in both unbid suits. You surely cannot expect partner to bid 3NT over 3♣ with

♠ A J x x   ♡ x x x   ◇ x x x   ♣ Q x x

Over your 2NT rebid partner can rebid spades if he has six of them, but if you rebid 3NT he should usually pass. Partner shouldn't jump to 4♠ on a weak six-card suit over 2NT just to say he doesn't like his hand! (I'll have much more to say later about Fast Arrival.)

Incidentally, most of the world disagrees with me about bidding 2NT with a singleton in partner's suit. The alternative is to rebid 3NT when you expect to win most of your tricks with a long suit. I prefer the 2NT bid (saving 3NT to show a solid suit) since it allows you to stop in a partscore when the long suit is not solid and when partner has a very weak response, perhaps with a singleton or void in your long suit. Also, it is hard for partner to evaluate his hand for slam purposes when he doesn't know whether a 3NT rebid is based on a solid or broken suit.

OPENING IN THIRD OR FOURTH POSITION

When should you open light in third or fourth position? As a general rule, players who are aggressive in first or second position tend not to open very light (maybe with one point less than normal) in third or fourth position. Those who are heavy openers tend to open lighter when partner has passed. There is no doubt that opening the bidding makes it more difficult for the opponents to bid when they have good hands. To some players, this justifies a strategy of opening in third position with almost anything. The trouble is that you don't know whether the opponents have most of the remaining strength or if partner has his fair share.

My feeling is that you should open most balanced 12-counts and tend to open in third position when you have a good suit like

♠ x x   ♡ x x x   ◇ K Q J x x   ♣ K 10 x

When you hold that hand, it is likely that the opponents will play the hand, and you would like a diamond lead whatever the final contract. The disadvantage is that if the next hand passes and partner bids 1♠ you have 'lost your bet' that the next hand will bid and buy the contract so that your lead-directing bid might pay off. Now you should pass 1♠ — and hope the opponents will reopen, since partner won't like playing 1♠ with Qxxx opposite your two small no matter what the rest of his hand is. However, you could make it much worse by bidding again since partner may also bid again. Even if partner goes down three in 1♠, the opponents can undoubtedly make a partscore, but if you rebid anything and partner bids 2NT or even jumps to game, you could be in real trouble.

In contrast, I think opening the bidding on

♠ x x x   ♡ K J x x   ◇ Q x   ♣ K Q x x

invites disaster (if not on this hand, then on a later deal when partner remembers that you did open this collection and compensates for the possibility). The argument for bidding is that you have a 'better than average hand' — more than 10 points — so the odds are that you will be plus. But I don't agree that you have a better than average hand. You do have 11 points, but they are terrible points. How often will your doubleton queen take a trick? Even more important, your left-hand opponent may hold one of these hands

♠ K Q 10 x x   ♡ x x   ◇ K 10 x x   ♣ x x

♠ K J x x x   ♡ A 10 9 x   ◇ x   ♣ x x x

With either of these holdings, if you had passed, he would have passed the deal out. Now, though, he will overcall 1♠ since he has, in my opinion, a better hand than yours; indeed, the odds are that the opponents will successfully outbid you because they have playing strength while you don't. *Far from obstructing the opposition, you have made it easier for them to bid.*

In fourth position the lead-directional factor is of less importance, but still of some value since the opponents may buy the contract. Naturally you won't open unless you think the odds favor bidding and making something your way, but you must also be prepared for things not to go as you had hoped they would.

WEAK TWO-BIDS

There is a vast disagreement among experts regarding the types of hand that justify a weak two-bid. Traditionally, a weak two-bid showed a good suit and 1½ to 2 quick tricks. Typical hands would be

♠ K Q 10 x x x   ♡ x x   ◇ A x x   ♣ x x

♠ K x   ♡ K Q J x x x   ◇ x x   ♣ x x x

At one time the tendency was to be very restrictive. Your suit should be headed by two of the top three, or three of the top five, honors; you should not have support for an unbid major; a singleton was undesirable; and 6421 distribution or a void was absolutely forbidden. Now the trend is the other way. Some players will open with almost any six-card suit and less than an opening bid. Others don't even require a six-card suit; they might open a non-vulnerable weak two-bid with either of these holdings:

♠ x x ♡ K Q x x x ◇ x x x ♣ x x x

♠ x x ♡ Q x x x x x x ◇ x x ♣ x x

They would justify their bid on the first hand by saying it might interfere somewhat with the opponents' bidding and will probably get partner off to the best opening lead. They would justify their bidding on the latter hand by saying they never pass with a seven-card suit, and they hate to bid at the three-level with such a poor playing hand.

Perhaps it is just a sign of old age, but I strongly disagree with bidding a weak two (or anything else) on either hand. But I might open a weak two with a very strong five-card suit and a singleton in the other major:

♠ x ♡ A Q J 10 x ◇ Q 10 9 x ♣ J x x

This hand, despite the five-card suit, has roughly the same playing strength as the typical weak two-bid. If I pass, the bidding may be at 2♠ or higher by the time it gets back to me. It is far safer and more effective to open 2♡ than to wait until the opponents get to 2♠ and then bid hearts. But if my spades and clubs were interchanged, I would be reluctant to open a weak two-bid since we might belong in spades, and a weak two-bid makes it hard to find a fit in another suit (and dangerous even to look for the fit since you may not find it).

There is a school of players including Mike Passell, the Kirkhams, and probably the Granovetters and Zia, who would open 2♠ with

♠ Q J 10 9 x x ♡ x ◇ A J 8 x x ♣ x

I think this hand is much too strong offensively since as little as the king of spades and the king-queen of diamonds from partner will be enough for game. Traditionally, the weak-two bidder is not allowed to bid again unless his partner invites him to. However, those who open 2♠ on hands like this plan to rebid diamonds if they get a chance, and they figure that most of the time there will be more bidding and they will get that chance.

Many players open a weak two-bid in fourth position to show an intermediate hand — about 13-15 points with a six-card suit. That doesn't make sense to me. Obviously, you have the option of passing the hand out with a minimum weak two-bid, but suppose you hold

♠ K Q 9 8 x x ♡ A x ◇ J x x ♣ x x

Probably everyone at the table has about ten points, but you have the spades and a six-card suit. Why pass the hand out when the odds favor your side being able to make 2♠? However, you really don't want either partner or the opponents to bid. Also, if you open 1♠ and rebid 2♠ over partner's response, he may play you for a better hand and bid again. If you are going to get to 2♠ anyway, it is better to bid it immediately while showing no interest in getting to game. Thus a fourth-position 1♠ opening followed by a 2♠ rebid should show at least a sound opening bid, allowing partner to raise spades or rebid 2NT. So even with

♠ K Q x x x x   ♡ Q x   ◇ Q J x   ♣ K x

since your chances of making game are remote opposite a passed partner, you should open 2♠, rather than 1♠ followed by a 2♠ rebid. However, most 13-point hands are too strong for an opening two-bid. Of course, if your suit is hearts rather than spades, and you decide to open in third or fourth chair, there is even more reason to make a mild preempt in the hope of not being outbid in spades.

Most people play new suits as forcing over a weak two-bid on the theory that there is no assurance of finding a better fit, so if responder has a weak hand there's no percentage in being a trick higher on a misfit. Thus the only time they bid a new suit over a weak two-bid is when they are interested in a game or slam in the new suit. But a few players play that all good hands or invitational hands bid 2NT, in which case new suits are not forcing. Marty Bergen plays that way, probably because his weak two-bids are so weak and are frequently made with only a five-card suit.

After a weak two-bid and a 2NT response, there are two schools of thought on what opener should rebid. One is that he should rebid his suit with a minimum, and otherwise show a feature (usually a high honor if he has one). In fact, if new suits are forcing, the 2NT response shows at least some interest in game in opener's suit, and with no feature, say

♠ A K J 9 x x   ♡ x   ◇ J 10 x x   ♣ x x

opener can jump to game. With a suit as good as AKQxxx he can bid 3NT, which responder will pass with a suitable hand.

The other way of rebidding over 2NT is for opener to show what he has in steps: 3♣ shows a bad hand and bad suit; 3◇ shows a good suit (two of the top three honors), but a minimum weak two-bid (perhaps AQ10xxx or KQJxxx and nothing else); 3♡ shows a bad suit with a good hand; 3♠ shows a good hand with a good suit. Again, 3NT shows a six-card suit headed by the AKQ. Some players employ the step principle but change the meanings of the steps: for example, the first step might show that opener has only a five-card suit.

No matter which system of rebids you play, when responder bids 2NT followed by 3NT, opener has the option to revert to his suit. After

Opener	Responder
2♠	2NT
immaterial	3NT
?	

with

$$\spadesuit\,Q\,J\,10\,x\,x\,x \quad \heartsuit\,x \quad \diamond\,K\,J\,10\,x \quad \clubsuit\,x\,x$$

he should bid 4♠. So if responder has something like

$$\spadesuit\,x \quad \heartsuit\,A\,Q \quad \diamond\,K\,Q\,J\,10\,x\,x \quad \clubsuit\,A\,10\,9\,x$$

or

$$\spadesuit\,— \quad \heartsuit\,A\,x \quad \diamond\,Q\,10\,x \quad \clubsuit\,A\,K\,Q\,J\,x\,x\,x$$

he should bid 3NT directly over 2♠ to avoid giving partner the 4♠ option.

Except at unfavorable vulnerability, responder should raise to the three-level almost any time he has three-card support with 0 to a bad 15 points, just to make it harder for the opponents to get to their best contract. Obviously the single raise is not invitational. In fact, it bars opener unless he has a peculiar hand, like

$$\spadesuit\,A\,J\,x\,x\,x\,x \quad \heartsuit\,x\,x \quad \diamond\,— \quad \clubsuit\,A\,10\,9\,x\,x$$

with which I personally would have opened 1♠ rather than 2♠.

In the previous discussion I assumed that we were talking about weak two-bids in the majors. What about an opening 2◊ bid? A good number of players use 2◊ as a weak two-bid also. Some North Americans and probably most Europeans play it as Multi (showing a weak two-bid in either major or some sort of strong hand like a balanced 20+ or a good three-suiter). Others play that it shows a weak two-bid in either major with no strong alternatives. The main advantage of Multi is that it creates problems for the opponents, who don't know which major opener has (this is also its main disadvantage, since responder doesn't know either). It also frees the 2♡ and 2♠ openings to show other types of hand. Typically 2♡ is used to show a two-suiter, with hearts being one of the suits (usually only a five-card suit), while an opening 2♠ bid can be assigned various meanings. If one of the possible hands for an opening 2◊ bid is 20-22 balanced points, a 2NT opening can show a preemptive hand with at least 5-5 in the minors. I'll leave it up to you to explore your options if you want to play something like this. I won't try to describe all the possible variations or recommend defenses against them. (I have an excuse not to discuss defenses since this book is about uncontested auctions. Besides, the ACBL has approved and printed recommended defenses which the opponents must provide for you if they use Multi, since it is a Mid-chart convention, which is only permitted in some Flight A or National events.)

FLANNERY

There are two other frequent uses for an opening 2◇ bid. My first choice is Flannery, since it fills a gap in your constructive bidding. Suppose you hold

♠ Q J x x   ♡ A Q x x x   ◇ K x   ♣ x x

and open 1♡. Partner bids a forcing one notrump; what do you rebid? Forty or fifty years ago Roth and Stone suggested 2♡ as the least of evils. However, most players like to play that a 2♡ rebid over a one-level response (either 1♠ or 1NT) shows six hearts, so they would choose to rebid 2♣ on their double-ton, which can work out badly if responder passes or raises clubs.

There is another problem in Standard bidding. This general subject will be discussed in detail later in the book, but most experts like to raise a response of one of a major with good three-card support and a ruffing value. When you open a five-card heart suit and partner responds 1♠, you automatically have a ruffing value when you hold three spades since you must be either 3-2 or 4-1 in the minors. Most experts would therefore raise a 1♠ response to 2♠ with either of these hands:

♠ K x x   ♡ A K x x x   ◇ K x x   ♣ x x

♠ Q x x   ♡ A K x x x   ◇ K x x x   ♣ x

A 1NT rebid with the first hand is undesirable with the weak club holding and a ruffing value (if you play in spades). The latter hand is too weak to bid 2◇ and show spade support later. For these reasons responder should avoid responding 1♠ with four small spades. A 4-3 fit at a partscore level may be quite playable when the four-card suit is fairly strong (AQxx oppo-site Kxx, KQxx opposite Axx, etc., especially when you expect to ruff first with the three-card holding) but I don't like to play xxxx opposite Kxx at any level. However, if you don't bid your spades with four small and part-ner has ♠AKxx, for example (and is too weak to reverse) you could miss a good spade contract.

Playing Flannery, an opening 2◇ bid shows exactly four spades and (usually) five hearts with a hand too weak to reverse. It is described on your convention card as 11-15 HCP although some 11-point hands are too weak for Flannery — for example

♠ Q J x x   ♡ Q J x x x   ◇ K x   ♣ Q x

doesn't even come close — and some 16-point hands are too weak for a reverse. If you decide to open a sub-minimum hand like

♠ Q J x x   ♡ A J 9 x x   ◇ Q J   ♣ J x

in third or fourth position, you should open 1♡ rather than 2◇. If you open 2◇ and partner has a hand worth a game try, you won't be able to stop short of 3♡. If you open 1♡, then after a Drury response you will be able to stop in 2♡.

I said Flannery shows five hearts usually, but I do recommend opening 2◊ with

♠ A K x x   ♡ Q 10 x x x x   ◊ Q x   ♣ x

To use Flannery with six hearts, you should hold a minimum hand with rather poor hearts. If you open 2◊ with

♠ A x x x   ♡ A K J x x x   ◊ Q x x   ♣ —

you could easily miss a game when partner holds

♠ K x   ♡ x x x   ◊ A x x   ♣ J x x x x

or even

♠ K x x   ♡ Q   ◊ K J x x   ♣ J x x x x

since it would not occur to him to make a forward move in either case. Indeed, with the latter hand he would bid 2♠ over 2◊, not only missing a good game but also playing in the wrong suit.

There are various responses and rebids one can use after a Flannery opening. Everyone plays that a 2♡, 2♠ or 3♣ response is natural, non-forcing and non-invitational. Only an unusual hand will tempt opener to bid again over these responses, although over a 2♡ response I suggest rebidding 3♣ with

♠ A x x x   ♡ A K Q x x   ◊ —   ♣ J 10 x x

since responder needs so little for game if his cards are in the right place (and after this bidding he should be able to tell which of his honors will be valuable). You can also gain if partner has bid 2♡ with something like

♠ x x   ♡ x x   ◊ J x x x x   ♣ K Q x x

since you will get to your best trump suit.

Opener	Responder
2◊	3♣

is ambiguous. Responder may have as little as

♠ x x   ♡ x   ◊ Q x x   ♣ J 10 9 x x x x

(what else can he bid?) or as much as

♠ x x   ♡ x x   ◊ K x x   ♣ A K 10 x x x

As opener I would bid 3NT over 3♣ with

♠ K x x x   ♡ A Q x x x   ◊ A x   ♣ Q x

hoping that partner had the latter type of hand (and that he would return to 4♣ with the weaker hand).

A direct 4♣ response to Flannery is Roman Keycard Blackwood for hearts, while 4◊ is RKB for spades. Some play that a 3◊ response transfers opener to hearts and initiates a slam invitational sequence; others play that it is natural but invitational since responder could pass with a weak hand and long diamonds.

Some people play a 3♡ or 3♠ response as invitational; others play it as preemptive. I don't see much need for a preempt at this level after RHO has passed, so I play it as natural and forcing, showing interest in a slam and asking opener to show a fragment if he has one. Showing a fragment is much more helpful than bidding a control since if responder has Axx of one minor and KQx of the other, he likes his hand much better when the singleton is opposite his ace rather than opposite the king-queen. With 2-2 in the minors, the cheapest bid by opener shows the best hand, so over 3♡, 3♠ is more encouraging than 3NT, and 4♡ shows a very poor hand. Over a 3♠ response a 3NT rebid shows a better hand than 4♡ or 4♠. (Perhaps 4♡ here should show the ace of hearts and deny the king, which will allow responder to evaluate his hand upward when he has a singleton heart.)

Responses of 4♡ and 4♠ are to play. That leaves 2NT for all game-invitational hands or hands that might make game in a 5-2 heart fit or in notrump (depending on opener's distribution) or game or slam in a minor. Over 2NT, opener bids his three-card minor at the three-level and (with a non-minimum hand) his four-card minor at the four-level. With 2-2 in the minors, a 3♡ rebid shows a minimum hand for hearts, but if partner converts to 3♠ you could raise with

♠ K Q x x   ♡ J 9 x x x   ◊ A x   ♣ A x

A 3♠ rebid over 2NT ostensibly shows 4-5-2-2 and a minimum for spades but accepts any invitation in hearts, perhaps with one of these hands:

♠ J x x x   ♡ K Q J x x   ◊ A x   ♣ K x

♠ Q x x x   ♡ A J 9 x x x   ◊ x   ♣ A x

Regarding the last example hand (which is 4-6), showing a minimum or maximum for the two major suits has precedence over showing your fragment, since two cards are not much of a fragment. Besides, if partner is considering a game or slam in a minor, you don't want to encourage him.

What I have just described is 'standard' Flannery. Some players from the Washington D.C. area (and perhaps elsewhere) play 'Extended Flannery,' in which 4-6 or even 5-6 in the majors is permissible. Now if responder bids 2♡ or 2♠, opener is allowed to bid more with these distributions because of the extra playing strength. It sounded wild to me, but

I tried it with one partner, at her suggestion, and we didn't run into any difficulties. At the least, it avoids problems Standard bidders have when holding hands like

♠ A Q x x x   ♡ K J x x x x   ◇ x   ♣ x

since if they open 1♡, they may not be able to show spades at a reasonable level. If they do get in a later spade bid, they will inevitably be misleading their partner regarding high-card strength. Meanwhile if they open 1♠ they are likely to play in the wrong suit.

Everyone has an opinion about Flannery; either you love it or you hate it. Incidentally, some people play a 2♡ opening as Flannery, perhaps because they play 2◇ as Multi or as showing a singleton or void in diamonds (when playing a strong club system with five-card majors). Since responder can pass 2♡, this convention is harder to defend against, but of course it gives up the natural weak-two opening in hearts.

THE THREE-SUITED 2◇ OPENER

The other popular use of an opening 2◇ bid is to show a three-suiter. Some play it strong, but most play it as a minimum range opener. Some play it as any three-suiter; others play that it always guarantees spades. When playing a strong club system it may specifically show a singleton or void in diamonds, as otherwise you may have to open 1◇ on those hands. The following treatment is my second choice (after Flannery) for an opening 2◇ bid.

An opening 2◇ shows a three-suiter, including both minors, with 10-13 points: in other words 4-0-4-5, 4-0-5-4, 4-1-4-4, 0-4-4-5, 0-4-5-4 or 1-4-4-4 distribution. If there is a five-card suit, it is always a minor. All non-jump responses are to play and will be passed, except for the bid of opener's short major. Jump responses are invitational — 3♡ or 3♠ invites game even when partner has a singleton in the suit.

A 2NT response asks opener to describe his hand further. It will be harder to defend a final contract when the 2◇ bidder is dummy since he will have described his distribution while his partner's hand pattern remains a secret from the opponents. So the following rebids over 2NT make sense in allowing responder to be declarer — and that may help you to remember what the rebids mean: 3♣ says opener's shortage is in hearts, and he has a minimum opening; 3◇ shows a minimum with shortage in spades; 3♡ shows a maximum with a shortage in hearts; 3♠ shows a maximum with a shortage in spades.

With no real game interest, responder bids his cheapest playable suit, assuming opener has four of them. Suppose responder bids 2♡ and opener has a shortage in hearts. With a minimum he rebids 2♠; with a maximum he rebids 2NT. In either case the final contract will probably be three of a minor — again played by responder. But there is a good reason for showing minimum or maximum since even when the hands purport not to fit, there could still be a game. Here's why: suppose, when partner opens 2◇, you hold

♠ J 10 x x x x   ♡ J x x   ◇ A x   ♣ K x

The probability is that partner's shortage is in spades. If so, 2♡ will be your best contract — not a great contract, but the best available. However, if partner's shortage is in hearts, you have a good chance for game. So you should respond 2♡! With short spades, partner will pass. About 80% of the time 2♡ will be the final contract, and you will probably make it. At the very least, it will be better to play 2♡ than 3♡, and better for the hand with three hearts to be concealed. When partner is short in hearts, he will bid either 2♠ (minimum) or 2NT (maximum). If he bids 2♠ you may still have a game, and you can invite by bidding 3♠. Partner will realize that honors in spades will be more valuable than honors in the minors, so he will be able to evaluate his hand accurately. If he bids 2NT, showing a maximum, you will jump to 4♠. If your hand were slightly weaker, you would pass 2♠ but invite over 2NT.

Similarly, when responder holds both majors with a hand too weak for game no matter what opener has, he should also bid 2♡, which affords the best chance to make 2♡ or 2♠ the final contract. However, if he holds something like

♠ J x x x   ♡ K Q 10 x   ◇ A x x   ♣ K x

he is too strong to bid 2♡ and risk it being passed when opener is short in spades. But a 2NT response would force the bidding to the three-level, which might be too high if opener does turn out to be short in hearts, so the best response is 2♠. When the bidding starts

Opener	Responder
2◇	2♠
?	

opener rebids 2NT with a maximum and a singleton spade, or 3♣ with a minimum. He is more likely to want to play 2NT with a maximum than with a minimum.

Suppose, when opener bids 2◇, next hand overcalls a major. A double should show at least four of the other major *and an interest in game*. With no interest in game responder can simply bid the other major with four or more, gambling that the overcaller has bid opener's shortage — a pretty good gamble. It isn't practical for the opponents to psyche an overcall, unless they have an illegal agreement that partner can't raise no matter what he has. On the rare hands when the overcaller has bid opener's major and responder doubles, opener will, of course, pass the double. (That is another reason why the overcaller can't afford to psyche an overcall with a singleton or doubleton.) If the bidding starts

Opener	Oppt.	Responder	Oppt.
2◇	2♡ or 2♠	pass	pass
?			

opener can make a reopening double with shortage and a maximum. His distribution is good for defending, and if his partner is too weak or short in the opponent's suit to pass the double he almost always has a safe runout. If the opponents overcall in a minor, a double by responder is for penalty.

To summarize, the three-suited 2◇ bid is relatively safe since partner has three chances to find a fit (including passing 2◇). It is hard for the opponents to bid over 2◇ since they may suspect, but can't know for sure, which your major is. Also, opener's 4441 or 5440 distribution means that when the opponents find an eight-card fit, it is sure to break no better than 4-1.

PREEMPTS AT THE THREE-LEVEL AND HIGHER

That takes care of the one- and two-levels except for 2♣ opening bids, which will be discussed shortly, and notrump openings, which will be discussed in a chapter of their own. How about opening bids at a higher level? Preempts at the three-level seldom help you to find your best contract — unless you play very disciplined preempts with good suits and little, if any, outside strength. (But who plays disciplined preempts these days?) Their primary purpose is to interfere with the opponents' bidding. When the opponents have most of the high cards, preempts usually work well by forcing them to guess whether they should attempt to penalize you or whether they belong in game or slam, and, if so, in which suit. When partner has most of the high cards, preempts usually work badly since you have lost at least two rounds of bidding.

When I started to play bridge, the 'Rule of 2 and 3' was the accepted guideline for preempts: you could overbid by two tricks when vulnerable, and by three tricks when not vulnerable. The theory was that you never risked more than a 500-point penalty, which was roughly the value of game, and that wasn't much of a risk since if the opponents could set you 500, they could almost surely make a game or slam of their own. This was true because your preempt showed a good suit — perhaps KQJxxxx. I had a rude awakening about thirty years ago when I was playing with Paul Heitner and, at favorable vulnerability, passed as dealer with ♣KQ98xx and nothing else. Paul was livid when the opponents got to a slam and he pointed out the problems they would have had if I had opened 3♣. This club suit was scarcely worth 4 tricks, and he wanted me to undertake a contract to take nine — a clear-cut violation of the Rule of 2 and 3!

When I discovered that most of the top players were preempting with hands like that, I decided to become a modern player myself, especially when the vulnerability was favorable. Perhaps one time in seven your left-hand opponent has a mediocre hand and good clubs, your right-hand opponent has a good hand and doubles when your partner passes, and LHO leaves the double in. Usually that will result in a bad score for your side, but not always. Partner may have seven or eight points, so perhaps you only go down three for -500 when the opponents could score 600 or 630 their way. If they can't double you and defend, there are many ways your preempt can gain. When the opponents each have balanced hands and about 13 points, you may even escape undoubled for -150 when they are cold for a game. Sometimes an opponent won't leave his partner's double in when he should (on a double-dummy basis) and other times he will leave it in when he shouldn't. Or they may simply get to the wrong game.

Most of my partners preempt more unsoundly than I do, and I sometimes almost wish for a bad result to discourage them from doing so — but we don't get a bad result as often as we should. I think it is Larry Cohen's fault that people think you can bid at the three-level any time you have a seven-card suit (treating 9875432 and KJ109653 the same way) — not that Larry, himself, is unaware of the difference. Even when the opponents don't catch you for a big penalty, you may lose occasionally because partner will be afraid to raise your 3♠ bid to game with

♠ K ♡ A Q x x ◇ A J 10 x x ♣ x x x

not knowing whether the preempt was based on

♠ Q J 10 x x x x ♡ K x ◇ x x ♣ x x

or

♠ Q x x x x x x ♡ x ◇ x x ♣ J x x

You may miss a game by preempting, but only when partner is short in your suit. If you open 3♠ and he has

♠ x ♡ A K x ◇ A Q x ♣ K J x x x

you could easily lose three trump tricks in spades and partner may take a pessimistic view and pass. Then if you happen to hold ♠KQJ10xxx (instead of ♠Q10xxxxx) you may miss a game. However, when partner has three or more trumps, he will tend to raise almost regardless of strength. If he has a good hand he is hoping you will make game; with a bad hand, his length in your suit cuts down what little defensive strength you might have, and he raises to make it harder for the opponents to get to their best game or slam. Everyone agrees that you deny side strength (no more than a king, if that) when you preempt. Nor should you have a solid suit of your own unless you open four of a major. We probably come out ahead in the long run with these 'unsound' preempts.

Players like Kerry Sanborn and Karen McCallum, who tend to open at the three-level on almost nothing, also tend to open at the four-level very optimistically. In the old days you could open 3♠ with

♠ A Q J x x x x   ♡ Q x   ◇ x x x   ♣ x

expecting partner to raise when you belonged in game. Now many pairs would open this hand 4♠, which does not appeal to me. However, I see nothing wrong with opening 4♠, whether vulnerable or not, with

♠ Q J 10 9 x x   ♡ x   ◇ A J 8 x x   ♣ x

This was the hand shown earlier on which some people would open 2♠, intending to bid diamonds later (if they got a chance). What does partner need to make a game? If he just has the king of spades and the king-queen of diamonds, game will be laydown, and with the help of a winning finesse you may succeed opposite even less. Partner would never raise to game with those few high cards (especially without length in spades). Partner could also have a lot more high cards, but we might have no play for game if they are in the wrong place. Since it is so difficult to be scientific with this type of hand, and since the opponents can often make a game of their own if we can't make 4♠, I think it is an ideal 4♠ opening.

Many people avoid opening a preempt with a two-suiter like my last example. What if we go down in 4♠, they ask, when we are cold for 6◇? All I can say is, 'That's very unlikely.' If partner has a singleton or void in spades, my hand will be worth very little in a diamond contract. It is unlikely the spade suit can be established and used without giving up two spade tricks. If we are going to lose two spade tricks, why not play the hand in spades? It would be an entirely different matter if the spades were ♠AJxxxx(x). In that case the hand could easily play much better in diamonds if partner were short in spades. This same principle is involved in deciding whether to open a weak two-bid. With either of these hands:

♠ A Q x x x x   ♡ Q x x x   ◇ x   ♣ J x

♠ A K x x x x   ♡ Q 10 x   ◇ x   ♣ x x x

I would not open 2♠, except opposite a passed hand, because we would frequently belong in hearts. But with

♠ K Q J 10 x x   ♡ Q x x x   ◇ x   ♣ J x

I see nothing wrong with a 2♠ bid. I doubt that there is one hand in twenty that will play better in hearts than in spades opposite this hand.

Once you preempt you are not supposed to bid again. Suppose you hold

♠ x   ♡ A K Q J x x x x   ◇ Q J x   ♣ x

and open 4♡ on the grounds that there is a greater danger of being outbid if you open 1♡ than that you will miss a slam by preempting. But you might miss a slam if partner has just the right cards. Worse still, supposing an opponent bids 4♠ over 4♡, partner doesn't know that the king of diamonds and any ace will be enough for you to make 5♡. Nor does he know that even when he has almost a yarborough, you probably have a good sacrifice in 5♡. Many pairs use Namyats (Stayman spelled backwards) openings to show this type of hand: 4♣ shows a good 4♡ bid; 4◇ shows a good 4♠ bid. The usual continuation is that bidding the in-between suit (4◇ over 4♣) shows some interest in slam, or at least in competing further in case the opponents bid. When the in-between bid is followed by a new suit, the latter is a cuebid; when a new suit above partner's suit is bid immediately, it is an asking bid. (In steps opener shows no control, second-round control or first-round control in the asking bid suit, except that the cheapest notrump bid shows the king.)

Like most conventions, Namyats has a downside. When an opponent opens 4♡, if you double (primarily for takeout) and partner has a weak hand, he may have a choice of letting the opponents make 4♡ doubled with an overtrick or of taking a big set himself by bidding. So there is danger in doubling. But if the opponents open 4♣ to show a good 4♡ bid, you can make a light takeout double with little risk, holding something like

♠ K x x x   ♡ x   ◇ K J x x   ♣ A x x x

The reason there is little risk is that the opponents are unlikely to be able to make 4♣ doubled and even more unlikely to know when to try to make that contract. With a better hand you can double immediately and double again when the opponents bid 4♡. In the unlikely event that you have a penalty double of 4♡, you can pass 4♣ and double when someone bids 4♡. My primary purpose in raising this issue was not to show you how to defend against Namyats since the subject of this book is uncontested auctions, but to point out that Namyats, like most conventions, can sometimes backfire. It isn't a perfect solution to the problem.

Almost everyone plays new suits as forcing in response to any high-level preemptive bid, A three-club opener can raise a three-heart response (for example) with three small or a doubleton honor, and if he happens to have something like

♠ x x   ♡ J x x   ◇ x   ♣ A K x x x x

he should bid 4◇, a splinter bid.

How does responder invite a game in opener's minor, since a raise of 3♣ to 4♣ continues the preempt and is not invitational? The logical way to invite game in a minor is to bid the other minor (3◇ by responder over 3♣, or 4♣ over 3◇). It is extremely unlikely that you would want to play in the other minor, so you might as well give it this meaning. I don't know who originated the idea, but a treatment that many experts play is that over 3♣, 3◇ is a puppet to 3♡. Responder may prefer to play in a heart partscore with, say

♠ A x x   ♡ K Q J 10 x x   ◇ Q J x   ♣ x

but he is not interested in game and doesn't want to hear a 4♣ rebid when opener can't raise hearts. After the 3♡ rebid, responder now can bid 3♠ to play with an appropriate hand. However, if he bids 4♣ over opener's forced 3♡ rebid, he is inviting 5♣. There are no gadgets after 3◇-4♣, which simply invites game in diamonds.

Since new suits are forcing over a preempt, a jump in a new suit should be an asking bid. In steps, the preemptor shows no control, second-round control or (very unlikely) first-round control in the suit bid. Over four of a major, since it is extremely unlikely that responder wants to play a different suit at this high level, a new suit without a jump should be an asking bid. You probably shouldn't make this bid without having discussed it, since you can't rely on partner's logic to reach this conclusion.

A recent bad experience with a preempt prompts me to say more about when you should and when you should not preempt at high levels. With both sides vulnerable, my partner *du jour* opened 5♣ with

♠ 10 9 x   ♡ x   ◇ x   ♣ K Q J x x x x

To be fair, he would have opened 4♣ if that bid had been available to him, but we were playing Namyats. Sometimes you are forced by your system to choose between two bids, both of which are less desirable than the one you would like to make. With his hand I would open 3♣ rather than 5♣; when you contract to take eleven tricks despite holding only seven, the odds are very much against you. It is true that when the opponents have almost all of the missing high cards and a good suit, your 5♣ bid may make it almost impossible for them to get to their slam, but it is unlikely that they have one. If you open 5♣ with this hand, the best you can reasonably hope for is that partner has two aces and nothing else. Then you will take nine tricks for -500 if you are doubled, while the opponents can probably make 4♡ or 5◇, and your sacrifice gains 4 IMPs. If partner has just one ace you will go for 800 and lose 4 IMPs unless they can make a slam (which may depend on exactly which ace he has). But the tricks your side can take on offense are usually quite different from the tricks it can take on defense. If partner has QJx of any suit except yours, it is probably worth one trick on defense but is of no value to you in 5♣ doubled; likewise KQ10x opposite your singleton is often worthless on offense and worth two or three tricks on defense.

I will admit that partner was rather unlucky on this hand. I held

♠ Q x   ♡ Q J x x x   ◇ A K J x x x   ♣ —

The opponents picked partner clean before he could get a discard on the king of diamonds, and an overruff held him to six trump tricks rather than seven. Minus 1100 on a hand where the opponents couldn't even make game! In fact (this was on OkBridge) several pairs had taken big sets in 4♡ doubled their way since the hearts split 5-1.

Because of the level, I would guess that a double of five of a minor is left in 85% of the time. A vulnerable five-bid should therefore probably show about 9+ tricks, and partner might raise 5♣ to six with something like

♠ J x x x x x   ♡ A K   ◇ A Q x   ♣ J x

gambling that opener has a singleton or void in spades.

THE STRONG 2♣ OPENING

The only opening suit bid we haven't discussed so far is 2♣, which most people play as strong and artificial. There is not much to say about the opening bid itself except that I think it should be used more often than it is. With a balanced hand, 22 points is the usual minimum for opening 2♣. That looks okay to me, and I have no opinion on whether the minimum should be almost any 22 points or a good 22. A 2♣ opening followed by a 2NT rebid over a negative or waiting response can, of course, be passed. Similarly responder can transfer and pass a below-game bid or use Stayman and pass opener's rebid with a shortage in clubs. Most players treat a rebid by opener of his original suit over a second negative as non-forcing. Again I have no strong feelings about that; sometimes it works well, and sometimes it doesn't. Suppose you hold

♠ A K J x x x   ♡ A x   ◇ K Q J x   ♣ x

(which most players would consider far too weak for a 2♣ bid). The bidding starts:

You	Partner
2♣	2◇
2♠	3♣

(cheaper minor is second negative). So you bid 3♠ and partner passes with

♠ x x x   ♡ x   x x   ◇ 10 x x   ♣ J x x x

The ♠Q drops singleton or doubleton and you take ten tricks. I suppose the chances of a diamond ruff make 4♠ a tad under a 50% contract (I'm not even sure of that), but I don't feel particularly triumphant for having stopped below game. However, my main point is that I think you should open 2♣ with this hand. You belong in slam opposite either of these hands:

♠ x x x x x   ♡ K x x   ◇ A x x   ♣ J x x

♠ Q x x   ♡ x x   ◇ A x x x x   ♣ Q x x

You may not get there even if you open 2♣ but you have a much better chance than if you open 1♠. You don't make every contract you bid, so why should it be more embarrassing to be set when you open 2♣ than in other bidding sequences? The test should be whether an opening 2♣ bid will enable you to bid a good game or slam.

1. Partner opens 4♡, with neither side vulnerable. What call do you make with

   ♠ Q 9 7 6 4   ♡ K Q 7   ◇ A K Q 2   ♣ A

2. What call do you make as dealer, both sides vulnerable, with

   ♠ 9   ♡ K Q J 10 6 5   ◇ K 7   ♣ A K Q 6

3. What call do you make as dealer, vulnerable against not, with

   ♠ K J 9 5 4   ♡ A 6   ◇ K 7 3   ♣ 8 7 5

4. You open 3♣ with

   ♠ J   ♡ Q 6 5 2   ◇ 8   ♣ A Q J 7 6 5 4

   and partner bids 3◇. What is your rebid?

5. You are playing Flannery. Partner opens 2◇, you bid 2NT and part-ner bids 3♣. What call do you make with

   ♠ K 5 3   ♡ Q 9   ◇ A 7 6 5   ♣ A 8 6 2

6. You are playing the three-suited 2◇ opener which guarantees both minors. Partner opens 2◇ with neither side vulnerable and RHO over-calls 3◇. What call do you make with

   ♠ K J 7 6   ♡ 8 5   ◇ Q 5 2   ♣ K 7 3 2

7. With both sides vulnerable, partner opens 2♠ and RHO overcalls 3♣. What call do you make with

   ♠ Q J   ♡ A Q 9 4   ◇ A J 6 4   ♣ 7 6 4

8. With both sides vulnerable, partner opens 2♡ and RHO passes. What call do you make with

   ♠ A 7   ♡ Q J 7 6   ◇ J 9 5 4 3   ♣ 8 5

9. You open 2♡ with

   ♠ J x   ♡ K Q J 9 x x   ◇ J 10 x   ♣ x x

   and partner responds 3◇. What would you rebid?

10. Partner opens 3♡ at favorable vulnerability. Next hand passes and you hold

    ♠ 10 8   ♡ Q 8 7 6   ◇ K J 5 4   ♣ Q 5 3

    What call do you make?

my answers

1. If you adopt my suggestion about asking bids, you should bid 4♠. If partner shows second-round control, either the king or a singleton, you can bid 6♡. If he shows first-round control (almost surely a void), you can bid 5NT (Grand Slam Force with graded responses); if you don't play graded responses to 5NT, you can just gamble on bidding 7♡ — it is unlikely that partner has opened 4♡ with

   ♠ A   ♡ J 10 9 x x x x x   ◇ x   ♣ K Q x

   If you are not playing asking bids, I would gamble on bidding 6♡ anyway. Partner probably has a singleton spade and, if not, perhaps spades won't be led.

2. Many people will disagree, but I think you should open 2♣. If partner has nothing but the jack of clubs you have a finesse for game, and any two aces will give you a play for slam. If you opened 1♡, would you expect to get to slam opposite one of these hands:

   ♠ J x x x   ♡ A x x   ◇ x x x   ♣ A x x
   ♠ J x x x   ♡ A x   ◇ A x x x x   ♣ x x

3. I probably wouldn't open this hand, but I consider it very close. Larry Cohen thinks opening is clear-cut, and I'm sure Meckwell would ask, 'What's the problem?' Larry argues, rather convincingly, that if the strength is evenly divided, or even if the opponents have a majority of the high cards, you can't be hurt at the two-level when partner has three-card spade support. It is very unlikely that you will be doubled, and if you can't make 2♠ the opponents can surely make something their way. The Law of Total Tricks protects you. (Of course, partner may not have spade support but, even so, it is very unlikely that the opponents will be able to penalize you severely).

4. Bid 3♠. There are three main possibilities. Partner may plan to invite game in clubs (and, if so, you will surely accept). Partner may want to sign off in 3♠ and, if so, he can pass. Or (least likely in view of your hand and RHO's pass), he may want to play 3♡. If he wanted to play 3♡, you have enough to bid 4♡, and your 3♠ bid will force him to 4♡; if that is the case, it may confuse the opponents, who are probably cold for 4♠. There is also a fourth possibility. Partner may be interested in a club slam, intending to bid 5♣ over your (almost forced) 3♡ bid. If he were not interested in slam, he would have bid 5♣ immediately.

5. Bid 4♡. You might have bid 3NT if partner had shown 4-5-2-2 distribution, although that choice is not clear-cut. Since partner has a singleton diamond and a diamond will almost surely be led, it looks as though 4♡ on the 5-2 fit is your best chance for game.

6. You should double for penalty. Almost certainly partner's four-card major is hearts, not spades, and even if partner has four spades, game will not be a cinch. With a total of only six trumps, the opponents should not do well in diamonds.

7. Without an overcall, you probably would have bid 2NT, intending to bid game if partner showed a maximum. After the overcall, you have to guess what to do. Since partner is vulnerable, and since a finesse in either red suit is likely to work, I think the odds favor bidding a game. Game will probably be a laydown if partner has a singleton club and will have at least a 50% play if he has a doubleton small club.

8. You are almost positive the opponents can make 4♠. The Law says you should bid 4♡, but I think the odds are about 10 to 1 that if you do, LHO will either bid 4♠ or will double, in which case RHO will bid

4♠. My inclination is to bid 2NT as though I were interested in game. If LHO has a choice of bidding 4♠ or passing, he will surely bid 4♠. If his choice is between bidding 3♠ or 4♠, he might bid 3♠ and his partner, not knowing whether or not he is stretching, might pass. I actually believe that the opponents will get to 4♠ whatever you do, but I think bidding 2NT gives you your best chance to talk them out of bidding a game.

9. If your hearts were headed by the ace you would raise to 4◊. If your hearts were headed by the ace and you had a singleton in a black suit, you would bid your singleton, hoping partner could bid 6◊. With your actual hand, I don't think you should encourage partner by raising diamonds, but if you bid 3♡, partner might pass with something like

   ♠ A K x   ♡ x   ◊ A K Q x x   ♣ x x x x

   With such good hearts and length in diamonds, I think you should bid 4♡.

10. Many players would be more aggressive, but I would simply raise to 4♡. The opponents should have about 25 points between them; if they are almost evenly divided, LHO might pass over 4♡ (and if he passes, RHO surely will). LHO can't tell whether you are bidding 4♡ to make or as an advance sacrifice, while if you bid 5♡ he will know it is a sacrifice. And while it is unlikely, it's possible that 5♡ doubled will go down four; if so, your -800 will be a poor result, even though the opponents are cold for a slam. You know that 4♡ doubled will be a better score than 5♡ doubled, and it is not a cinch that the opponents will bid 4♠.

CHAPTER 2

responses and rebids

THE FIRST RESPONSE

The first question you have to decide is how little you need to have for a response to partner's opening one-bid. The general guideline is 6 HCP, or 5 HCP with a five-card suit which you can bid at the one level, or as little as a king with a six-card major. Many players bid with less on the theory that even if they get too high as a result of bidding on 'nothing,' the opponents can make something anyway and the light response will make it more difficult for them to get into the auction. Sometimes it works that way, and sometimes when you keep the bidding open on nothing, partner bids too much with a good hand. As a result, you go minus on a deal where you were entitled to a plus.

The safest times to bid with sub-minimum values are when you have three- or four-card support for partner's major suit (and consequently a total of eight or nine trumps). Suppose partner opens 1♡, RHO passes, and you hold

♠ x x x　♡ Q x x x　◇ J x x　♣ x x x

If you pass, LHO will almost surely enter the bidding and may outbid you successfully. If you respond 1NT, unless LHO has a good suit or most of the outstanding high cards, he will probably pass. Suppose partner rebids 2♣ or 2◇ and you take a preference back to hearts. Partner needs a very strong hand to bid again, so you may buy the contract for 2♡, down one, when the opponents could make 140 or 130 their way. Strangely enough, a 1NT response is 'more preemptive' than a raise to 2♡. When one side has a fit, the other side usually has a fit too, and the opponents are therefore more likely to compete after you show a fit. Your 1NT response *could* be based on 10 or 11 points with a misfit for hearts (I will suggest later that it could be even stronger than that), and that makes this a very dangerous auction for opponents to enter.

However, if you hold

♠ J x x x　♡ x x　◇ Q x x x　♣ Q J x

I suggest passing partner's 1♡ bid despite your six points. This hand is primarily defensive, and it is extremely unlikely that keeping the bidding open will help you to get to a better contract. With your smattering of strength and spade length, it is very unlikely the opponents will get to or make any game contract. For that matter, it is very unlikely that your side has a game. Even if partner has 20 points with 5332 distribution, there is no assurance that you can make either 4♡ or 3NT, especially when the weak hand is declarer and the strong hand is exposed. I also recommend passing partner's 1♡ bid with

♠ J x x ♡ x ◇ K J 10 x x x ♣ J x x

Again the chances of making game are remote, and your best chance to play the hand in 2◇ is to pass at this point; if LHO doubles, you can bid 2◇ at your next turn. You have a good chance to buy the hand, and partner will not get too excited. Bidding 1NT instead risks a very likely 3♡ rebid from partner.

Bidding up the line?

There are not many players who, like me, have been playing bridge for almost sixty years. But players who started playing even thirty or more years ago learned to respond (and many still respond) 'up the line' when they hold two or three four-card suits. However, that's not the modern style.

Why is this so? Why would you skip over any chance to find a fit? It is because you are guarding against being preempted, while doing a little preempting yourself. In the old days there was a tendency to stay out of the bidding once the opponents had opened. Nowadays there is much more competitive bidding (and rightly so, since partscores are important, and the first side that discovers a major-suit fit often prevails when the strength is evenly divided). Suppose you hold

♠ K J x x ♡ x x ◇ A x x x ♣ x x x

and partner opens 1♣. If partner has a minimum balanced hand, you probably belong in 1NT or 2♠. If you respond 1♠, that will often shut LHO out of bidding hearts, but if you bid 1◇, LHO will frequently bid 1♡, getting a favorable lead if partner plays a notrump contract, or perhaps enabling the opponents to outbid you. Worse, if you respond 1◇ and LHO makes a preemptive overcall of 2♡, partner may be too weak either to double or bid 2♠ with a minimum hand. Now if the bidding is passed around to you, 2♠ would be a tremendous overbid; if you find a fit you can probably make 2♠, but there is no way to play there since your 2♠ bid is forcing. There is an even greater danger of being shut out of hearts if you don't bid 1♡ at your first opportunity with

♠ x x ♡ K x x x ◇ A J 10 x x ♣ x x

since if you bid 1♢ and LHO overcalls 2♠ or 3♣, partner may be shut out. (If LHO bids spades at the one-level, many players have the agreement that opener's double shows four hearts.)

About 40 years ago Richard Walsh and his disciples concluded that most hands should play in a major suit or notrump, and they skipped over minor suits. I think they carried this philosophy to an extreme since they would respond 1♠ on four small spades rather than 1♢ with ♢AKJxxx (unless they were strong enough to force to game), but the general idea was sound. As a result, if the bidding went

Opener	Oppt.	Responder	Oppt.
1♣	pass	1♢	pass
?			

opener wouldn't bid a major with

♠ A J x x ♡ K x x ♢ x x ♣ A Q x x

or even

♠ A J x x ♡ K x x x ♢ x x ♣ A J x

since he assumed that partner didn't have a four-card major (unless he was strong enough to show it later, which would be forcing to game). Opener would only rebid a major if he had a singleton or void somewhere, not with a balanced or semi-balanced hand.

What I just described is 'pure' Walsh. However, I believe that the following recommendation represents what a majority of today's experts do. *Do not* open 1♣ and rebid a major with only a three-card club suit. *Usually* rebid 1NT rather than a four-card major with a balanced hand. But with 4-2-2-5 or 2-4-2-5 distribution or with strength concentrated in two suits — like

♠ A Q J x ♡ x x ♢ x x x ♣ A K 10 x

— you should rebid your major at the one-level. There are two reasons for this. First, with two unstopped suits, if you get to a notrump contact it is better for partner to be the declarer, especially when you have a worthless doubleton in an unbid suit. Second, with such strong suits, a spade contract may be quite playable in a 4-3 fit. (Give responder

♠ K 10 x ♡ J x ♢ A K x x x ♣ Q x x

and a good partnership, upon discovering weakness in hearts, may well choose to play 4♠).

The main reason for not opening 1♣ and rebidding one of a major with only a three-card club suit is that you don't want partner to take a preference to clubs with either three or four clubs.

♠ x x   ♡ A x x   ◇ A x x x x   ♣ J x x

What do you want responder to bid with this hand after opener bids 1♣ and rebids 1♡ over a 1◇ response? Not 1NT with a worthless doubleton in spades. From responder's point of view, a preference to 2♣ looks best. After all, opener might have five or six clubs while he is not likely to hold more than four hearts. If opener holds

♠ K J x x   ♡ Q x x x   ◇ K x   ♣ A x x

then 2♣ will not be a very elegant contract. It would be bad enough if opener held

♠ K J x   ♡ Q x x x   ◇ K x   ♣ A x x x

with which I, along with many people, recommend a 1NT rebid.

My comment about the Walsh players carrying their theory to an extreme implies that with a weak four-card major and a good diamond suit, e.g.

♠ x x   ♡ J x x x   ◇ A Q x x x   ♣ Q x

I would bid 1◇ over 1♣. But wouldn't this cause us to miss our 4-4 heart fit when opener rebids 1NT with

♠ K 10 x   ♡ K x x x   ◇ K x   ♣ A J x x

Yes, it would! But bridge is a game of percentages. When there is no 4-4 heart fit, the 14-point hand, with tenaces, will often make an extra trick in a notrump contract, as compared to when the weaker hand is declarer. I already mentioned the problem that responder might take a preference to clubs with three-card support. Also, it is harder for the opponents to defend well when you rebid 1NT rather then showing your four-card major — sometimes the opponents lead your suit when you haven't warned them by bidding it. Finally, when the hands are both balanced, the 4-4 major fit does not always play better than 1NT, and you have to play a trick higher. There are many advantages to bidding notrump with a balanced hand and letting partner, if he is unbalanced, look for a suit fit.

The following example shows what can go wrong when you bid 'up the line.'

Partner	Me
♠ A Q x x	♠ K J x
♡ x x x	♡ x x x
◇ Q J x	◇ A K x
♣ A x x	♣ K J x x

Partner opened 1♣. Also, we were playing a 2NT response as invitational, rather than forcing, so that was not an alternative; if I bid notrump, I would have to bid 3NT. I preferred, if the contract was to be 3NT, for partner to be the declarer, and it would be really embarrassing to bid 3NT and find him with a singleton heart. So I bid 1◇. Partner rebid 1♠ and I bid 2♡, fourth suit forcing. Partner bid 3◇, and now I visualized him with 4-1-3-5 distribution — or just possibly 4-2-3-4 with concentrated values in his suits and no heart stopper. At matchpoints I might have bid 3♠, looking for a 4-3 fit, but at IMPs, it would be weird never to support clubs. So I bid 5♣ to show good clubs, hoping that with the right hand partner would bid 6♣. Needless to say, this was a terrible contract, while 3NT was cold unless the opponents could take the first five heart tricks.

Partner violated two rules. He bid clubs and then spades with only three clubs, and he didn't rebid 1NT with a balanced hand. I could have raised immediately to 2♣, an inverted minor raise, but I bid 1◇, to make it easy for him to rebid 1NT with a balanced hand. Besides, since we show stoppers after an inverted raise, we probably would have discovered we had no heart stopper and might well have got to the same contract by a different route. I still think 1♣-1◇, 1NT-3NT is the best way to bid these hands.

You may wonder why I blamed partner for not bidding notrump without a heart stopper despite not bidding notrump myself because I had no heart stopper. It was because of the bidding level. If either of us bids 1NT, there is room for further investigation. If I could bid 2NT, forcing, I might do that (but probably would not). As you will soon learn, there is a gadget that would allow opener to bid 3♡ with a singleton or void in hearts over a 2NT response, but there is no chance to discover whether partner has a balanced or unbalanced hand over a 3NT response.

Finding a 4-4 major fit is not my most important objective in life. In fact, with

♠ Q x   ♡ J x x x   ◇ K J x x   ♣ J 10 x

I would respond 1NT to partner's 1♣ opening. If we don't have a heart fit, I have a sure double stopper in spades (if a spade is led) when partner has ♠Axx and a probable double stopper when he holds ♠Kxx. The decisive factor is that a 1NT bid may preempt the opponents and keep them from bidding spades. If we have a 4-4 heart fit and partner has four or more clubs for his bid, partner is likely to be short in spades. With an eight- or nine-card spade fit the opponents might outbid us in spades if we make it easy for them. Bidding up the line, or designing a system where you never miss a 4-4 major-suit fit, may work well in a bidding contest, but bidding up the line does not work nearly as well at the table where the opponents are likely to compete.

Here is still another situation where I think it best not to bid the cheaper four-card major suit. Partner opens a minor and you hold

♠ A Q x x　♡ x x x x　♢ Q 10 x　♣ J x

If you play the Walsh style where partner almost never raises your response with three-card support, it probably won't cost to bid 1♡. But if partner would raise with

♠ J x　♡ K x x　♢ K x x　♣ A Q x x x

I think it is better to respond 1♠, at least at IMPs. If you find a 4-4 heart fit, you will usually do a trick better in hearts than in notrump, which is important at matchpoints, but you don't belong in a heart game unless partner is strong enough to reverse into hearts or rebid 2NT. If you bid 1♠, you are almost sure to get a plus whatever the final contract may be, while if partner raises hearts with three-card support or you get a bad break in hearts, you may lose 4 or 5 IMPs in a heart contract. Also it is possible that partner has two four-card majors, and if he has

♠ J 10 x x　♡ Q x x x　♢ x　♣ A K Q x

you want to play in spades rather than hearts.

It is also dangerous to bid a weak suit with a strong hand. Suppose partner opens 1♢ and you hold

♠ A K x　♡ 10 x x x　♢ A Q J x　♣ A x

If you bid 1♡, partner may insist upon a 6♡ contract with

♠ J　♡ A Q x x　♢ K x x x x　♣ K Q x

when 6♢, or even 6NT, would be better. (I think responder should bid 2♢ if playing inverted raises, and ignore the hearts completely.)

NEW MINOR FORCING AND CHECKBACK

The problem of missing a 4-4 major fit need only arise when responder has less than game-invitational values. With 12 or more points, or a good 11, responder can use some form of New Minor Forcing (NMF) or Checkback, and discover any 4-4 or 5-3 major fit which may have been temporarily skipped over. In the simplest form of NMF, after a one of a minor opening, a one of a major response and a 1NT rebid by opener, a bid of the other minor by responder at the two-level is artificial and asks opener to describe his hand further. With three-card support for responder's major, he bids two of that major (with a minimum opening) or three of that major with a maximum for his 1NT rebid. With only two cards in partner's major (or possibly one if it doesn't bother you to rebid 1NT with a singleton in partner's suit), opener makes the cheapest bid (except that 2♡ shows hearts when responder's first bid was 1♠) with a minimum and bids more with a maximum. For example,

Opener	Responder
1◇	1♡
1NT	2♣
?	

With

♠ Q J x   ♡ J x   ◇ K Q x x x   ♣ K J x

bid 2◇. In Walsh you are not supposed to have four spades when you rebid 1NT over 1♡, even with

♠ 10 x x x   ♡ Q x   ◇ A Q 10 x   ♣ K J x

But the really bad feature of NMF is that if the bidding goes

Opener	Responder
1♣	1♠
1NT	2◇

since 2♡ ostensibly shows a four-card heart suit, opener has to bid 2NT to show a minimum without three spades and 3NT to show a maximum. That doesn't work well when responder has something like

♠ K 10 9 x x   ♡ x   ◇ K Q x x   ♣ Q 10 9

and only wants to be in game opposite three-card spade support and a maximum (without which he would like to play in 2♠ or 2◇).

I think it is always better to play 2♣ as Checkback, no matter which minor partner opens. Eddie Kantar convinced me to play that way forty years ago and I still think it is right. You give up the chance to play 2♣ — you have to bid 3♣ directly to play in a club partscore — but the opponents seldom allow you to play 2♣ when that is the only contract you can make. Using 2♣ as Checkback gains in several ways, and while you lose 2♣ as a natural bid, you gain 2◇ (by responder) as a natural bid.

Opener's first priority is to show four of the unbid major if he has it; second priority is to show three-card support, either maximum or minimum; he bids 2◇ when lacking the appropriate major lengths. In the 2◇ auction, he doesn't have to show whether he is minimum or maximum since he can't stop short of two of responder's major or 2NT anyway. With three-card support for responder's major suit, instead of jumping to the three-level with a maximum, he can bid 2NT as an artificial bid. This leaves more room below the 3NT level for responder to further describe his hand, by showing another suit or support for opener's suit when he is interested in slam.

This is the new sequence we have available:

Opener	Responder
1♣	1♠
1NT	2♣[1]
2◇[2]	?

1. Checkback.
2. Denies three spades or four hearts.

If responder now bids two of his original major, he must have a good five-card suit or a six-card suit to want to play opposite a doubleton (or conceivably a singleton). This bid is still mildly invitational since he could have rebid his suit at the two-level directly over 1NT if he had no interest in game. If responder bids 2NT instead, opener will pass or bid 3NT, depending on how strong his hand is. Responder probably has a weak five-card suit; otherwise he would have just raised to 2NT directly over 1NT. Either the suit is too weak or the hand is too balanced for responder to want to play in his major opposite a doubleton.

With an unbalanced hand and a skimpy invitation, responder can stop at the two-level when he receives an unfavorable rebid. With

♠ K 10 9 x x   ♡ x   ◇ K Q x x x   ♣ Q x

he can pass 2◇, knowing that will be the safest contract when opener has only five cards in the majors. With

♠ K J x x x x   ♡ x   ◇ A J x   ♣ x x x

he can issue an invitation by bidding 2♣ followed by 2♠ rather than an immediate 3♠. (Playing old-fashioned NMF, opener bids 2NT to show a maximum with fewer than three spades and without four hearts.) After the 2♣ Checkback bid, new suits are forcing, and if responder jump rebids his suit, it is forcing since

Opener	Responder
1♣	1♠
1NT	3♠

would have been invitational. A checkback 2♣ followed by 2♡ from responder is forcing for one round since he could have bid 2♡ directly over 1NT to show a weak hand with both majors, and a 3♣ rebid is forcing since responder could have signed off in clubs by bidding 3♣ directly over 1NT.

In Southern California, two-way Checkback seems to be the most popular choice. The original concept was that a 2♣ rebid over 1NT showed an invitational hand unless responder intended to pass 2◇. Opener was forced to rebid 2◇ and the next bid showed what kind of invitation responder had. A 2◇ rebid over 1NT was game-forcing and the bidding was natural after that. These are some of the good features of this method:

You can play 2◇ when responder has a weak hand with long diamonds. You can distinguish between good suits and bad suits. With

♠ A Q J x x   ♡ K Q J x x   ◇ J x   ♣ x

you can respond 1♠ and rebid 3♡. With

♠ K J x x x   ♡ A J x x x   ◇ x   ♣ A x

you can rebid 2◇ as a game force and bid hearts later (even though opener denied a four-card heart suit by not rebidding 2♡ over 2◇).

If you hold

♠ A Q J 10 x x   ♡ A x   ◇ x x   ♣ K x x

you can respond 1♠ and rebid 3♠ over a 1NT rebid to show good spades, and you can bid 2◇ followed by 3♠ with

♠ A J x x x x   ♡ A x x   ◇ A x   ♣ x x.

Jumps should be forcing since you could rebid 2♣ on all invitational hands. However some people play just the opposite.They play jumps as invitational since if you wanted to force to game you would have bid 2◇ over 1NT. I don't like the latter variation.

The disadvantage of playing two-way Checkback is that opener's forced 2◇ rebid over 2♣ doesn't provide any distributional information. So far as locating a trump suit is concerned, it just wastes half a round of bidding. In the following sequence:

Opener	Responder
1♣	1♠
1NT	2♣
2◇	2♠

does responder show 11 points with a good five-card suit? A longer suit with fewer points? A balanced or unbalanced hand? Some players try to solve this problem by rebidding two of responder's major over 2♣ with three-card support rather than making an automatic 2◇ bid.

This has been a rather long-winded discussion of the reasons I don't like two-way Checkback. My own preference is for Eddie Kantar's idea: always use 2♣ as Checkback.

FOURTH SUIT FORCING

When the bidding goes

Opener	Responder
1◇	1♠
2♣	2♡

what does 2♡ show? In this particular sequence no one can tell. Responder might have hearts and he might not. The modern interpretation is that if he bids 2♡ here, there is an inference that responder probably has neither a heart suit nor a heart stopper for notrump!

Why does bidding the fourth suit, hearts in this case, suggest that he doesn't have hearts? Because (a) if he had a *four*-card heart suit, he would not expect partner to have four-card support after bidding both minors, presumably showing at least nine cards in the minors; and (b) if he had either four hearts or a stopper in hearts, and was strong enough to make an encouraging bid, he would probably bid either 2NT or 3NT, depending on his overall strength. The only time he will have real hearts is when he holds a two-suiter, probably 6-5 or 5-5 in the majors.

With very few specific exceptions, a jump by responder on the second round is invitational rather than forcing. Some examples are

Opener	Responder	Opener	Responder	Opener	Responder
1♣	1♡	1♣	1♡	1♣	1♡
1♠	3♣	1♠	3♡	1♠	3♠

Since these are not forcing sequences, what does responder do when his hand is too strong for a mere invitation? He bids the fourth suit and follows up with a bid showing why he wanted to force. When the bidding starts

Opener	Responder
1♣	1♡
1♠	?

responder might hold

♠ A x   ♡ K J x x x   ◇ J x   ♣ A J x x

A 3♣ bid directly over 1♠ would not be forcing, so he has to bid 2◇, planning to bid 3♣ next round. With a strong one-suiter he may have to make a fourth-suit bid followed by a jump. In the same auction, with

♠ K x   ♡ K Q x x x x   ◇ A x x   ♣ Q x

responder is too strong to risk stopping under game, but his suit is not good enough to play 4♡ opposite a singleton or void. Since 3♡ would not be forcing, responder must bid 2◇ followed by 3♡ to give opener a choice of game contracts.

Note that when the unopposed bidding goes

Opener	Responder
1♣	1♦
1♡	1♠

the 1♠ bid is not considered fourth suit forcing, but presumably shows spades and is forcing for one round. Instead, a jump to 2♠ is fourth suit forcing (and because of the level, *forcing to game*).

There is a box to be checked on your convention card to say whether fourth suit is forcing for one round or forcing to game. According to *Bridge World* Standard, it is just forcing for one round, and that is my choice also. After the first two rounds in all of these sequences, such as

Opener	Responder
1♣	1♡
1♠	2♦

if opener bids 2♡, 2♠ or 2NT, these bids are therefore invitational rather than forcing. Suppose responder holds

♠ Q x x   ♡ K J x x x   ♦ J x x   ♣ A x

What can he bid over 1♠? Yes, 2NT is right on strength, but the diamond 'stopper' is a bit skimpy. If opener bids 2♡ (probably with a doubleton honor or three small), or 2NT (minimum balanced hand with a diamond stopper), responder can and should pass. With perhaps only 24 points and no fit (and probably a single stopper in diamonds), it will be hard to take nine tricks. A plus score on this board should be well above average since many pairs won't have the machinery or discipline to stop under game. The way I play, if opener has something like

♠ A J x x   ♡ x x   ♦ A K x x   ♣ x x x

(no club stopper, no heart support, nothing he hasn't already shown) he should bid 2♠, the cheapest bid, allowing responder to pass or bid 2NT, which opener would pass. Later we will consider 'default' bids in more detail.

Remember, however, that the purpose of bidding fourth suit forcing is often to make a forcing bid later. Since

Opener	Responder
1♣	1♡
1♠	3♣

would be invitational,

Opener	Responder
1♣	1♡
1♠	2◇
2♡	3♣

must be forcing. According to *Bridge World* Standard,

Opener	Responder
1◇	1♠
2♣	3♡

is forcing, while

Opener	Responder
1◇	1♠
2♣	2♡
2NT	3♡

is not. Paul Soloway suggested reversing that procedure and having the first auction show an invitational 5-5 or 6-5. Opener can pass, and responder is allowed to pass a preference to 3♠. When the fourth-suit bid is *not* a jump, according to Paul all bids at the three-level are forcing to game. With a good hand responder wants more room since he might be interested in slam, and it will help him to hear opener's rebid.

What I have just described is the 'standard' way to play fourth suit forcing. According to *Bridge World* polls, partner of the fourth-suit bidder needs at least Jxx of the fourth suit to bid notrump, and preferably better than that. If the bidding starts

Opener	Responder
1♣	1♡
1♠	2◇

responder has at least invitational values, and opener with

♠ K Q x x   ♡ A x x   ◇ x   ♣ A J x x x

should bid 3♡, both to avoid being passed in 2♡ and to describe his hand in case responder is interested in slam. In fact, he should probably make the same bid with one fewer club and one more diamond. After a fourth-suit bid, any jump by either partner is forcing. When the fourth suit bid is at the three-level, e.g.

Opener	Responder
1♡	1♠
2◇	3♣

it is forcing to game. But if you play Soloway's way, the fourth-suit *jump* to the three-level is not.

Note that in all my examples, responder's first bid was at the one-level. I haven't discussed two-over-one bids yet, but after a two-over-one response to a major (except for responder rebidding his own suit), I play any below-game bid by responder as forcing (with rare exceptions to be discussed later). Consequently there is little need for fourth suit forcing after a two-over-one response, and it should not be used when there is some natural bid that would be more descriptive. Also, it is illogical for a passed hand to drive to game. Consequently, fourth-suit bids by a passed hand are natural (and non-forcing). They usually show 6-5 in the two suits or, if only 5-5, very strong suits. There is much more to say about fourth suit forcing, but I shall return to the subject in the next chapter after discussing two-over-one sequences.

XYZ

There is an alternative method of describing these difficult responding hands after a one-over-one response, called XYZ. The concept was created by California's Joe Kivel and involves transfers. It is not a simple convention, however, because when responder makes a transfer bid, opener does not have to accept the transfer. However, if you understand the purpose of the convention and generally how it works, you can figure out what to do and not have to rely on memory alone.

If, in an uncontested auction, opener's second bid is at the one-level, the convention applies. According to Joe, there are ten such uncontested auctions: 1♣-1◇, 1♡; 1♣-1◇, 1♠; 1♣-1◇, 1NT; 1♣-1♡, 1♠; 1♣-1♡, 1NT; 1♣-1♠, 1NT; 1◇-1♡, 1♠; 1◇-1♡, 1NT; 1◇-1♠, 1NT; 1♡-1♠, 1NT. In each of these three-bid auctions, the first bid is called X; the second is called Y and the third is called Z. In addition to these ten sequences, there are many more when the opponents compete. In this case doubles and redoubles by opener or responder count as Y or Z bids. For example, these are all XYZ sequences:

Opener	Oppt.	Responder	Oppt.
1♣	dbl	1♡	dbl
redbl			

Opener	Oppt.	Responder	Oppt.
1♣	1♡	dbl	pass
1♠			

Opener	Oppt.	Responder	Oppt.
1♣	1♠	dbl	redbl
1NT			

After an XYZ sequence, 2♣ by responder is a transfer to diamonds and shows either a desire to play 2◊ or an invitational hand of some kind if responder bids again. An immediate 2◊ by responder is artificial and forcing to game. This is a lot like two-way Checkback, the difference being that opener doesn't have to bid 2◊ over 2♣. This makes sense, because after a 1NT rebid responder knows much more about opener's hand than opener knows about responder's hand, and if he asks opener to bid 2◊, opener must comply. After a suit rebid, opener's hand is not yet closely limited as to strength or distribution, and if he would not pass a natural, non-forcing 2◊ rebid from responder, he can make his normal bid over 2♣. So if the first four bids were

Opener	Responder
1♣	1◊
1♠	2♣
?	

opener would bid 3♣ with

$$♠ A Q x x \quad ♡ A x \quad ◊ x \quad ♣ A Q 10 x x x$$

and 3◊ with

$$♠ A x x x \quad ♡ x x \quad ◊ K Q x \quad ♣ A K x x$$

and so on[1].

After this start:

Opener	Responder
1♣	1♡
1♠	?

2♡ would be weak and 2NT would be invitational with a balanced hand. If responder bids 2♣ on the second round and 2NT on the third round, it shows roughly the same strength as a direct 2NT, but is more unbalanced, perhaps with

$$♠ x \quad ♡ Q x x x \quad ◊ K J x \quad ♣ K Q x x x$$

and if opener also has a weakness somewhere he might look for a better spot than 3NT. Some people play that in this sequence responder guarantees four clubs.

Two disadvantages of any of these Checkback conventions are that you can no longer play in a 2♣ contract and that someone might double the artificial 2♣ bid for a lead. In my opinion a more serious disadvantage is

---

1.   In Chapter 4, you will see that I recommend opening 4432 hands with one of a minor when the hand includes four spades (not hearts) and a worthless doubleton, even when it falls within the range for a notrump opening.

that responder can't take a preference to clubs with a weak or mediocre hand. When the bidding starts with

Opener	Responder
1♣	1♡
1♠	

what can responder bid with either of these hands:

♠ J x   ♡ A J x x x   ◇ x x x   ♣ Q x x

♠ J x x   ♡ A Q 10 x   ◇ x x   ♣ 10 x x x

Opener promises at least four clubs in this sequence, and 3♣ would be an attempt to sign off in clubs. But neither 1NT nor 3♣ appeals to me — if opener has a suit-oriented hand, I want to be able to bid a natural 2♣. If the 'Z' bid is 1NT, I prefer to play only 2♣ as the checkback bid for the reasons previously stated.

One of the advantages of the convention is that, with suits other than clubs, you can often sign off at the two-level rather than the three-level. Look at these hands:

Opener	Responder
♠ A Q x x	♠ K x x x
♡ x x x	♡ A Q x x
◇ x x	◇ Q J x
♣ A Q x x	♣ x x

Standard bidding would be

Opener	Responder
1♣	1♡
1♠	3♠
pass	

XYZ bidding would be

Opener	Responder
1♣	1♡
1♠	2♣
2◇	2♠
pass	

Note that 3♠ in the Standard auction is by no means safe. Also you can find out about your fit (or non-fit) at a low level, leaving more room for slam investigation.

So as with everything, there are pros and cons. Although my preference is *not* to play XYZ, I have tried to present both sides fairly so that you can make your own choice.

RAISING PARTNER'S MAJOR

For the purposes of the following discussion, assume that you are playing five-card major openings in first and second position and a forcing notrump response.

Some players play 'constructive' raises of major suits; that usually means 8-10 points, counting something for ruffing values. Others, including me, don't claim to be playing constructive raises, but with a minimum or sub-minimum balanced hand they bid 1NT anyway (a less encouraging response) and take a preference back to opener's suit, which purportedly shows 6-10 points with two trumps but may instead be 5-6 points with a balanced hand and three- or four-card support.

According to so-called Standard bidding, a double raise is a limit raise, showing a good 10 to a poor 12 points with at least four-card support. The key here is proper hand evaluation. Over a 1♡ opening, this hand

$$♠ J x x \quad ♡ K Q J x \quad ◇ Q x x \quad ♣ J x x$$

is far too weak for a limit raise. Unless you get a 4-0 trump break your ♡KQJx is probably worth no more than ♡KQxx, and your unguarded honors may all turn out to be worthless. Change your ♣J to the ♣Q, and the hand is still worth only a single raise. Change your hand to either of these:

$$♠ A x x \quad ♡ K x x x \quad ◇ K 10 x \quad ♣ x x x$$

$$♠ A x x \quad ♡ Q x x x \quad ◇ x x \quad ♣ K 10 9 x$$

and the hand is easily worth a limit raise.

Responder can show a three-card limit raise (needing a little extra in high card points to compensate for having only three trumps) by bidding a forcing notrump and taking a jump preference to the three-level in opener's first suit. However, if responder has passed originally, a 1NT response is not forcing (and, in my opinion, should not even be semi-forcing). Drury or Reverse Drury (explained later) can take care of all invitational hands with support for opener's major, and there is no need for a forcing or semi-forcing notrump.

Game tries over a major raise

Suppose the bidding has started with one of these simple sequences:

Opener	Responder	Opener	Responder
1♠	2♠	1♡	2♡

Of course opener may pass now with a poor hand or jump straight to game with a really good one, but if he is uncertain, how does he make a game try? The 'standard' way is to make a 'help-suit' game try. He bids the suit where partner's holding is most important, usually where he wants partner's strength to be, although a singleton with four-card trump support may be equally valuable. At one time 'short-suit' game tries, where opener bids his singleton or void, were also popular. Bob Hamman claims that the short-suit game try is his favorite convention — provided it is used by his opponents! It makes the defense extremely easy. Others suggested two-way game tries: the cheapest bid might initiate a short-suit game try sequence while other bids were help-suit game tries.

I think the following method, combining three types of game try, is far better. In most sequences opener (who will be the declarer) provides no information about his distribution. Usually responder doesn't need it, and it only helps the opponents, not only on opening lead but also throughout the rest of the hand.

The first game try is a simple raise to the three-level:

Opener	Responder		Opener	Responder
1♠	2♠		1♡	2♡
3♠			3♡	

These bids say, 'I have (or I am pretending to have) weak trumps. So don't take me to game unless you have very good trump support. Nothing but good trumps (and aces) will be of any value to me.' About two-thirds of the time when opener makes this bid, he actually has good trumps himself! After a single raise, when he holds

♠ A K Q x x x   ♡ x x   ◇ x x   ♣ Q J x

or a similar hand with hearts (especially with hearts!) he has little defense, and he wants to make it difficult for the opponents to compete with a reopening bid or double. Partner won't have good trumps when you have good trumps, so he won't accept your 'invitation.' This is a modified one-two-three-stop approach. But opener *could* hold

♠ J x x x x   ♡ A K   ◇ K Q 10 x x   ♣ x

In that case, if responder holds ♠KQxx or ♠Q10xx with a side ace, he will raise to game. But if he has the king-queen-jack of clubs and the queen-jack of hearts, he will realize they are worthless cards. Needless to say, responder must alert the opponents to the two possibilities.

The second type of game try is with a true two-suiter. After a raise of his 1♠ bid, opener holds one of these hands:

♠ A Q x x x   ♡ A Q 10 x x   ◇ J x   ♣ x

♠ A x x x x x   ♡ Q J 9 x x   ◇ —   ♣ K x

If responder holds both major-suit kings, you belong in game. So you bid

3♡ (the only sequence where opener describes his distribution) and partner knows that honors in your two suits plus aces figure to be useful, while all other high cards are of dubious value.

The third type of game try is used for all other invitational hands, whether they are balanced or unbalanced. These auctions

Opener	Responder		Opener	Responder
1♠	2♠		1♡	2♡
2NT			2♠	

both say, 'I am interested in game. If you have a poor raise, sign off in three of our suit. If you have a good raise, bid game. If you have an in-between hand, bid the cheapest suit in which you would *reject* a short-suit game try.' That is roughly equivalent to saying, 'Show me where you have a concentration of strength.' So for example, after 2NT, responder's 3♢ says, 'If you made a short-suit game try in clubs, I would accept. If you made a short-suit game try in diamonds, I would reject.' Responder might hold

♠ Q x x   ♡ K x x   ♢ K J x x   ♣ x x x

Most of the time, that is all opener needs to know. On rare occasions, he can now bid 3♡ to ask, 'Would you accept a short-suit game try in hearts?' However, opener might not have a short suit. He might hold something like

♠ A K x x x x   ♡ K x   ♢ A x x   ♣ J x

so that when responder bids 3♢, opener likes his hand. He will probably find (among other values) the diamond king or queen (or better still, two diamond honors) in his partner's hand, and he would rather partner have honors in diamonds than honors in the other two suits. So if opener bids game over 3♢, the opponents don't know whether it is because (a) he would have accepted a short-suit game try in clubs, or (b) because he has scattered strength and a good enough hand to bid game if responder was strong enough to accept any game try, or (c) whether he had

♠ A Q x x x x   ♡ K J x x   ♢ —   ♣ A K x

and thought he might have a slam until he got the disappointing diamond response, showing a duplication of values. Incidentally, if the bidding goes

Opener	Responder
1♡	2♡
2♠	2NT

responder is saying, 'I would have rejected a short-suit game try in spades.' He can't bid 3♠ to reject a short-suit game try in spades, since the 3♠ bid would force the bidding to game. Similarly

Opener	Responder
1♡	2♡
2NT	

shows a two-suiter with spades being the other suit.

Drury

The Drury convention, a bid of 2♣ over partner's third- or fourth-seat major-suit opening, is used to show a limit raise or better with three or more trumps. Some players play two-way Drury where 2♣ shows four-card or longer trump support and 2♢ shows three-card support (or vice versa). Still others play some form of Drury and also 'fit-jump' bids at the three-level, and they play all of their Drury-type bids in competition. For example

West	North	East	South
pass	pass	1♠	2♣
dbl			

shows that without the overcall West would have bid 2♣; 2♢ is still three-card Drury, etc. I think the simple 2♣ version is sufficient to show an invitational hand in support of partner's suit since various follow-ups can determine both opener's and responder's degrees of enthusiasm. I don't want to give up several natural calls in an effort to increase the effectiveness of my raise system by 1% (even if it would accomplish that objective).

When Eric Murray and Sami Kehela first popularized Drury, it just showed a maximum for having passed, but not necessarily a fit. Opener's 2♢ rebid said he had a sub-minimum opening, and the bidding was natural after that, with responder pulling in his horns a bit. The way it is invariably played now is called 'Reverse Drury,' and it promises at least three-card trump support. A rebid of opener's suit shows a sub-minimum hand, or conceivably a rock-bottom minimum with only a four-card suit. A 2♢ rebid is artificial and guarantees a normal opening bid; however, there is no general agreement on the meaning of subsequent auctions. What follows is my own suggestion.

Because 2♣ guarantees a fit, this kind of auction is frequent:

Opener	responder
	Pass
1♠	2♣
4♠	

This tells the opponents nothing about opener's distribution. It just says, 'You invited me to game and I accept.' After the 2♢ rebid (which means that opener is uncertain), responder usually bids two of the major, but with a super-passed hand, he too can go straight to game. With an average-plus hand (for the Drury bid) and four trumps, and no singleton or void, he can bid three of the major, strongly inviting a game, and with a good hand including a singleton or void, he can bid the singleton or void at the three-level (or at the two-level if his shortage is in spades). This permits opener to evaluate the fit.

There is another possibility. After opener rebids 2◇ and responder bids two of opener's major, opener can make a game try with 2♠ (over hearts) or 2NT (over spades) as described above (but with a different range, of course). When responder bids Drury over 1♠, a 2♡ rebid by opener is natural and forcing. It costs nothing to show responder his second suit (except for making the defense easier) and responder might jump straight to game with

$$♠ Q\ 10\ x\ x \quad ♡ K\ x \quad ◇ A\ x\ x \quad ♣ x\ x\ x\ x$$

since his hand is very good opposite a major two-suiter.

It is not at all farfetched for opener to be interested in a slam after a Drury response.

If opener rebids three of his major, he shows an interest in slam, not just game, and a 2NT bid over a Drury 2♣ has a similar implication. Jumping to three of the major asks responder to show a source of tricks, like KQxxx, and 2NT asks for short suits — responder would show a short suit at a minimum level with three trumps and jump (like a normal splinter) with four trumps. If opener jumps in a new suit, he shows a powerful two-suited hand so that responder can tell which of his high cards will be valuable and which will not.

Bergen and Jacoby raises

Larry Cohen and Marty Bergen have both written about the Law of Total Tricks. Both contend that when you discover a nine-card fit you can 'safely' bid to the three-level. The rationale is that if you can't make nine tricks, the opponents can probably make something in a suit of their own. Therefore they urge you to bid to the three-level before the opponents get into the bidding and find a fit. Consequently, when opener bids a five-card major and responder has four-card trump support, Bergen advocates an immediate three-level bid.

Playing Bergen major-suit raises, a single raise is constructive and shows three-card support. When holding only three-card support and 6 or 7 points, responder bids 1NT (forcing) and, in most sequences, takes a simple preference to opener's major suit. With a bad hand (0 to 6 HCP) and four-card support, responder jumps to three of opener's major as a preempt. With a constructive four-card raise (7 to 9+ HCP), responder bids 3♣. With a limit raise and four-card support, he bids 3◇ .

With a balanced hand, opening bid values and four-card support, responder bids 2NT. Oswald and Jim Jacoby first suggested this idea, which gives the partners a lot of room for slam investigation. You may have noticed that I said a 2NT response shows a balanced hand. Some players pay no attention to this restriction. Since there is no way to show a single-ton or void later, I don't see how they can get by with this (unless respon-der holds something like

♠ A x x x   ♡ x   ◇ A K Q J x   ♣ K Q x

and intends to take control of the bidding later and just bids Jacoby to set the trump suit for Keycard Blackwood). Over the 2NT bid a new suit at the three-level *by opener* shows a singleton or void, and a jump in a new suit to the four-level shows 5-5 distribution. Some people say that the jump must show a *good* five-card side suit. I think it is more important for it to deny two quick losers elsewhere. With

♠ A Q x x x   ♡ Q x   ◇ x   ♣ K Q x x x

you should just bid 3◇ to show your singleton. With

♠ A Q x x x   ♡ K x   ◇ x   ♣ K 10 x x x

you should bid 4♣. The rationale for this treatment is that when opener shows a five-card suit at the four-level and denies two quick outside losers, responder can evaluate his hand. Aces and honors in opener's two suits will be valuable; other honors are often worthless. Cohen and Bergen play different responses: opener's 3◇ shows any singleton (except in the agreed major, of course) and a not very good hand; 3♣ shows any singleton with a better hand. If responder wants to know where the singleton is, he can ask by making the next cheapest bid.

Over the 2NT response, opener's weakest rebid is four of his suit, with 3NT showing a medium balanced hand and three of the agreed major showing a good balanced hand. Since the 2NT response is unlimited, I don't really like the jump to game to show the weakest hand. Even the weakest hand may be enough for a slam if the honors mesh. I once sug-gested that opener's initial rebid should simply show whether he had an absolute minimum or somewhat more. Then responder could ask for a fur-ther description of strength and distribution if he was still interested in slam. Not showing his distribution (or even whether he had a balanced or unbalanced hand unless the hands are within the possible slam range and responder decides to ask for more information) would conceal opener's hand and make the defense more difficult. However, my suggestion did not go over well with my friends and partners: for one thing, it was very com-plicated and perhaps not worth the mental effort. So I gave up, but I do suggest that a regular partnership work out something along these lines.

Now let us return to our discussion of Bergen raises. The main feature of Bergen raises is jumping to the three-level with four-card support, whether the overall strength is poor, mediocre, or good. My first reaction was that it was a mistake to commit to playing in 3♠ with 7 to 9 points. When you are down one, even if the opponents can make a three-level contract, they won't always be able to bid it. But it does help you to tell whether to bid game or not and/or how high to compete if the opponents bid. You can show more ranges: preemptive, constructive, limit, and forcing instead of just forcing, limit and worse (without showing whether you have three- or four-card support). Incidentally, I may treat four-card support for partner in a 4-3-3-3 hand as three-card support. If partner opens 1♠ and I hold

♠ J x x x   ♡ K x x   ◇ K x x   ♣ J 10 x

I raise to 2♠ rather than bidding 3♣. When my hand is balanced, the other hands tend to be balanced also (this is not superstition on my part — it is really true), and no one can make as much as you would normally expect. So you will often be down one at the three-level, when the opponents cannot make nine tricks of their own (and are unlikely, with balanced hands, to get into the bidding at this level).

The main advantage of Bergen raises is that, if it is the opponents' hand, it is very dangerous for one of them to enter the bidding at the three- or four-level. If he does bid, it is hard for his partner to know whether to raise with 7 or 8 points. However, there is one thing you should know about Bergen raises: they don't go well with two-over-one forcing to game. There should be some way for responder to show a long suit with an invitational hand, as compared to a long suit with a weak hand. According to *Bridge World* Standard, when partner opens 1♡ you would bid 1NT followed by 3◇ (over his 2♡ rebid) with

♠ x x   ♡ x   ◇ Q J 9 8 x x x   ♣ K J x

and 2◇ followed by 3◇ with a stronger hand that is more suitable for notrump. As you will soon become aware, some two-over-one forcing-to-game bidders jump to the three-level immediately to show an invitational one-suiter. Over 1♠ they would bid 3◇ (rather than 2◇ and then 3◇) with

♠ x x   ♡ A x   ◇ K Q J 9 x x   ♣ x x x

and 3♡ (rather than 2♡ and then 3♡) with

♠ x   ♡ K J 10 9 x x   ◇ K x x   ♣ Q J x

If you play a rebid of responder's suit by him as invitational rather than forcing after an initial two-over-one, there is no conflict between Bergen raises and *Bridge World* Standard, but you are in lots of trouble if your two-over-one is unconditionally forcing to game.

Other responses to a major-suit opening

Almost everyone today plays splinter bids over a major-suit opening. After a 1♠ opening, 4♣, 4♢ and 4♡ all show a singleton or void with spade support and roughly the same strength as a 2NT response (except that a 2NT bid denies a singleton or void). So what should a 3NT response over 1♠ or a 3♠ response over 1♡ show?

Some people claim that 3NT over either major shows 13-15 points with, depending on your agreement, either two- or three-card support for partner's major. However, there is no way to find out whether 3NT or four of the major is the superior contract. I think it best to use this bid instead to show a mini-splinter. Suppose partner opens 1♠ and you hold

♠ Q x x x x   ♡ x   ♢ Q J x x   ♣ K J x

That may or may not be enough to make game, depending upon the degree of fit, but I can't imagine bidding so delicately as to stop short of game. If partner has

♠ K J x x x   ♡ J 10 x   ♢ K x x   ♣ A x

you are cold for game, and if he has a very good hand you might have a slam. You can use 3♠ over 1♡ and 3NT over 1♠ to show this type of hand, and if partner is interested, he can ask where your singleton or void is. For example,

Opener	Responder
1♡	3♠
3NT	

asks where the shortness is, and a 4♡ response shows that the singleton is in spades. Over 1♡, 3NT shows a regular splinter, not a mini-splinter, in spades, perhaps with

♠ x   ♡ K Q x x   ♢ Q x x x   ♣ A J x x

When one hand has 5332 distribution and the other has 4333 distribution (the four-card suit not being partner's five-card suit), 3NT is usually a better contract than four of the major. I have no statistics to prove this assertion, but that is what my experience tells me. It is quite likely that, with no ruffing value, you can make as many tricks in notrump as in the major. If the same number of tricks happens to be nine, 3NT is definitely superior. So how can you tell when one hand has 5332 distribution and the other has 4333?

In the old days the bidding might start 1♠-2NT (natural, 13-15). With 5332 (or 4432) opener would rebid 3NT. With 5422 distribution opener would rebid his four-card side suit instead; responder would bid 3♠, showing three-card support (or possibly a strong doubleton in spades with a weakness in one of the unbid suits), and the bidders could make an intelligent choice between 3NT and 4♠. Now, of course, the 2NT bid is no longer natural, but Jacoby.

So how can responder, with 4333 or occasionally 4432 — the doubleton being in opener's suit — offer opener a choice of contracts? By bidding 1NT, forcing. On the next round he will usually bid 3NT with a doubleton spade (or conceivably a singleton). But a jump in the other major, e.g.

Opener	Responder	Opener	Responder
1♠	1NT	1♡	1NT
2♣	3♡	2♦	3♠

is forcing and shows a balanced hand, purportedly with three-card support for opener's major. Occasionally responder can bid this way with strong two-card support to suggest that four of opener's major might be better. For example,

♠ K J   ♡ J x x   ◇ K Q x x   ♣ A x x x

Opener	Responder
1♠	1NT
2◇	?

opener might have a singleton (or worthless doubleton) in either hearts or clubs, in which case 4♠ might be a superior contract. Responder should bid 3♡, purportedly showing three spades. Why wouldn't 3♡ in this sequence show an invitational hand in hearts? Because with an invitational hand in hearts responder would have bid 2♡ and then 3♡, the latter bid being non-forcing. (This will be explained when we get to Chapter 3.)

What do you think these auctions show:

Opener	Responder	Opener	Responder
1♠	1NT	1♡	1NT
2◇	4NT	2♣	3♠
		3NT/4♠	4NT

These sequences would be similar to bidding

Opener	Responder
1maj	2NT
3NT	4NT

in the old days. The 2NT response was game-forcing, usually a balanced 13-15, and 4NT (the Miles convention) corrected that to a good 18 or 19 points. The second sequence above would guarantee three-card heart support, which could be important if opener's hearts were just headed by two top honors (AQxxx opposite Kxx is much more likely to take five tricks than AQxxx opposite Kx). I have to admit this is my own idea and not a treatment widely adopted. But why not? If you are playing a forcing notrump, why not use it?

Here is another treatment where I differ from the mainstream. Partner opens a major in third or fourth position and you hold a good 11 or bad 12 balanced points (or perhaps something like

♠ J   ♡ K J x   ◊ K x x x   ♣ A 10 x x x

when the opening bid was 1♠). I think you should bid 2NT, which denies three or more of partner's suit (with which you would start with Drury). 'What if partner has opened light in third or fourth seat?' people ask. Too bad! I am not afraid to get too high occasionally in an effort to bid to game. Why should this sequence be treated differently? Most players would bid 1NT. Then opener, with 14 points, can bid a three-card minor to give responder another chance, and responder can now bid 2NT or 3NT. The result of this treatment is that when opener holds

♠ A x x x x   ♡ A   ◊ x x   ♣ K x x x

he is reluctant to bid 2♣ over a 1NT response to get to a safer contract for fear that responder will bid 2NT or 3NT, getting to an even more dangerous contract. Since most players say there is no hand where you should bid 2NT by a passed hand as a natural bid, they invent some exotic meaning such as 5-5 in the minors or the sort of hand with which I would bid 3♣ since 2♣ would be Drury:

♠ x   ♡ K x   ◊ Q x x x   ♣ K Q 10 x x x

You have to rebid a three-card minor sometimes when partner bids a forcing notrump, but when partner bids 1NT as a passed hand, I think a rebid of a new suit should guarantee at least a four-card suit and an unbalanced hand.

Bidding opposite a passed hand

Having concluded this brief excursion, I shall return to the mainstream. Suppose you open 1♠ in third or fourth position and partner bids either 2♡ or 2◊. Neither bid is forcing, and if you have a minimum opening with at least two-card support, you should probably pass. Even with a singleton, it may be right to pass, unless you have a good suit of your own. Suppose you hold

♠ A K x x x x   ♡ x   ◊ A J x   ♣ x x x

With a six-card major and a full opening bid you don't want to pass partner's 2♡ bid. Since he failed to open a weak two-bid, he is far more likely to have five good hearts than to have six or seven. Is your 2♠ rebid forcing? I don't see why it should be. Partner has less than an opening bid and you haven't found a fit. If the two hands are

♠ A K x x x x   ♠ x x
♡ x   ♡ K Q 10 x x
◇ A J x   ◇ K x
♣ x x x   ♣ Q 10 x x

where do you want to play? Some players would bid 1NT over 1♠ with this hand, but I would be delighted to have the opportunity to show a good heart suit without overstating my strength. And with

♠ x   ♡ A J x x   ◇ K 10 9 x x x   ♣ J x

I'd be glad I could make a natural, non-forcing 2◇ bid. Opposite a 2◇ response, opener, with

♠ Q 10 x x x   ♡ K x   ◇ A Q x   ♣ K x x

could bid 3NT, gambling on finding his partner with six diamonds to the king and an outside ace. While playing as I recommend, he would pass a 1NT response. Opposite any passed hand two-over-one response, opener must bid the full value of his hand. Opposite a 2♡ response by a non-passed hand, he would raise to 3♡ (forcing) with

♠ A K x x x   ♡ A J x   ◇ x   ♣ Q x x x

But the latter hand is much too strong to bid anything other than 4♡ when partner is a passed hand. With one more diamond and one fewer club, a raise to 3♡ would be just right.

If a passed hand makes a one-over-one response in a major suit, opener should pass with a sub-minimum hand or even a bad 13 points with three-card support and a ruffing value like

♠ J x x   ♡ K x   ◇ A J x x x   ♣ K J x

if the response was 1♠. If you raise to 2♠ there is a greater chance of getting too high than of getting to a good game. Likewise, if you rebid 1NT there is a chance of getting too high or of taking one fewer trick. Change the spades to ♠Q10x and you would raise to 2♠ since you might belong in game opposite a distributional hand such as

♠ K J x x x   ♡ x x   ◇ x   ♣ A Q x x x

Also the raise makes it more difficult for the opponents to enter the bidding. If your hand were

♠ J x x   ♡ K Q x   ◇ A J 10 x   ♣ x x x

you should definitely pass. You don't know whether spades or notrump would be better, but the more important factor is that you don't want your partner to raise to 2NT.

BART

When the bidding goes

Opener	Responder
1♠	1NT[1]
2♣	?

1. Forcing.

what should responder bid now with

♠ x x ♡ K J 10 x x ◇ A x x ♣ Q x x

There could be an easy game if partner's hand is either of these:

♠ A J x x x ♡ Q x x ◇ K x ♣ K J x

♠ A K x x x ♡ A Q x ◇ x ♣ Q x x x

so it is tempting to bid 2♡. But what should opener do over 2♡ if his hand is

♠ A K x x x ♡ x ◇ K x x ♣ A J x x

Some players would bid 2♠ because of the singleton heart, hoping responder would bid a minor with a singleton spade, but if responder had

♠ x ♡ K J 10 9 x x ◇ Q x x ♣ K x x

2♡ would be a superior contract. The problem is that opener can't tell whether responder holds five or six hearts. Bart Bramley suggested that an artificial 2◇ bid by responder in this sequence would help to solve this problem (and other problems). A direct 2♡ bid now shows six hearts so that opener's percentage call would be to pass with a singleton or void, while the 2◇ bid implies five hearts — and a fairly good hand considering that responder did not make a two-over-one response in the first place. With a three-card heart holding (5-3-2-3 or 5-3-1-4 distribution), opener rebids 2♡, 3♡ or 4♡, depending on how strong he is. If he bids 2♡, perhaps with a doubleton honor, and responder bids 2♠, it means that responder has 9 or 10 points with a doubleton spade (better than the typical 6-8 points with a doubleton spade). There are other hands responder could show, including a real diamond suit, a strong raise in clubs, or 9-10 points with a doubleton honor in spades, but the main purpose is to distinguish between a five- and six-card heart holdings.

RESPONDING TO A MINOR-SUIT OPENING

A 1◇ opening bid should show 4+ diamonds unless you have precisely 4-4-3-2 distribution (in that order). Since that is a fairly uncommon distribution, you should assume, for bidding purposes, that a diamond opening shows four. A 1♣ bid shows three or more clubs. (That means that with ◇AKQ alone and three small clubs, you would still open 1♣ rather than 1◇.)

At the expert level, inverted minor raises are more popular than old-fashioned raises, as indicated by a *Bridge World* poll. Most people who play inverted raises treat a single raise of a minor as forcing to 2NT or three of that minor. With ten points or less, it usually shows five or more of the suit (especially in clubs), but with a game-forcing hand or better, it may show only four if you have the sort of hand where you would prefer to have partner, rather than you, play the hand in a notrump contract. Not everyone agrees on how the subsequent bidding should go. Some people, at IMPs, play that you can't stop in 2NT and that you have to get to three of your minor.

Most play that inverted raises do not apply in competition and some players, including me, think they should not apply by a passed hand. When you are not a passed hand, there is no upper limit to your bid, and when you might have anywhere from 10 to 20 points (or more), you often need some way to force without bidding a three-card major, which creates problems of its own. Besides, after both opponents have passed, you don't have a strong need for a preemptive double raise. When your original pass limits your hand, I hardly think it is worthwhile to save a single raise to show 10 or 11 points. (With 12 points and a five-card suit you probably would have opened.) Playing inverted raises can cause difficulties when you hold something like

♠ A x   ♡ x   ◇ J x x x   ♣ Q x x x x x

and partner opens 1◇: would you bid 1NT, 2♣, 2◇ or 3◇? However, the ease of bidding good hands compensates for the terrible problems you may have on rare occasions. But when you can't have a 'good' hand, why invite trouble by giving up the natural single raise?

The raise to either the two- or three-level is supposed to deny a four-card major, but with

♠ x   ♡ J x x x   ◇ K Q 10 x x x   ♣ x x

I can't imagine *not* bidding 3◇ if partner opens 1◇, or *not* bidding 2◇ with

♠ x x x x   ♡ A x   ◇ A Q J 10 x   ♣ A x

With the first hand, preempting the opponents when they have spades is far more likely to gain than showing your very weak heart suit. With the latter hand, if you stop in game, your best contract is probably 3NT, not 4♠, even if there is a 4-4 spade fit. Since you seldom (some people say never) hold a four-card major when you give partner a single raise, the assumption is that major-suit bids now show stoppers. *Opener* can, of course, hold a four-card major, but since responder is not expected to, there is no point in bidding a major to look for a fit. So after 1◇-2◇, 2♠ suggests, unless opener does something inconsistent later, that he has a spade stopper but no heart stopper. With both he probably would have bid either 2NT or 3NT, depending on whether he is minimum or slightly above. You don't worry much about a stopper in the other minor since if responder has length in any side suit, it is almost certainly the other minor.

One method, based upon the way most of my friends and partners play inverted raises, is for opener to bid notrump (either two or three, depending upon his strength) with stoppers in both majors or to bid the major he has stopped if he only has one stopper. An alternative method, which might be as good or better, is to rebid notrump whenever opener has a balanced hand, especially when he opened a three-card minor as on one of these hands:

♠ A K x x   ♡ x x x   ◇ K J x   ♣ Q x x

♠ A K x x   ♡ 10 x x x   ◇ K J x   ♣ Q x

From his point of view, a good major-suit fit is impossible, and 3NT is the most likely game. Why disclose the location of his stoppers to the opponents? Responder can issue a warning if his hand is very distributional. This approach works well when both hands have three small of a suit, like the deal I mentioned earlier, on which my partner and I missed 3NT with

♠ A Q x x	♠ K J x
♡ x x x	♡ x x x
◇ Q J x	◇ A K x
♣ A x x	♣ K J x x

The 2NT response — forcing or invitational?

Now let's look at hands where responder does not raise partner's minor-suit opening. For reasons that will be discussed soon, I don't think the auction 1◇-2♣ should be forcing to game or even beyond 2NT. It is different over a major suit, since with a hand not strong enough to insist on game you have the forcing 1NT available. Over 1♣ you have a 1◇ bid available, even if it is a three-card suit when you have 3-3-3-4 distribution, or an inverted raise with an invitational or game-forcing hand. But over an opening 1◇ bid you have no convenient bid with a balanced 11 or 12 points and 3-3-3-4, 3-2-3-5, or 2-3-3-5 distribution since bidding a three-card major can cause all sorts of problems. That is why most people play a 2NT response as non-forcing over 1◇. Because people are lazy and don't want to strain themselves by treating two similar sequences differently, they usually play 2NT non-forcing over 1♣ also.

I don't know whether Mike Lawrence has changed his mind since his book entitled *Mike Lawrence's Bidding Quizzes — The Uncontested Auction* was published in 1990, but in that book he expressed the view that a 2NT response to either minor should be played as forcing and that a 2♣ response to 1◇ should be forcing only to 2NT. The sequences 1◇-2♣, 2◇-2NT and 1◇-2♣, 2NT were both non-forcing, and that seems to me the best way to play them. Over 1◇-2♣, a rebid of two of a major showed at least a good 14 points and forced the bidding to game.

This treatment avoided the problem of how responder shows a balanced hand in the 13-19 HCP range. You could hardly have a 3NT response cover such a wide range. If 2NT is forcing, it presumably shows 13-15 HCP; so 3NT shows a good 15-17, and with 18-19 you can bid 2NT and bid again (usually 4NT, but possibly returning to partner's suit at the four-level to show a ruffing value in case partner wants to accept an invitation to slam). So with

♠ A K   ♡ K x x   ◇ K J x x   ♣ A 10 x x

you would bid 2NT over an opening bid in either minor suit, followed by bidding 4♣ or 4◇ (whichever was partner's suit) over a 3NT rebid. With a minimum, balanced hand partner would sign off in 4NT. With just a bit more than a minimum balanced hand or with almost any unbalanced hand, partner would bid 6♣ or 6◇.

When the opening bid is a major suit, the forcing notrump response allows responder to make a two-step response to show an invitational hand. These auctions are typical examples:

Opener	Responder	Opener	Responder
1♠	1NT	1♡	1NT
2♣	3♠	2◇	2NT

But if two-over-one responses are forcing to game, even with a few exceptions, how can you show an invitational hand over a 1◇ opening? There is no problem if you can make a major-suit response:

Opener	Responder	Opener	Responder
1◇	1♡	1♣	1♡
1NT	2NT	1♠	3♣

But what if you don't have a major suit? With either of these hands

♠ x x   ♡ K x x   ◇ K J x   ♣ A x x x x

♠ x x x   ♡ K x x   ◇ K J x   ♣ A x x x

some players would respond 1♡ anyway. If opener raises hearts with ♡Jxxx or with good three-card support (perhaps at the three-level in competition), it causes problems. After making a heart raise, is opener supposed to pass any notrump rebid, regardless of the rest of his hand, on the assumption that a notrump bid after one's suit has been raised denies having a four-card suit? I have heard players who bid that way say they never have a problem, but I find that hard to believe. The most common solution to the problem is to play that 1◊-3♣ is merely invitational, and that 1◊-2NT is also invitational, showing 10-12 or 11-12 HCP. Of course that makes the wrong hand declarer in notrump when responder has a worthless doubleton. And if a 2NT response shows 11-12 HCP, what does one do with 13-15? With 16-17? With 18-19? For these reasons, it seems to me that 1◊-2♣ should not be forcing to game.

Timo Ercok, a Turkish player now residing in the United States, liked to play that after 1◊-2♣, an artificial 2♡ rebid by opener suggested (unless he did something inconsistent later) that he had an absolute minimum. The bid allowed the bidding to terminate below game. With a minimum 2♣ bid responder would bid 2♠, allowing opener to sign off in 2NT. He said that treatment was quite popular in Europe, and it worked well for us.

Mike Lawrence recommends that these:

Opener	Responder	Opener	Responder	Opener	Responder
1◊	2♣	1◊	2♣	1◊	2♣
2NT		2◊	2NT	2◊	3♣

should all be non-forcing sequences, but that if opener rebids anything except 2◊ or 2NT, the partnership cannot stop short of game. Playing Mike's way, after 1◊-2♣, opener would rebid 2NT rather than 2◊ with

♠ A Q x x   ♡ K x   ◊ Q J x x x   ♣ J x

for two reasons: (a) balanced hands tend to bid notrump at the first opportunity, and (b) 2♠ would be forcing to game (showing at least a good 14 points). The 2NT bid allows responder to pass with

♠ K x x   ♡ J x x   ◊ x x   ♣ A K x x x

With a sixth club he would raise to 3NT since the 2NT rebid shows a balanced hand and no misfit for clubs. Admittedly

♠ A Q x x   ♡ K x   ◊ Q J x x x   ♣ J x

opposite this hand would offer almost no play for 3NT, especially with a heart lead, but many other 13-point hands containing either three clubs or the doubleton queen would offer adequate chances.

After the 2NT rebid, 3♣ by responder is forcing, showing either an unbalanced hand or an interest in slam (or both). According to Mike, over 2♣, opener can bid 2NT with a minimum 4-4-4-1 hand. Then if responder bids 3♣, an opener with at least two clubs bids 3◊ with a minimum, 3♡ or 3♠ with a maximum (a good 13 or a bad 14 points), and 3NT with 4-4-4-1 distribution. I like the idea of bidding the major where the majority of strength is, but I don't like the idea of rebidding 2NT with a minimum plus a misfit. With

♠ A Q x x   ♡ K x x x   ◇ K x x x   ♣ x

I think it is better to rebid 2◇, just as you would with

♠ A Q x x   ♡ Kx x   ◇ K x x x x   ♣ x

in order to allow the bidding to stop short of game when responder has

♠ x x   ♡ Q x x   ◇ x x   ♣ A K J x x x.

Rebidding diamonds with a four-card suit can create complications when responder has both minors, but now that inverted minor raises are popular, unlike in 1990, responder, with

♠ x   ♡ Q x   ◇ K Q x x x   ♣ A J 9 x x

can raise to 2◇ and rebid clubs later.

Many players want to avoid complications and prefer to play all two-over-ones as forcing to game: that is why they play a 2NT response as invitational rather than forcing. I think these complications are worthwhile so that you don't either have to respond 2NT over 1◇ with

♠ x x   ♡ J x x   ◇ Q J x   ♣ A K x x x

or make a 3NT response with as wide a range as 13-19 points (or respond in a three-card major). Let's look at a few examples to see how Mike's system (slightly modified by me) works.

For the following hands, the bidding starts

Opener	Responder
1◇	2♣
?	

♠ A Q x x   ♡ K 10 9 x   ◇ A Q x x   ♣ x

I think you should rebid 2NT. The hand looks as though it should play in notrump, and your extra values compensate for the misfit. If partner raises to 3NT with

♠ K x   ♡ x x x   ◇ x x   ♣ A Q J x x x

you will probably need a 3-3 club break or the doubleton ♣K on side. At least four times out of five, responder intends to bid game when he responds 2♣, so you don't want to treat most responses as non-forcing, which may create problems when responder has a good hand.

♠ A Q x x   ♡ 10 x x x   ◇ A Q x x   ♣ x

Bid 2◇ so that you can pass a 2NT or 3♣ rebid by partner.

♠ A Q x x   ♡ J x x   ◇ A K Q 10 x   ♣ x

Bid 2♠. If partner has a heart stopper you probably belong in 3NT. There are no guarantees, but partner's clubs may run, or you may win five diamond tricks. If partner bids 3♣, denying a heart stopper, you will bid 3◊. Now if partner has solid clubs, he will bid 5♣. If he has a singleton heart, he will probably bid 5♣ or raise diamonds. If he bids 4♣, it seems to me that you should be allowed to pass.

Now let's look at some hands where the bidding starts

Opener	Responder
1◊	2♣
2NT	?

♠ x x ♡ J x ◊ x x x ♣ A K Q x x x

Raise to 3NT. The clubs should run. It is reasonable to hope opener can furnish three tricks before the opponents can take five.

♠ x ♡ A x ◊ Q x x ♣ A K Q x x x x

Bid 4♠, a self-splinter. If opener bids 4NT, showing a lot of wastage in spades, you should pass; otherwise you will bid 6♣.

♠ K J x x ♡ Q x ◊ x ♣ A K x x x x

Bid 3♠. Remember, if opener had

♠ A Q x x ♡ K x x ◊ A x x x ♣ x x

he would rebid 2NT not 2♠, which would be forcing to game. If opener doesn't have four spades, he will bid 3NT.

♠ A x x ♡ Q x ◊ x ♣ A K Q x x x x

Bid 3♣, forcing after the 2NT rebid. Since you are going to get at least to game, opener will not be as concerned about whether he has exactly 12, 13 or 14 points as with whether he has good controls. With

♠ K J x ♡ K J x ◊ K Q x x x ♣ J x

he would bid 3◊, showing a minimum. With

♠ K Q x ♡ A x x ◊ A x x x ♣ x x x

he would bid 3♠ to show a maximum with more values in spades than in hearts. If opener bids either 3♠ or 3♡, you plan to bid 6♣. If he bids 3◊, you are still strong enough to cuebid, but would pass if he then bids either 3NT or 5♣.

The auction after a 2NT response

If your 2NT response to one of a minor, whether by a passed hand or non-passed hand, is not played as forcing, what rebids by opener are forcing? It is generally agreed that rebidding opener's minor is non-forcing; it just shows a hand unsuitable for notrump. There are pros and cons to treating 1◇, followed by a non-forcing 2NT, and a 3♣ rebid as forcing. Without discussion I think it should be treated as forcing to 3◇, 3NT or 4♣, although I don't feel strongly about it if the partners wish to agree to something different.

Since I don't believe that inverted minor raises should apply by a passed hand, how should responder show a good hand (for having passed)? I think the double raise should show a good hand for notrump (like KQxxxx of the minor and an ace) while a jump shift to the other minor (1◇-3♣ or 1♣-2◇) should show a good distributional raise.

Eddie Kantar and I used to play that after a 2NT response to a minor opening a bid of a higher-ranking suit at the three-level showed 0, 1, or 5 cards of the suit. In effect, this was a splinter bid played before splinters became popular. (Obviously a splinter was several times more common than a five-card suit.) This kept us out of 3NT contracts with Axx or Qxx opposite a singleton. If responder bid 3NT anyway, showing that the suit was well stopped, and if opener happened to have 5-6 distribution, he knew there was a great fit for his second suit. We actually played the 2NT response as forcing, but even if you play it as merely invitational, I like the splinter rebid whenever opener is strong enough to bid again. As I recall, 1◇-2NT, 3♣ was a two-way bid, either showing a club suit or a splinter, and opener could rebid 3◇ to find out which, but I don't consider that variation as important as the others.

REVERSES

There are several problems regarding reverses.

What is a reverse?
It is a rebid made in a higher-ranking suit than your first bid, forcing the bidding one level higher if partner prefers the first suit. So when the initial response was at the one-level, reverses by opener must show quite a bit better than a minimum opening bid —

♠ x   ♡ A K x x x   ◇ K Q x x x x   ♣ x

would be a minimum — such as 6-5 distribution with the points in the two suits or, with 5-4 or 6-4 distribution, 17 points, and perhaps slightly less when opener's two suits are the majors. Reverses after a two-level response will be discussed in the next chapter.

Should reverses be forcing to game?
No, not after a one-level response, because you would seldom have a good enough hand to show your second suit if game-forcing values were required. (Even the 17 point or 6-5 requirement makes them fairly rare.)

Does the reverser guarantee another bid?

Most players would say yes, which means that responder, with a very weak hand, should not take a preference to opener's first suit. He has to make a warning bid, after which he can pass opener's rebid. Let's look at some examples.

Opener	Responder
1♣	1♠
2♦	?

If responder holds

♠ K 10 x x x   ♡ J x x   ♦ Q x x   ♣ x x

he should rebid 2♠. He might make the same bid with another ace or so, since the bid is forcing, but it is potentially weak. This time he plans to pass either a 2NT or 3♣ rebid.

With

♠ K 10 x x   ♡ Q J x   ♦ x x x x   ♣ x x

he should bid 2NT. This bid is also potentially weak, and he plans to pass if opener bids 3♣. But he does have a heart stopper, and if opener has

♠ x x   ♡ x x   ♦ A K x   ♣ A K Q x x x

he will rebid 3NT. Responder could have a better hand since 2NT is forcing (or put it another way, opener has promised a rebid).

With

♠ K 10 x x   ♡ J x x   ♦ Q x x   ♣ x x x

responder should bid 2♡. When the fourth suit can be bid at the two-level, bidding 2NT shows a stopper and bidding the fourth suit denies one. But if the bidding had gone

Opener	Responder
1♣	1♠
2♡	?

responder would bid 2NT with

♠ K 10 x x   ♡ Q J x   ♦ x x x   ♣ x x x

despite the lack of a diamond stopper. It wouldn't make good sense for responder to bid 3♦ to say he was too weak to bid 3♣. Perhaps you noted that in the previous example opener reversed into 3♦ with a three-card suit. That is permissible and a good idea when opener just needs a stopper in the fourth suit to bid 3NT since it shows where he needs help.

Suppose the bidding has gone

Opener	Responder
1◇	1♠
2♡	?

and responder has

♠ Q J x x x   ♡ Q x x x   ◇ x   ♣ x x x

Not only does he hold a very weak hand, but he is not positive that opener has a four-card heart suit (although he probably does). Responder
should bid 2♠. Then if opener bids 2NT or 3◇, he can bid 3♡ to show a
weak, non-forcing raise. Change his hand to

♠ A J x x x   ♡ Q x x x   ◇ x   ♣ x x x

and he would have bid 3♡ directly over 2♡, since he is willing to force
to game.

Responder, as well as opener, can reverse. With

♠ A J x x x   ♡ K Q x x x x   ◇ x   ♣ x

he would bid 1♡ in response to one of a minor and bid 2♠ next time. That
bid is surely forcing for one round; whether it is forcing to game is a matter of partnership agreement. You probably noticed that whenever a player reversed, his first suit was longer than his second. That is certainly the
'rule,' but I believe there could be exceptions. Suppose you hold one of
these hands

♠ A J x   ♡ x x   ◇ A K x x   ♣ A Q 10 x

♠ A 10 x   ♡ x x   ◇ A K x x   ♣ A K J x

and you open 1◇. If partner responds 1♡, you have an easy rebid — 2NT.
But suppose he responds 1♠. Now what? Many players would rebid 2NT,
hoping for one of three things: a) that partner has high cards or length in
hearts; b) that hearts won't be led; c) that with a five-card spade suit, partner will make some sort of checkback bid, permitting you to discover a
5-3 fit in spades. Another possibility is to rebid 3♠, despite holding only
three-card support. A third possibility is to anticipate the problem and
open 1♣ in the first place. Then you could bid 2◇ over 1♠ and later show
your three-card spade support (but be willing to play 3NT if partner bids
it). This could get you a trick too high if partner has only five or six points,
but at least you should get to the right denomination.

On these hands, you have to lie about something. A 2NT rebid shows
stoppers (and certainly not two small) in all unbid suits; a raise to 3♠ shows
four spades; the reverse shows more clubs than diamonds. Which lie is likely to do the least harm? It is better to lie about your club length than your
spade length. And I don't expect a checkback bid if partner has 5-3-3-2 distribution. You could use this same sequence with

♠ A Q x   ♡ x   ♢ A J x x   ♣ A K x x x

or

♠ K Q x   ♡ x   ♢ A K x   ♣ A J x x x x

With

♠ J x   ♡ x x   ♢ A K x   ♣ A K Q x x x

you should open 1♣ and rebid 2♢, hoping partner can bid 2NT (which in this sequence promises a heart stopper) so that you can raise to 3NT. In most cases the least of evils is to lie about your minor-suit length(s) since you or partner will choose a minor-suit contract only as a last resort.

I said earlier that a reverse by opener with both majors might be made slightly lighter than with any other two suits. After 1♡-1NT, if you have four spades and you don't bid spades now, you may never get another chance. Furthermore, if you find a fit in either major, you need only ten tricks, rather than eleven, to make game. So that justifies stretching slightly to show the spade suit. But I don't think this particular sequence (1♡-1NT, 2♠) should require opener to bid again. Responder would bid 2NT with

♠ x x x   ♡ x x   ♢ Q J x x   ♣ K x x x

and opener should be allowed to pass. Or responder would bid 3♡ with

♠ x x   ♡ K x   ♢ Q J x x   ♣ x x x x x

or

♠ x x x   ♡ Q x x   ♢ J x x x x   ♣ x x

and opener should be allowed to pass. But three of a minor should be forcing, since with

♠ x x x   ♡ K x   ♢ K J 10 x x x   ♣ J x

or

♠ Q x x   ♡ Q x   ♢ x x   ♣ A J 10 x x x

it is important to be able to look for the best game.

After a two-over-one response, what do you need for a reverse? Let's defer a discussion of that question until the next chapter. The problem is not that you lack the values for game; it is possible that you do, but very unlikely. The problem is that a reverse may mislead partner regarding your strength, and he may invite or bid a poor slam. As has already been mentioned, I don't think 1♢-2♣ sequences should be forcing to game in any event. Mike Lawrence suggests that bidding two of a major over this starting sequence should show a good 14 points (or more) and be forcing to game. I agree. That leaves a 1♡ opening, a minor-suit response and a 2♠

rebid as the only two-over-one reverse sequence left to discuss, but we will save that for the next chapter.

THREE-CARD RAISES

Three-card raises are standard when partner has shown a five-card (or longer) suit and they require no comment by me. When partner may have only a four-card suit, or probably has only a four-card suit, we enter a controversial area. In the original Walsh style, if responder bids a suit at the one-level, opener was not allowed to raise with three-card support unless he had a singleton (and even then, he was supposed to avoid a raise if there was a reasonable alternative). For example, if the bidding started

Opener	Responder
1♣	1♡
?	

opener would rebid 1NT rather than raise hearts with

♠ x x   ♡ A Q x   ◊ A x x   ♣ K x x x x

That almost makes me ill. Also, with

♠ Q x x x   ♡ A J x   ◊ x   ♣ K J 9 8 x

he would rebid 1♠ rather than raise hearts. This latter action is not that unusual, and many players today would rebid 1♠ on this hand. The difficulty is that if responder now bids 1NT, a 2♡ rebid shows extra values, and if responder bids 2NT or 3♣, there is a real problem: 3♡ would be forcing, which wouldn't work out well if responder had a four-card suit with about 11 points. I think that opener should raise to 2♡ immediately with his minimum hand.

There is another problem. Should this auction be forcing?

Opener	Responder
1♣	1♡
2♡	3♣
?	

I say no. The 3♣ bid should be invitational, and with four-card support for hearts opener should bid 3♡ or 4♡, but with only three-card support, I think he should be able to pass since there is no eight-card major fit.

So what does responder do with a hand like this:

♠ x x   ♡ K x x x   ◊ A J x   ♣ A Q x x

He has to bid 3◊, not 3♣, over 2♡. (With the same distribution, but a stronger hand, with which responder wants to suggest a 6♣ contract, responder would have bid 2♠, fourth suit, followed by a club raise.) Walsh players might bid 4♡ directly since their partners are less likely than the rest of the world to have raised with three-card support. With

♠ x x ♡ A Q x ◇ A x x ♣ K J x x x

or

♠ A x x ♡ A Q x ◇ x x ♣ K J x x x

they would have rebid 1NT in the first place. Most experts would raise to 2♡ with either hand for several reasons:

a) Responder may have a long heart suit with a marginal hand. If so, the raise, guaranteeing a fit, will be more encouraging. He would pass a 1NT rebid with

♠ K x x ♡ K x x x x ◇ x x ♣ A x x

but would invite game over a heart raise.

b) If the hand ends up in notrump, quite likely it will play better from partner's side since he may have a tenace opposite the worthless doubleton.

c) At the partscore level the hand may play much better in hearts when there is a 5-3 fit and responder is too weak to bid again.

d) At either the game or partscore level, the hand may play better in a 4-3 heart fit than in notrump — for example if responder holds

♠ x x x ♡ K J x x ◇ x x x x ♣ A x

When the hand with three hearts can ruff something, it usually gains a trick.

Most experts agree that with good three-card support and a worthless doubleton, a raise is automatic in this kind of sequence

Opener	Responder
1♣	1♡
?	

Even when the doubleton is Ax, they also tend to raise. With Kx or Qx their tendency is to rebid notrump. There is a corollary for frequent three-card major raises: when responder has a four-card suit with an invitational hand, he should bid where his values are. Suppose responder holds

♠ K J x x ♡ A x x x ◇ K x ♣ x x x

His partner opens 1◇ and raises the 1♡ response to 2♡. A pass at matchpoints is not unreasonable, but if he bids again, he should bid either 2♠ or

2NT. When this hand came up, responder was sure that the final contract would be either 3♡ or 4♡, and he bid 3♣ in the hope of avoiding a club lead or misleading the defenders. I especially disapprove of a phony 3♣ bid in this sequence because in fact responder doesn't know whether the final contract will be in hearts or notrump. Opener's actual hand was

♠ x x   ♡ J 10 x   ◇ A J x x   ♣ A Q 10 x

If responder had bid 2NT, opener would have passed. If responder had bid 2♠, opener would have bid 2NT, which responder would have passed. By not bidding where his values were, responder made it impossible to get to notrump, which is where they belonged.

Suppose opener has

♠ A Q x   ♡ x x   ◇ A K J x x   ♣ A x x

and opens 1◇, over which responder bids 1♠. On this type of hand, with the minors reversed, opener might rebid 2◇ after having opened 1♣, and then raise spades on the next round, but that option isn't available here. Some might gamble on a 2♣ rebid, even though it wouldn't be forcing, in the hope of having a similar sequence. Kit Woolsey and many of his followers play what they call Cole, where the 2♣ rebid shows either real clubs or three-card support for responder's major (or possibly both!). Responder can bid 2◇ now to find out more. I suspect that most players would rebid 2NT on this hand, gambling that partner has a stopper in hearts or that hearts won't be led, or that responder will make some sort of checkback enquiry if he has a five-card spade suit. The third possibility is to raise to 3♠. The trouble with bidding 3♠ is that responder, with a good hand or fair hand but only a weak four-card spade suit, may simply bid 4♠, assuming that you have shown four-card spade support. I really think the best solution is to bid 3♠ after reaching an agreement that responder will consider bidding 3NT with only a four-card spade suit and an appropriate hand, like

♠ K x x x   ♡ K x x   ◇ Q x x   ♣ Q x x

so as to give you a choice of contracts. Even without this understanding, I think that the odds favor the raise to 3♠, but not many players would agree with me.

In the bidding sequences discussed so far, there were two factors favoring a three-card raise. Whenever partner had a five-card suit or longer, the raise would usually lead to the best contract, and it would often be the best contract when he had only four. But suppose the bidding has been

Opener	Responder
1♣	1♡
1♠	?

and you (responder) hold

♠ K J x   ♡ A x x x x   ◇ x x   ♣ J x x

In this sequence the odds are at least 20 to 1 that partner has only a four-card spade suit. So what should you do? You could easily miss a game by passing. Rebidding 1NT with a worthless doubleton in the unbid suit can't be right. The orthodox bid is 2♣ (unless you are playing XYZ). At IMPs this would be the *safest* bid: partner might have five or six clubs but only four spades and even if partner has only four clubs, two clubs on a 4-3 club fit is as likely to make as two spades on a 4-3 spade fit, and the difference between +90 and +110 won't be crucial. But at matchpoints, 2♠ is better. If the opponents lead diamonds, the unbid suit, partner can ruff the third round with your three-card holding, keeping his four-card suit intact. Actually, even at IMPs I like 2♠ slightly better since your most likely game is in spades.

TENTATIVE BIDS

Bob Hamman is supposed to have said, '3NT ends all auctions.' *If* he said that, he was probably joking or being sarcastic. For example, you hold

♠ A J x x x x   ♡ x   ◇ x   ♣ J 10 x x x

Partner opens 1◇ and you respond 1♠. He rebids 2♣ and you raise to 3♣. Partner then bids 3NT. Would you pass? Of course not!

If partner holds

♠ x   ♡ K 10 x   ◇ A K x x x   ♣ K Q x x

where will he get his tricks? Although partner didn't know it, you were not inviting 3NT. You were inviting 5♣, with the secondary motive of preempting the opponents out of hearts. Nor is 3NT likely to make. So you should bid 4♣ now. Then, if partner has the right sort of hand, he can bid 5♣. Another example: the bidding goes

Partner	Oppt.	You	Oppt.
1◇	1♡	1♠	2♡
3◇	3♡	pass	pass
3NT	pass	?	

and you hold

♠ A Q x x x   ♡ x x   ◇ x x   ♣ Q x x x

If partner couldn't bid 3NT last round, he is not likely to make it. The only possible explanation for partner's apparently inconsistent bidding is that he holds something like

♠ x   ♡ K x   ◇ A Q 10 9 x x x   ♣ A J x

or

♠ J x   ♡ A x   ◇ K Q J x x x x   ♣ A x

He has a good enough hand to compete to the four-level, and if your values include a high honor in diamonds to solidify partner's suit, 3NT will probably be cold. But you know you don't have what he needs, and 3NT would be a poor gamble, at best, so you should retreat to 4◇ (even if you had a singleton diamond!). Here is one more example:

You	Oppt.	Partner	Oppt.
1♣	2◇	dbl	pass
2♡	pass	3♣	3◇
pass	pass	3♡	pass
?			

You hold

♠ A K   ♡ Q x x x   ◇ x x x   ♣ A 10 x x

What do you think partner's distribution is? Probably 4-3-1-5 or 4-3-2-4 (more likely the former). Partner actually holds

♠ J 10 x x   ♡ A x x   ◇ x   ♣ K Q x x x

He certainly has sufficient values to compete to 4♣, but he suggests a 4-3 heart fit in case your hearts are good, or even a 4-4 spade fit in case you are 4-4 in the majors but were too weak to cuebid 4◇. With ♡KQxx, perhaps even with ♡KJ10x, you would be willing to pass (at matchpoints). On your actual hand, since you don't want to play in a 4-3 heart fit with such bad hearts, you should bid 4♣.

JUMP SHIFT RESPONSES

Almost everyone agrees that jump shifts in competition should be weak, or at least weaker than non-jumps. After either an overcall or a takeout double the likelihood of a slam is decreased, and you want more ways to compete. For example, after partner opens 1◇ and RHO overcalls 1♠ you want to show your heart suit when you hold

♠ x x   ♡ A Q 10 x x x x   ◇ J x   ♣ x x

and bidding 3♡ shows a weaker hand than 2♡ followed by 3♡. The question is whether jump shifts should be weak in an uncontested auction. Most two-over-one players play that jumps to the three-level (like 1♡ -3♣) are not strong; they are either natural and invitational or they are conventional Bergen raises. Since most auctions starting with a two-over-one response are forcing to game, there is no great need for strong jump shifts to the three-level[1]. But what about the two-level? For example, what should 1♣-2♡ mean?

There is no doubt that you get to use weak jump shifts more often than strong jump shifts, especially considering the way most players who use strong jump shifts play them. With a first time partner it is much easier to play weak jump shifts since no discussion is needed. If you require 19 points (or the distributional equivalent) and a strong suit for your strong jump shifts, I'll admit that they are rare enough to be hardly worthwhile. But I think strong jump shifts in a modified Soloway style are quite desirable since they make your slam bidding more accurate. And accuracy at the slam level is more important than accuracy at the partscore level, even at matchpoints. Bidding a good slam in the right suit or avoiding a bad slam is worth at least half a board compared to the alternative. Making the theoretically wrong decision at the partscore level may cost little or nothing. For example, by not making a weak jump shift you may miss out on a 300-point sacrifice against a game, but with good defense you score -420 while most pairs your direction are -450, so you get well above average anyway.

The basic requirement for a strong jump shift is that the hand is strong enough to make a slam opposite a well-fitting minimum opening. The bidding becomes much simpler when partner knows right away that you are in the likely slam zone. Scattered queens, jacks, and tens may be valuable in 3NT contracts, but are seldom helpful in slam contracts. Partner also knows that bidding a weak suit in a slam auction can only cause confusion. After 1♣-1♡, opener would rebid 1♠ with

$$♠ J x x x \quad ♡ x x \quad ◇ A K x \quad ♣ K Q 10 x$$

but there would be no purpose in showing such a weak suit after 1♣-2♡. According to Paul Soloway and Mike Lawrence, a jump shift shows one of three types of hand:

- a good hand with a very strong suit
- a good hand with a pretty good suit with which responder plans to rebid notrump
- a good hand including a pretty good suit and at least four-card support for partner's suit

In other words, it denies a two-suited hand unless the second suit is the one partner has bid. So if the bidding in an uncontested auction starts:

---

1. The main advantage of weak jump shifts when the opponents haven't entered the bidding is that they create problems for fourth hand. After 1◇-(pass)-2♠-(?) the next player has a problem with ♠ K x ♡ A Q x x x ◇ x x x x ♣ A Q

Opener	Responder
1◇	2♠
2NT	3♡

responder is showing a spade suit, at least four-card support for diamonds, and a *singleton or void in hearts*. In other words, responder's second bid shows a splinter rather than a second suit. That makes it easy for opener to evaluate his hand, and with

♠ K x ♡ x x x ◇ A Q J x x ♣ K x x

the only question is whether the final contract should be 6◇ or 7◇. A typical responding hand would be

♠ A Q 10 x x ♡ x ◇ K x x x ♣ A J x

If responder's second round bid had been 3◇, it would have shown a good hand for diamonds but no singleton. No matter how you play it, this type of hand — strong support for opener's suit — will occur more frequently than the other two types combined. But you will get many more jump shifts if you drop the requirement for a good five-card or longer suit when *responder intends to show support for opener's suit.* Suppose responder's hand is

♠ A Q 10 x ♡ x ◇ K x x x x ♣ A J x

Many players who would respond 2♠ with

♠ A Q 10 x x ♡ x ◇ K x x x ♣ A J x

say that a jump shift must show at least a good five-card suit; otherwise opener can't count his tricks. I find that it almost never matters whether responder has a five-card suit of his own with four card-support for opener or a four-card suit of his own and five-card support for partner. So I would bid 2♠ with either hand.

Needless to say, it won't work well for opener to raise the jump shift to 3♠ with ♠xxx. In fact, I have had undisciplined partners bid 4♠ over 2♠ with three small spades and a balanced 12 points — a sort of 'Fast Arrival.' It worked in a sense: we *immediately* got to almost the only game contract we couldn't make. It is desirable to allow responder to describe the type of hand he has for a jump shift below the 3NT level. For that reason my recommendation is that opener make the cheapest bid, artificially (which must be alerted), unless he has an unusual hand. Thus over 1♣-2♡, opener should bid 2♠ with

♠ J x x ♡ Q x ◇ A K x ♣ K x x x x

If responder bids 3◇ (showing a singleton or void and club support) opener can bid 3NT since he has a minimum opening including the king of diamonds, which won't be a useful card for slam opposite partner's singleton or void.

If responder bids 3♠ (spade shortness and clubs) over the artificial 2♠, I think opener should bid 4♣ to confirm a good club suit (as compared to ♣Qxx or three small). Showing a good club suit, while at the same time bidding past the 3NT level, will be more encouraging to partner than showing a lack of a misfit for hearts. With a nine-card trump fit and useful honors, it is almost certain that the hands belong in slam. Perhaps partner will now be able to take control of the bidding.

The reason for making the cheapest bid is that, when the hands don't fit, it is possible to play 3NT. If the bidding had gone 1♣-2♡, 3♣ instead, responder would been forced to bid 4♣ with

♠ A x   ♡ K Q x x x   ◇ A x   ♣ Q J 10 x

bypassing 3NT, in order to show why he made a jump shift.

I said opener should make the cheapest bid unless he has an unusual hand. What is 'unusual'? It could be a good five-card side suit, a very strong holding in the suit opened, or Qxxx or better in the jump-shift suit. With the last holding, responder may choose to play in his own suit with AKxx, even though he had originally intended to play in partner's minor. But whatever the *final* contract may be, responder should show that his jump shift was based on a fit for opener's suit.

Suppose partner opens 1◇ and you hold

♠ A x   ♡ K 10 8 x x x   ◇ A Q x x   ♣ x

What would you respond? I consider it a serious mistake *not* to bid 2♡. If partner has a minimum with a fit, you will reach a cold slam. If you discover that the hands don't fit well, you can decide to play in 4♡, 3NT or 5◇. So you bid 2♡ and partner bids 3♡. That means he has four hearts headed by the ace, the queen or both top honors. But you still should still bid 4♣ to describe what type of hand you have for your jump shift — strong diamond support plus a singleton club. Now let's look at opener's hand for a moment. He holds

♠ Q x x   ♡ A Q x x   ◇ K x x x   ♣ J 10

I'm not sure I would have opened his hand in the first place, but on this auction it looks like a great hand. He has very good heart support with practically nothing wasted in clubs. His diamonds are not especially good, but at least he has a four-card suit. What should he bid now? Not 4♡, which could be passed. That is what he would bid with

♠ K J   ♡ A x x x   ◇ J x x x   ♣ K Q x

(very bad diamonds and/or duplication in clubs) or with

♠ Q J x x   ♡ A Q x x   ◊ K x x   ♣ J x

(only a three-card diamond suit). I think the best bid now is 4◊, which is encouraging (because opener didn't bid 4♡, risking a pass) and it guarantees at least a four-card diamond suit.

Notice that opener is not strong enough to take over and bid 4NT (Keycard for hearts). He doesn't want to be in slam when you have ◊Axxx or ◊AJxx plus a club loser, although, if your response is 5♡, showing two controls and no queen of hearts, he could pass 5♡. But even 5♡ *could* be too high with bad breaks. As will be mentioned in Chapter 6, if anyone uses Blackwood, it should be the strong, unbalanced hand, rather than the balanced hand.

Over opener's 4◊ bid, with either your actual hand or with something like

♠ A K x   ♡ K J x x x   ◊ A J x x   ♣ x

you would bid Blackwood *for diamonds*. With your actual hand you would bid 6◊ over a two-keycard response. (You don't even need the queen of hearts to have a good play for slam.) But with

♠ A K x   ♡ K J x x x   ◊ A J x x   ♣ x

you would pass a 5♡ response. Sometimes bidding or staying out of slam will require good bidding judgment. More often, there won't be a problem since the strong jump shift will make it easy to get to the right contract. These two hands (with the six-card heart suit) were held by our opponents, who bid to 6♡, as many pairs would. Although 6◊ was cold, 6♡ had no play after a club lead and continuation.

It's nice to show methods for bidding hands that fit perfectly and make a slam other players find hard to reach. But staying out of bad slams is just as important. In a recent bidding contest my partner and I were given approximately the following hands and asked to bid them at matchpoint scoring:

Opener	Responder
♠ J x x	♠ K Q
♡ A K J x	♡ x
◊ x x	◊ A K Q J
♣ K J x x	♣ Q 10 x x x x
1♣	2◊
2♡	3♡
3NT	pass

Holding a combined total of ten clubs, it was hard for Standard bidders to avoid a club contract once they passed the 3NT level. Our opponents had an accident and got all the way to 6♣. But it was easy for my partner to stop in 3NT when he knew that there was duplication in hearts.

I'll admit that this style has a few complications. Suppose the bidding starts 1◊-2♡, 3♡. If responder bids 3♠ or 4♣ now, he is showing a single-ton in that suit plus great support for diamonds. Whether the final contract will be in hearts or diamonds, he should describe his hand. But responder *might* have a one-suiter, something like

♠ A K x   ♡ A Q J 10 x x   ◊ Q x   ♣ J x

He knows the final contract will be some number of hearts, but at what level? He can't make the 'obvious' bid of 3♠ since that would show a sin-gleton with diamond support. So what should he do? The following gadg-et solves the problem: he should bid 3NT, artificial and forcing. This mere-ly says, 'I do not have four-card support for your suit this time.' Then each player should cuebid his first- or second-round controls up the line unless they discover that both first- and second-round controls of a suit are miss-ing. So with

♠ Q x   ♡ K x x x   ◊ A x x x   ♣ K J x

opener should bid 4♣, not 4◊. If opener bids 4◊ and responder has a great hand with two small clubs, he will stop at game, knowing the opponents have the ace-king of clubs. Or if opener bids 4♣ with the ♣AK and respon-der does not bid 4◊, opener knows there is no slam if he holds ◊Qx. Since aces, kings, singletons and voids are all cuebid up the line, then even when all suits have been cuebid, two aces could be missing. For example, both hands could have a diamond control, but one has the king and the other has a singleton instead of the ace. So, after finding out that there aren't two quick losers in any suit, either one of the pair can bid 4NT to find out whether two aces are missing. Presumably after a strong jump shift with a long suit, when opener has a great fit (Qxxx or better) in a notrump type of hand, the two hands should make a slam unless the opponents can take the first two tricks off the top.

As previously stated, the basic requirement for a strong jump shift is that responder must be strong enough for a slam opposite a minimum opening bid, provided the hands fit well. The exception is when respon-der has a long, absolutely solid suit like

♠ Q J   ♡ A K Q J x x x x   ◊ x   ♣ x x

or

♠ x   ♡ A K Q J x x x   ◊ Q J 10   ♣ Q x

With one of these hands he can jump to 2♡ over one of a minor followed by rebidding 4♡ over the usual relay of 2♠. This sequence shows a solid suit and 8+ playing tricks, but denies an ace or void or more than one king on the side. With more high honors on the side, responder would just bid 2♡ followed by 3♡, leaving room for both partners to show their features. This is a rare case where Fast Arrival makes good sense, although it also follows my principle that a jump should show good trumps and nothing to cuebid. Incidentally, since a jump shift followed by a jump in responder's suit shows a solid suit and at most one king on the side, if opener uses Blackwood, he is asking about the side king. Responder will rebid his suit with no side king or bid the suit where he has a king. Opener will pass after the double jump when he knows that too many controls are missing. But if he is interested in singletons or can't stand a 5♠ response to 4NT when the suit is hearts, he can bid a side suit as an asking bid. The cheapest response shows no control in that suit; the next shows a singleton, and the third step the king.

Some people claim that you need a suit with no more than one loser to make a jump shift (unless you have four-card support for partner or a notrump-type hand). With

$$♠ A K J x x \quad ♡ K Q x \quad ◇ J x \quad ♣ K J x$$

you would bid 2♠ over 1◇, planning to bid 3NT next round. But I recommended a jump shift to 2♡ a moment ago with

$$♠ A K x \quad ♡ A Q J 10 x x \quad ◇ Q x \quad ♣ J x$$

Whether partner opens 1♣ or 1◇, after you jump shift into hearts you can't rebid 3NT next round since you don't have all the unbid suits stopped, so you would have to rebid 3♡ even if you were missing the ten of hearts. This hand meets my liberal standards: it can make a slam opposite the right minimum opening — for example

$$♠ x x \quad ♡ K x \quad ◇ A K x x x \quad ♣ K x x x$$

— and if you wait for the perfect hand, you won't get many strong jump shifts. You certainly want to suggest a slam with this hand, and the best way is to make a strong jump shift, followed by a rebid of your suit. This gets your message across while allowing you to stop in 4♡ or 3NT when the hands don't fit. The alternative is to bid 1♡, followed by a spade bid on your three-card suit, followed by 4♡ (or 5♡). I prefer the simple way.

THE SEMI-FORCING NOTRUMP AND
THE KAPLAN INTERCHANGE

In all the discussion thus far, my assumption was that a 1NT response to a major was forcing for one round. However, a semi-forcing 1NT has gained popularity recently and is now part of *Bridge World* Standard. I think that is a big mistake. The way it works is that a 1NT response can be as strong as 11 HCP or perhaps a bad 12. Opener *usually* bids again but can pass with 12 or 13 points and 5-3-3-2 distribution. The obvious purpose in playing 1NT semi-forcing, rather than forcing, is to allow the final contract to be 1NT when both hands are balanced. But responder has to bid 1NT with many unbalanced hands. For example, what else could he bid in response to one of a major with

$$\spadesuit x \quad \heartsuit x x \quad \diamondsuit K J x \quad \clubsuit Q J 10 x x x x$$

Playing 1NT forcing, you could bid 1NT followed by 3♣ over any minimum rebid. Or suppose the opening bid is 1♠ and responder holds

$$\spadesuit K x x \quad \heartsuit x x \quad \diamondsuit A x x x x \quad \clubsuit K x x$$

or

$$\spadesuit K x x \quad \heartsuit x \quad \diamondsuit K x x x x \quad \clubsuit K x x x$$

Playing a forcing notrump responder could bid 1NT followed by 3♠ to show a three-card limit raise. If the notrump response is semi-forcing, opener would pass with

$$\spadesuit A Q x x x \quad \heartsuit x x \quad \diamondsuit K Q x \quad \clubsuit J x x$$

in which case you would probably take six or seven tricks in notrump, when you could take nine or ten tricks in spades. What is the remedy? Making the same limit raise with either three- or four-card support? Making the single raise super-constructive? I haven't even mentioned that this would require two-over-one responses on three- or four-card suits, and you couldn't plan to bid 1NT followed by four of partner's heart suit with trashy hands like

$$\spadesuit J x \quad \heartsuit Q 10 x \quad \diamondsuit K Q x x \quad \clubsuit K Q x x$$

because partner might pass 1NT.

As I said, the purpose of making the response semi-forcing is to allow the final contract to be 1NT. There is another way to alleviate that problem when the opening bid is 1♡: simply interchange the 1♠ and 1NT responses. Now 1♠ is equivalent to a forcing notrump and 1NT is equivalent to a forcing spade bid. (This only applies to non-passed hands and is off in competition.) After a 1♠ response to 1♡, opener can bid 1NT with a balanced minimum. He no longer has to rebid a three-card minor suit with 5332 hands, or possibly a two-card minor with 4-5-2-2 distribution. So, when he does rebid a minor, responder can safely raise or pass with four-card support. In Standard forcing notrump bidding, after a 1♡ opening, a 1NT response and a 2♣ rebid, responder might bid 2♡ with

♠ Q x x   ♡ x x   ◊ K x x x   ♣ J 10 x x

even though he has no chance for game, just in case opener has only a three-card club suit.

It is tempting to stop here, perhaps leaving you with the impression that nothing but good can occur by making this switch, which is referred to as the Kaplan Interchange or the Kaplan Inversion. (It was named after Edgar Kaplan, who either introduced the idea or promoted it.) But there is (as always) a dark side. If, over 1♡, responder bids 1NT, showing 5+ spades or a good four-card suit, opener may still have to bid a three-card minor unless he decides to bid 2♠ with three-card spade support and, of necessity, a ruffing value. As against this, responder will have a biddable spade suit far less frequently than a hand with no spade suit which he wishes to show (especially when playing Flannery), and, as I said, over 1NT opener may be able to bid (in effect, raise) spades with three. When he does bid spades, he has one of the same advantages that he would have after a notrump opening and a transfer response: the contract will be played by the stronger hand, which makes it harder to defend.

The other disadvantage is that, at the present time, the Kaplan Interchange is a Mid-chart convention in ACBL tournaments, supposedly because it might confuse the average player. Almost every year I send letters to the ACBL, asking that it be made a General Chart convention for several reasons, the main one being that other transfer responses are allowed, so why not this one? Other artificial bids, which are equally confusing to the average player (or were when they were first introduced) are Bergen raises, Namyats, Jacoby transfers, 2-way Drury, Rubens advances of overcalls, etc, all of which require the opponents to decide how to bid over artificial bids and transfer bids. It seems like Alice in Wonderland logic to say the Kaplan Interchange would be confusing because many players are not familiar with it, when the reason they are not familiar with it is that it has not been allowed. One of these days I believe the Kaplan Interchange will be made a General Chart convention. But whether or not that happens, I still don't like the semi-forcing notrump response. Nor do I like it as a passed hand, for reasons previously stated.

NEGATIVE INFERENCES

In an ideal partnership, if you could see partner's hand, you would know exactly how he would bid it. Also you would know that he would bid it that way consistently, not one way one time and another way another time. When that is the case, you can draw inferences from what partner bid *or didn't bid*. For example, take the auction 1◊-1♡, 4♡. What would the 4♡ bid mean in your partnership? Presumably it shows one of these hands:

♠ x x ♡ K Q x x ◊ A K J x x x ♣ Q

♠ A x x ♡ K Q x x ◊ A K Q x x ♣ x

♠ K x ♡ A K Q x ◊ A J x x ♣ Q x x

There is not much bidding room for investigation, so it is important for responder to know which type of hand his partner has. Ironically, for slam purposes, the last hand with 19 HCP (or 20 support points, counting a point for the doubleton) is the weakest. The first hand belongs in slam opposite

♠ A x ♡ A x x x ◊ Q x x ♣ x x x x

while the third hand needs a lot more. The second hand could make slam opposite as little as

♠ x x x ♡ A x x x x ◊ J x ♣ x x x

and is, by far, the best hand of the three. Most experts would bid 4◊ over 1♡ with the first hand to show a sort of gambling 4♡ bid with six diamonds and four hearts. The second hand is so good that responder should start with a 4♣ splinter and risk a 4♠ bid even if partner just bids 4♡. The third hand is a typical balanced raise to 4♡, not worth the acceptance of a slam try. (Partner would have to bid slam himself, perhaps after using Blackwood.) The balanced raise is even worse for slam purposes than this, for example:

♠ A x ♡ K Q x x ◊ A K Q 10 x ♣ x x

The latter hand would be enough to bid slam with over a 5♣ cuebid.

Since a reverse is forcing, 1♣-1♠, 3◊ should be a splinter in support of spades. Some play it as forcing to game; others play that a 3♠ bid can be passed. Their theory is that the splinter, with a hand like

♠ K J x x ♡ A x x ◊ x ♣ A Q x x x

is a more descriptive game try than merely raising to 3♠. Responder would accept the splinter invitation with

♠ Q x x x ♡ K x ◊ x x x x ♣ K x x

and reject it with

♠ Q x x x ♡ Q x ◊ K Q x ♣ x x x x

Opener *could* have a game-forcing hand, planning to bid game even if responder bids 3♠ and to try for slam if responder cuebids. A double jump (1♣-1♠, 4♦) would show a void.

What about 1♣-1♡, 3♦? Since a mini-splinter in spades is not available (because it would be a jump shift and forcing to game), some play that the 3♦ bid shows a splinter in either diamonds or spades (mini or otherwise). One can usually guess which suit partner is short in. For example, if responder has 1-5-4-3 distribution, it is almost a cinch that partner's splinter is truly in diamonds, otherwise someone would have bid spades. I'm neutral on this idea. When the short suit can be either of two suits, and the splinter is either forcing to game or merely invitational, there might be too much ambiguity for the partner of the splinter bidder to bid with confidence.

WHAT IS FORCING?

New suits by responder are forcing unless opener has rebid 1NT or unless responder has previously made a weak, non-forcing bid. For example,

Opener	Responder
1♡	1♠
2♦	2♠
2NT	3♣

If responder was willing to play 2♠, he can't be very strong. In fact, his hand is too weak to play 2NT, perhaps

♠ Q 10 9 8 x x ♡ x ♦ x ♣ Q 10 x x x

Reverses by opener are forcing (and usually guarantee a rebid). A jump shift by opener is forcing to game. If the bidding is forced to game, any non-game bid is, by definition, forcing. After a one-level response most jumps in a previously-bid suit are invitational but not forcing. For example,

Opener	Responder	Opener	Responder	Opener	Responder
1♣	1♠	1♡	1NT	1♦	1♠
3♠		3♡		3♦	

Most jump bids in notrump are only invitational:

Opener	Responder	Opener	Responder
1♣	1♡	1♦	1♡
2NT		1♠	2NT

In general, when the partner of an invitational bidder makes a further bid, he has accepted the invitation, and the bid is forcing to game. For example,

Opener	Responder	Opener	Responder	Opener	Responder
1◇	1♠	1♡	1♠	1♣	1♡
3♠	4◇	3♡	3♠	2NT	3♡

But there are a few conventions or treatments that modify the general rule. We have already discussed whether a 2NT response to a minor is forcing. If it is merely invitational, should these auctions

Opener	Responder	Opener	Responder
1♣	2NT	1◇	2NT
3♣		3◇	

be forcing? Most players agree that they should not.

Opener	Responder
1♠	1NT
2NT	?

In this auction 3♠ should certainly not be forcing, since responder shows a hand too weak to raise 1♠ to 2♠. But 3♡ by responder *should* be forcing since the probability of making a game in hearts is greater than that 3♡ is the only remaining contract that can be made. Whether 3♣ and 3◇ are forcing is a matter for partnership agreement. In the absence of agreement, they should not be forcing, since responder might hold

♠ — ♡ J x x ◇ x x x ♣ K J x x x x x

With a good club fit, opener would bid 3NT anyway.

You may have heard of the Wolff signoff. After

Opener	Responder
1X	1Y
2NT	?

a 3♣ bid by responder is a transfer to 3◇. The 3♣ bid is either a slam try or the start of a signoff. If responder bids 3Y (his original suit) over the forced 3◇ rebid, he wants his partner to pass. If, over 3◇, he bids 3NT, it is a mild slam try in opener's suit. If he bids the other major over 3◇, it is a slam try in the other minor. Here are a few examples.

Opener	Responder
1♣	1♠
2NT	3♣
3◇	?

With

♠ Q J 10 x x x ♡ x ◇ J x x x ♣ x x

responder would bid 3♠ to sign off. With

♠ K 10 9 x   ♡ x x   ◇ J 10 x x x x   ♣ x

he would pass 3◇. With

♠ A J x x x   ♡ x   ◇ A K x x x   ♣ 10 x

he would bid 3♡ (the other major) to suggest a slam in diamonds (or spades). With

♠ A x x x   ♡ K x   ◇ K x x   ♣ Q x x x

or

♠ A 10 x x x   ♡ x x   ◇ A Q x   ♣ Q x x

he would bid 3NT to suggest a slam in clubs. Neither hand is quite good enough to suggest a slam in notrump, but the ruffing value may produce the twelfth trick. Some players would not bid this way with the second hand because, first, the hand might play better in spades and, second, they think they need four clubs to invite a slam in clubs. But usually opener should reject the invitation with only a four-card club suit. A typical acceptance would be with one of these hands:

♠ K x   ♡ A J x   ◇ K x x   ♣ A K x x x

♠ Q   ♡ A K x   ◇ K x x   ♣ A K x x x x

Since the rebid of 3NT is a mild invitation and allows opener to pass, with a better hand responder could bid 4♣. (This would not be Gerber since, if responder wanted to ask about controls, he could bid 4♣ directly over 2NT rather than starting with 3♣.)

No matter which suit opener has bid, 3◇ is a checkback bid. In priority order, opener should bid the other major holding four, and three of responder's major with three-card support; otherwise he bids 3NT. Some players reverse the order here and show three of responder's major as the first priority, but this seems inferior to me. If the partnership finds a 4-4 fit in the other major, it is better to have the strong hand declaring. If the bidding goes 1◇-1♡, 2NT-3◇, 3♠-3NT, opener knows responder was looking for a 5-3 heart fit, and he can bid 4♡. The 3◇ checkback bid only allows responder to discover whether opener has three -card support for his original major or four of the other major. Thus if responder is 5-5 in the majors he should bid 1♠ followed by a direct 3♡ over 2NT since the checkback bid would not discover whether opener has three hearts. Likewise, if responder has six hearts and five spades, after bidding 1♡ initially, he should bid 3♠ directly over 2NT. Finally, as suggested much earlier when discussing Fast Arrival, a jump to game in responder's major (1◇-1♠, 2NT-4♠) shows a solid suit and slam interest. Opener will not be discouraged by a weak holding in the solid suit.

PASSING FORCING BIDS

Most players play a simple rule: never pass a forcing bid. You may gain on the hand, but you lose partner's confidence, so it isn't worth it. Perhaps they are right, but I think you should make the percentage bid on each hand, which means that you do pass on very rare and unusual occasions. For example, you hold

♠ 8 6 5 4 3   ♡ 10 6 4   ◊ 6   ♣ K Q 10 9

Partner opens 1◊. You respond 1♠ and partner rebids 2♡. His reverse is forcing for one round, and he guarantees a rebid. Most players would rebid 2♠. What else can they do? If partner has spade support, he is short in clubs, and your club honors won't be valuable. Perhaps he will bid 2NT or 3NT over 2♠. He *could* hold

♠ x   ♡ A J x x   ◊ A K Q J x x   ♣ A x

in which case you belong in 3NT. Or he could hold

♠ A x x   ♡ A K x x   ◊ A K Q x x   ♣ x

in which case you probably belong in 4♠ (although a 4-1 spade break may 'save' you if you stop below game). Or partner may have a three-card heart holding with solid diamonds, something like:

♠ x x   ♡ A Q x   ◊ A K Q J x x x   ♣ J

A pass may work out badly, but I think it is the percentage bid. Actually, when this hand was dealt, a heart partscore *was* your best contract since partner's high cards plus a diamond ruff or two made nine tricks while the rest of the field was getting minus scores. Eddie Kantar and I both recommend a pass at matchpoints, and I would even pass at IMPs. Fortunately, although I passed, I didn't lose my partner!

Here is a stranger auction. You open 1♠ with

♠ A Q J x x x   ♡ x x   ◊ x   ♣ K J x x

LHO bids 4♣ and partner bids 4◊. You bid 4♠ and partner bids 5♡. We had never discussed this sequence. Some players think 5♡ must be a cuebid in support of spades. I thought my partner's bid was natural, showing 5-6 in hearts and diamonds. In either event it must be forcing, so I bid 5♠. What else could I do? Partner then bid 5NT, obviously asking me to choose a slam. This was at IMPs, and I was sure that if partner had solid diamonds (six or seven headed by the AKQJ), he would simply have bid 6◊. If he had ♠Kx, he would bid 6♠ after I have bid spades three times. If his diamonds were less than solid, or if he had a singleton spade, I wanted no part of a slam, especially since West probably has an eight-card club suit, and partner's suits will not break well. Not only did I doubt that we could make a slam with my misfit hand opposite a red two-suiter with suits likely to break badly, but I thought the doubling might start if I bid again — so I passed 5NT! Partner certainly had his bids — he had

♠ K ♡ A K Q x x ◇ A K J 10 x x ♣ x

— but 5NT was our last makable contract, and even that could be set with a spade opening lead (rather than the actual jack of hearts from ♡J109x) since it forces dummy to cash three spades (or lose them), which establishes the setting trick for the defense. (The opening leader obviously had a void in clubs, which was not a great surprise since I had four and LHO probably had eight.) The 4♣ bidder had 1-2-2-8 distribution.

Passing is not an insult to partner. It isn't a case of not trusting him. You consider the hands he might hold, bidding logically, and if the odds are 10 to 1 that further bidding will cost, you simply play the odds by passing. Incidentally the player with my hand at the other table passed 5♡! Apparently he shared my philosophy regarding passing forcing bids, so we tied the board (660 for us, 650 for them). When the hand and auction were presented to a bidding panel, Eddie Kantar was the only one who chose to pass. Good for him!

PASS OR CORRECT

Most 'pass or correct' situations occur in competitive bidding. For example, if the bidding goes

Opener	Oppt.	Responder	Oppt.
1♠	pass	1NT	3◇
3♡	pass	?	

and responder holds one of these hands:

a) ♠ K J x ♡ K x ◇ x x x x ♣ A x x x

b) ♠ K x ♡ K J x x ◇ x x x x ♣ A x x

a slam is quite possible. Yes, opener will bid 3♡ almost any time he has 5-5 in the majors, even with a minimum in high cards, or with 5-4 and very little more than a minimum — but he may have a pretty good hand. In most uncontested auctions, responder can agree upon a suit and then cue-bid, but in this case 3♠, 4♡ and 4♠ are all non-forcing. So he should bid 4◇ as a general slam try in support of one of opener's suits.

What does opener do when he doesn't know which suit responder has good support for? Suppose opener has

♠ A Q 10 x x ♡ A J x x ◇ x ♣ K Q x

If responder has hand (a) 6♠ will be an excellent contract. Opener should bid 4♡, and if responder bids 4♠, he will bid 6♠, or at least invite 6♠. Suppose opener holds

♠ A J 9 x x   ♡ A Q J x   ◇ x   ♣ K Q x

or

♠ A x x x x   ♡ A Q x x x   ◇ —   ♣ K Q x

With either of these two hands, if responder holds hand (b) opener wants to get to a slam in hearts. So he should bid 4♠, rejecting any slam try in spades but accepting any slam try in hearts. This is a 'pass or correct' bid, forcing the bidding beyond game if responder returns to hearts.

While it occurs less frequently, a pass or correct situation may arise in an uncontested auction. Suppose partner opens 2◇, showing a weak two-bid in either major. You hold

♠ x   ♡ K x x   ◇ A x x x   ♣ A J x x x

If you had support for both majors, you could bid 2NT to find out which major partner had and then bid or invite game in that major. But you don't have support for both majors. If partner's major is spades, you don't want to get past 2♠, but if he has hearts, you have enough to bid game, or at least invite game. So you should bid 2♠. That means you are not interested in a game in spades, but have enough for at least an invitation if his suit is hearts. Knowing that, opener can bid 4♡ directly, or if he wants to give you a little leeway, he can bid 2NT or three of a minor to show invitational values. With a heart suit, Meckwell rebid in steps over 2♠ to show bad, medium or good hands.

Suppose you are playing Namyats. Since an opening bid of 4♣ or 4◇ shows a good preempt in hearts or spades, many Namyats players open 3NT to show a four-level preempt in either minor. If responder holds

♠ A J x x   ♡ A x x x x   ◇ x   ♣ Q x x

he wants to raise to game if opener's suit is clubs, but stop at 4◇ if his suit is diamonds. Again 'pass or correct' is the solution. Bid 4◇, and if opener's suit is clubs, he is forced to 5♣, which is just what you want. There are many other possible sequences where the 'pass or correct' principle solves your problem; some were discussed under the topic of the three-suited 2◇ opening.

SOME OPTIONAL TRADEOFFS

In Standard bidding 1♡/1♠-1NT, 2NT should show a good 17 to 18 HCP. Some people say 18 to 19, but 19 with a five-card suit opposite 7 should provide a good play for game. Since the range for a 1NT response, even for standard two-over-one bidders, is 6-11 (although with 11 responder normally bids again), it seems strange to have an invitational bid, asking partner to pass only with precisely six points, rather than with 6-7 or 6-8. While suit responses are often made with less than 6 points, 1NT seldom is (other than with a fit for opener's major suit as a semi-psyche). Anyway, after the raise to 2NT, three of a minor is a tentative sign off. I don't know what 1♡-1NT, 2NT-3♠ should mean — perhaps a three-card limit raise in hearts with 4333 distribution, giving opener the option of letting you play notrump with 5332 opposite 4333. Bidding three of opener's major means that responder bid a minimum or sub-minimum 1NT with three- or four-card support, and it is an attempt to sign off. The special case (which was discussed earlier) is 1♠-1NT, 2NT-3♡. This should be forcing since responder could have, for example

♠ x x   ♡ K Q x x x   ◇ K x x x   ♣ J x

in which case 4♡ might be greatly superior to 3NT.

Geir Helgemo thinks it a worthwhile trade-off to play 1♡/1♠ -1NT, 2NT as forcing to game and artificial. After

Opener	Responder
1♠	1NT
2NT	?

3♣ shows five or more cards in either minor, 3◇ shows four hearts, 3♡ shows five hearts, 3♠ shows two spades and 3NT shows both minors. Similar responses are used after a 1♡ opening. If they had been using that convention they could have reached 7♣ on these hands

♠ A K 10 9 x x	♠ J x
♡ x x	♡ A x
◇ A x	◇ 10 x x
♣ A Q 9	♣ K 10 x x x x

which he encountered in a tournament before adopting his new convention. This also takes care of 6-4 hands and other odd distributions. With a 5332 hand that would have bid 2NT as invitational, they simply jump to 3NT. It helps to be as good a player as Helgemo when you get so high in some of these contracts.

Jeff Goldsmith thinks it is worth giving up the ability to play in 3♣ in order to use various transfer responses after 1♡/1♠ -1NT, 2NT. Another idea — not mine — is to play a jump to 2NT as forcing to game after opening one of a suit and getting a one-over-one suit response. (The theory is that the 2NT rebid is seldom passed anyway.) This treatment allows opener to describe various distributions and distinguish strong 6-4 and 5-4 hands from 6-5 and 5-5 hands, which are shown by the old-fashioned jump shift. This is just a sample of things you can do by giving up one thing for another. Usually it is natural minor-suit bids, especially clubs, that you give up. Already you have 2♣ for Stayman or Drury, 3♣ as a Bergen raise or Stayman over 2NT, 4♣ as Gerber, and 5♣ as Super Gerber. Some players treat various diamond bids as artificial (like in two-way Drury, part of two-way new minor forcing, XYZ, etc.). My feeling is that there are too many conventional bids and not enough natural bids. But of course, exceptions should be made for the artificial bids *I* recommend! ⁄

RESPONDING TO 2♣

I have some strong opinions on this subject, and they differ from those of most other people. Let's start with some philosophical observations. How is it possible to bid to 7♠ with the following hands?

♠ A Q J 10 x x x	♠ K
♡ A	♡ Q x x x
◇ K Q J 10 x	◇ A x x
♣ —	♣ J x x x x

No matter what the strong hand tells the weak hand, the weak hand cannot know that 7♠ will be cold, but if the strong hand can find out that the weak hand has the king of spades and the ace of diamonds, he can easily place the contract. At the moment we are not concerned with how the strong hand will find out. The point is that the strong distributional hand should be 'captain' in order to place the contract. The hand that opens 2♣ presumably is the strong distributional hand (although, if he rebids 2NT, showing a balanced hand, the captaincy will revert to responder since when one hand shows a balanced hand within a narrow range, it is his partner who more or less places the contract).

So, in the usual case, the 2♣ bidder should find out whatever he can about responder's hand and responder should furnish information so that opener can make the correct decision. But what usually happens is that responder makes a non-descriptive (waiting) 2◇ bid, thereby wasting an opportunity to describe his hand, while opener has more features to show than he will have time to show before a final decision is made. Besides, responder is not the one who should make the final decision. It is important for him to start describing his hand immediately. Haven't you seen bidding sequences like the following? Responder has 7 or 8 points with either a balanced or unbalanced hand. He responds 2◇; opener bids his suit, and responder now bids his five-card suit (not showing whether he has 4 points or 10 points) and either passes when opener bids game or bids 4NT and places the final contract. Or, if he has a fit for opener's suit, he either raises once (showing better than a double negative, but anywhere from 4 HCP to 8 HCP) and drops the bidding later, or he uses Blackwood and places the final contract. Again the weaker hand takes control of the bidding and decides whether or not to bid a slam. This is *wrong*!

Some players respond 2♡ to 2♣ to show a 'double negative,' denying as much as a king or two queens. This isn't very helpful either. After the double negative response opener is afraid to rebid 3♡ with

♠ A K x   ♡ A K J x x x   ♢ A K x   ♣ x

for fear that responder will pass with nothing but three small hearts or two hearts and a pointed queen. So he bids 4♡, which shuts responder out of the bidding with

♠ Q J x x x x   ♡ x   ♢ x x x   ♣ J x x

While a double negative response tells opener that a slam is unlikely unless he has an exceptionally good hand, failure to show a double negative does not tell him whether responder has 4 points or 13 points and is not much help in getting to a slam. Surely it would be more helpful if the first response provided more information than whether responder holds (roughly) more or less than three points. Some people play that 2♢ shows 0 or 1 control (kings counting as one control, aces as two); 2♡ shows 2 controls; 2♠ shows 3, etc. However, this method, while better than an almost automatic 2♢ response, interferes with natural bidding. Is it more important to show the exact number of controls or to show whether responder holds a minimum of high card strength together with a six-card suit or a good five-card suit? (Showing controls over a strong *one* club bid is effective since there is more bidding room to show distribution later.)

Of course, I am prejudiced in favor of my own methods, but this is what I recommend. A 2♢ response *denies* two kings, or 7 points including an ace, or 8 points including a king. A bid of 2♡ shows too many high cards for a 2♢ response but no suit worth showing. I don't insist on a five-card suit with two of the top three honors to show a suit. That, perhaps, was a logical requirement before Roman Keycard Blackwood became popular. Now you can find out about missing honors in the trump suit by using that convention, so I think Q10xxx of spades (which you can show at the two-level) or any six-card suit with enough high cards on the side is a good enough suit to show. The other suits need to be slightly stronger because they take up more bidding room. (Note that 2NT is a positive response with at least five hearts and three of either minor is natural and positive.)

There are several advantages to this method. Suppose opener holds

♠ A K x   ♡ A Q x   ♢ K J 9 x x   ♣ A Q

If responder bids 2♢ he may have a yarborough, so opener will rebid 2NT. The most likely game is 3NT, and if responder has a very weak hand, he can pass 2NT. But if responder bids 2♡, game is a certainty, even if played by the weaker hand, so opener can afford to show his suit by bidding 3◊. Now responder, with diamond support and a ruffing value — a hand like

♠ x x   ♡ K x x x   ◊ Q x x x   ♣ K x x

say — can afford to raise diamonds and a very good slam will be reached. The rest of the field will bid 2♣-2◊, 2NT-3NT since the responding hand can only count a combined 30 to 32 points, hardly enough to try for 6NT.

Suppose responder holds

♠ Q x x x   ♡ x   ◊ x x x   ♣ Q 10 x x x

The bidding starts 2♣ -2◊, 2♠. Are you strong enough to make a splinter bid of 4♡? In Standard bidding you might be reluctant to make the bid for fear of giving partner too much encouragement, but if your 2◊ response placed an upper limit on your hand, I think it is logical to splinter.

Suppose opener has

♠ A K Q J x x   ♡ K x   ◊ A K Q   ♣ J x

and responder has

♠ x x x x x   ♡ x x   ◊ x x x   ♣ A Q x x

The bidding goes 2♣-2◊, 2♠-3♠. In Standard, where the 2◊ response is unlimited and 3♠ is encouraging, opener might be tempted to bid 4◊, and responder might think he was strong enough to cuebid 5♣. But there is no way responder can have the right cards for a good slam after a 2◊ response in my methods when he does not splinter on the second round. Consequently, the bidding would stop safely at the four-level. With these two hands, there is about a 25% play for slam and a 25% chance of being set at the five-level.

I have covered the main features of the 2♡ positive response. But there is more.

After you open 2♣ and receive a 2◊ response, most players would rebid 3NT with

♠ A Q x x   ♡ A K x   ◊ A Q x x   ♣ A Q

But if responder holds one of these hands:

♠ 10 x x x   ♡ x x   ◊ J x x x   ♣ x x x

♠ x   ♡ J 10 x x x   ◊ J x   ♣ J x x x x

then 4♠ or 4♡ will be a much better contract. With either hand, responder could do nothing but pass 3NT and hope for the best. Any attempt to improve the contract might result in just being one trick higher if no fit is discovered. Also, most players treat any bid over 3NT as a slam try. The Kokish convention allows opener to bid 2♡ over a 2◊ response, showing either a heart suit or a game-forcing balanced hand (25+). Responder is required to bid 2♠, after which opener bids 2NT with the strong balanced hand. If opener bids anything except 2NT, his bid is natural and retroactively confirms a heart suit. The 2NT bid is forcing, but otherwise responder bids as though his partner had opened 2NT. He can use Stayman with the first hand or bid 3◊, transferring to hearts, with the second. If no better contract is discovered, the final contract will be 3NT, but nothing has been lost by investigating alternatives. Note that if the response had been 2♡, a double negative, Kokish would not have been available, so playing 2♡ as a double negative along with Kokish over a 2◊ response makes little sense. When you need Kokish it is not available; when you don't need it (because you are too strong for a double negative) you can use it.

What would you expect 2♣-2◊, 3NT to show? It should show a hand with a long solid minor, but with controls on the side, something like

$$◊ K x \quad ♡ A J \quad ◊ A K Q J x x x \quad ♣ K x$$

After a 2◊ response you are not worried about missing a slam and want to get the notrump bid in first to protect your tenaces. If partner had made a positive response you would simply have bid 3◊ for two reasons: you might have a slam and don't want to preempt partner out of describing his hand, and you are no longer quite so worried about who should be the declarer.

What would you expect a 3NT response to an opening 2♣ bid to show? Not a good, balanced hand, since you have no need for the bid, and it leaves little room to discover where responder's values are. It is better to bid 2♡, allowing opener with a balanced hand to bid 2NT. Not only is it better for the stronger hand to be declarer, but you can use your whole system, including transfers and Stayman after 2♣-2♡, 2NT. The 3NT response to 2♣ shows a completely solid suit, good enough to lose no tricks opposite a singleton or void. The minimum suit strength for this bid is AKQJxx or AKQxxxx. Both suits give you a reasonable chance to avoid a loser opposite a void and very good chances to avoid a loser opposite a singleton. Opener should be able to tell what your solid suit is, and if he bids it, the bidding afterwards is natural. But opener can often place the contract after asking one more question. Suppose he holds

$$♠ A K Q x x \quad ♡ x \quad ◊ A K Q J x \quad ♣ Q x$$

Opener knows partner's suit is hearts. If partner has a singleton club or the king, he can bid 6♡ or 6NT with assurance. If partner has the ace of clubs or a void, he can bid a grand slam. So opener should bid 4♣, an asking bid. Responder bids the first step (in this case 4◊) to deny a control in clubs, the second step to show a singleton and the third step to show the ace or void. The cheapest notrump bid shows the king, and it is squeezed in, displacing the other bid. For example, if the asking bid were 4♠, 4NT would show the king and 5♣ would show no control.

A jump to the four-level over 2♣ shows a one-loser suit, missing the ace or king. It could be AQJ10xx or KQJxxxx, but not AK10xxxxx; that way, if opener has the ace or king, he knows there is no loser. If he merely has length (like three small), he will figure there is still a loser. While the jump to the four-level shows a one-loser suit, the one-loser suit is not the suit responder bids, but the one above it: 4◇ shows hearts, and 4♠ shows clubs. The same asking bids as after a 3NT response are available. When one holds a solid or one-loser suit it is imperative to show it, otherwise partner will assume that the suit is not that good. In other words, all of the recommended responses provide negative, as well as positive information. A 2◇ response denies two kings, or 7 points with an ace or 8 points with a king, but responder could have as much as a 12-count if he does not have an ace or king. The artificial 2♡ response denies a good suit, although if you are contemplating a bid of three of a minor, or 2NT to show a positive response in hearts, you need a better suit than you need to bid 2♠, and any ordinary suit response denies the ability to bid 3NT or to bid a suit at the four-level. An optional feature is to respond 3♡ or 3♠ with a six-card or longer suit headed by two of the top three honors. It is a close question whether showing this strong a major suit (and denying this strong a suit if you don't bid it) is worth the cost of preempting the 2♣ bidder out of showing *his* suit at a reasonable level.

What should the following sequences mean?

Opener	Responder	Opener	Responder
2♣	2◇	2♣	2♡
3♡	?	3♠	?

When the opening 2♣ bidder jumps, he not only sets the trump suit, but he indicates that a slam is likely. It depends upon where responder's high cards are located. In other words, he is asking for controls and he doesn't care about responder's distribution. These are typical hands for the bids are

♠ A Q J   ♡ A K Q J x x x   ◇ —   ♣ K Q J

♠ A Q J x x x x x   ♡ —   ◇ K Q J 9   ♣ A

In the first example, after a 2◇ response, partner can't have both the king of spades and the ace of clubs, but if he has either of these cards, it will be enough for a small slam. The second hand is a bit more of a gamble since with a bad spade break there could be two (or three!) losers in spades, and the ◇9 could also be a loser, but I think most players would be willing to gamble on a small slam if partner had one of the two critical high cards or a grand slam with both. In principle, opener can also jump to 4♣ or 4◇ if his long suit is a minor, but he has to be careful that the wrong response won't get him too high.

Over the jump bid the king of trumps counts as an ace. If responder has one ace he should bid it. With two (or more!) aces, he jumps to the cheapest ace. In the first example, if responder bids 4♣ (ace of clubs), opener will just bid 6♡ since responder can't have an ace and a king, but if his first response had been 2♡ and if responder had bid 4♣ opener would bid 4♠ to ask about the king of spades. With no aces or kings, responder would raise opener's suit; in this case he would bid 4♡. (A 5♡ bid would show the ace or king of hearts but no other ace.) With no aces, but one or more kings, responder would bid 3NT and opener could ask about kings. In this case, if responder had bid 3NT over 3♡, opener would bid 4♠ to ask about the king. In the second example responder would jump to 5♢ if he had the ace of diamonds and either the ace of hearts or king of spades. Since opener couldn't tell which, he would bid 5NT and responder would bid 6♡ with the ace of hearts or 6♠ with the king of spades (or bid 7♠ with the king of spades to save a round of bidding). The king of trumps can't be wasted but the ace of hearts might be useless.

1. **Partner**   **You**
   1♢   1♠
   2♣   ?

   ♠ K Q 10 8 5 4   ♡ Q 9 8 6 3   ♢ —   ♣ 10 7
   What call do you make?

2. You are vulnerable vs. not and partner opens 1♣. You hold

   ♠ K 10   ♡ J 6 4 3   ♢ Q 10 6   ♣ Q 5 4 2
   What call do you make?

3. What call do you make with?

   Partner   **You**
   1♢   2♢¹
   2♡   ?
   1. Inverted.

   ♠ J   ♡ Q J 7   ♢ K Q 6 4 2   ♣ A Q 6 2

4. Partner opens 1♣. You hold

   ♠ 8 6   ♡ 10 9 6 5   ♢ 7   ♣ K Q J 8 7 3
   What call do you make?

5. **West**   **East**
  ♠ A Q J 7 4   ♠ K 9 3
  ♡ Q 10   ♡ K J 8 3
  ◊ A K 6   ◊ J 9
  ♣ Q J 3   ♣ 10 8 7 2

  1♠   2♠
  4♠   pass

The contract is defeated by two high clubs and a club ruff. Whose fault is it?

6. **West**   **East**
  ♠ A K 7 5 4 2   ♠ J 10 8 3
  ♡ 6   ♡ A J 7 4 2
  ◊ 10 9 6   ◊ 8
  ♣ A K 5   ♣ Q 10 3

  1♠   3♠¹
  4♠   pass
  1. Limit raise.

Whose fault is it that a good slam was missed?

7. **West**   **East**
  ♠ K J   ♠ A Q 8 6 2
  ♡ 8 7   ♡ 6 4
  ◊ A Q J 5   ◊ K 8 3
  ♣ 9 7 6 5 4   ♣ A J 2

  pass   1♠
  1NT   pass

Whose fault was it for not getting to game (in spades, of course)?

8. **West**   **East**
  1◊   1♠
  2♣   3◊
  3♠   ?

East holds

  ♠ Q 6 5 4   ♡ 9 2   ◊ K Q 7 5   ♣ A 9 8

What call should he make?

9. **You**   **Partner**
   1♣   2♠
   2NT   4♡
   4NT   5♣[1]
   ?
   1. 0 or 3 keycards.

   ♠ K 7   ♡ J 7 6   ◇ K Q 2   ♣ K Q 6 5 4
   Your call.

10. **Partner**   **You**
    1♣   1♡
    1♠   3♣
    3♡   ?

    ♠ K 9 8   ♡ Q 6 4 2   ◇ 9   ♣ A J 8 7 3
    Your next call?

11. **Partner**   **You**
    1♣   1♠
    2◇   ?

    ♠ A J 6 4 3   ♡ 8 6   ◇ K 5   ♣ K 8 6 5
    What do you bid now?

12. **You**   **Partner**
    2♣   2♡
    ?

    ♠ A Q J 7   ♡ A Q 8   ◇ A K 10   ♣ K Q 2
    Your bid.

13. **Partner**   **You**
    2◇[1]   3♠
    4◇   ?
    1. Flannery.

    ♠ K J 9 8 6   ♡ 7   ◇ —   ♣ A K Q 8 6 4 3
    What call would you make now?

14. **West**   **East**

♠ A K J 10 9 5 2   ♠ 7 4
♡ 4   ♡ A K Q 9 8 6
◊ A K 8   ◊ J 6
♣ A Q   ♣ 9 7 5

2♣   2NT
3♠   4♡
4NT   5♠[1]
7♡

1. 2 keycards plus the heart queen.

This is not a grand that you want to reach. Who was at fault?

15. Partner opens 1♣. Which of the following hands justifies a strong jump shift response?

♠ K 10 8 7 5 4 3   ♡ A K   ◊ A   ♣ Q 4 2

♠ A K   ♡ Q 10 9 5 2   ◊ J 10 7   ♣ A Q J

16. Partner opens 1♡ and you hold

♠ A K J 6 3   ♡ K 10 6 4 3   ◊ 7 6   ♣ 10

What would you respond?

17. **Partner**   **You**
2♣   2♡
2♠   ?

What would you bid now with each of these hands?
(a) ♠ 8 7 6   ♡ K Q 5   ◊ K 6 4 3   ♣ J 6 2
(b) ♠ K 9 5   ♡ A 8 7 3   ◊ 9 7 6   ♣ K J 5

my answers

1. Just bid 2♠. A bid of 2♡ would be forcing and unlimited and would almost certainly cause you to get to game unless partner bids 2♠ or 3♠. It's unlikely that he will do either of these things, and even if he does, you gain nothing as compared to bidding 2♠ yourself. A bid of 3♡, showing an invitational two-suiter, is possible, but too aggressive, I think.

2. Bid 1NT. You barely have enough for this bid, but it may prevent an overcall in spades, which is more important than bidding the weak heart suit.

3. Bid 3♠, a splinter of course. The fact that partner apparently lacks a spade stopper makes your hand look good for slam purposes. If partner has the ♡AK, ◇A and ♣K you are probably cold for a slam.

4. Bid 3♣ at any vulnerability and any form of scoring.

5. West was at fault. It couldn't cost him to bid 2NT. East would then have bid 3♡, showing secondary values in hearts, which is all West would have needed to know to bid 3NT. If East makes any other bid over 2NT, West can't be blamed for bidding 4♠, but it costs nothing to investigate.

6. Both players are at fault. East has too good a hand to invite game; he should insist on game — not that he is sure it will make, because he can't tell how well the hands will fit, but ten tricks are more likely than nine. So he should have bid 3NT, a mini-splinter, and this time West should ask where the splinter is. If it is anything but diamonds, he will sign off in 4♠. When he discovers the splinter is in diamonds, he can use Blackwood, knowing there are many chances to avoid a club loser. However, over 3♠, opener could still have bid 3NT (a Mathe asking bid), asking responder to show a singleton.

7. Not everyone will agree with me, but I think West should bid 2♣, Drury, as the least of evils. The top cards and potential ruffing value compensate for the missing spade. After pass-1♠, 2♣-2◇, 2♠-? I think East has just about enough for 2NT, followed by bidding 4♠ over a 3◇ bid by West. But even if they don't get to game, a spade partscore is obviously better than 1NT.

8. Opener's 3♠ is only a tentative bid, allowing responder to bid 4♠ with a five-card suit or a good four-card suit. Since responder has a weak spade holding, he should return to 4◇. A bid of 4♣ would imply a singleton heart and be too encouraging.

9. You should bid 7♣. Partner has

    ♠ A J 10 x x   ♡ —   ◇ A x x   ♣ A J x x x

    A 3♡ bid on the second round would show a singleton, so 4♡ must show a void.

10. You should bid 3♠ for two reasons. First, your hearts are too weak to play in a 4-3 fit: perhaps partner's spades are strong, and if not, he can return to clubs. The second reason is that you would rather

have partner ruff diamonds with your three-card spade holding instead of you ruffing diamonds with your four-card heart holding. Partner has

♠ A Q x x ♡ A J x ◇ x x ♣ K Q x x

He followed my recommendation in a later chapter to avoid opening 1NT with four spades and a worthless doubleton.

11. You should jump to 4♣, showing good trumps and no control in hearts. (What 'good trumps' are varies, of course, depending upon the previous bidding.) A bid of 3♣ is forcing, of course, but your hand is so good that you almost surely belong in slam if partner has a heart control. Your 4♣ bid shows a good enough hand that partner can Blackwood if he has a heart control and perhaps get to a grand slam with

♠ K ♡ A x ◇ A Q x x ♣ A Q x x x x

12. Just bid 2NT, which allows you to play the system (Stayman, transfers, etc.). Usually, when partner makes what he thinks will be the final bid, you will bid one more. For example, if he bids 3NT, you will bid 4NT; if he uses Stayman and signs off in four of a major, you will bid five. This means you have extra values that you didn't show the previous round since it would have crowded the bidding.

13. It is hard to be scientific with this distributional hand, especially when there are so few rounds of bidding available. Perhaps I am influenced since I know the actual hands. Partner has shown 4-5-3-1 distribution and, if he has wasted values in diamonds, even the five-level may not be safe. You are missing three critical cards (♠AQ and ♡A), and you need to find partner with two of them for a good slam. My suggestion is to bid 4♠. Your 3♠ response already showed an interest in slam, and if you have lost your interest, it is probably because partner bid 4◇ rather than 4♣. So if partner has most of his values in diamonds, he will be willing to pass 4♠, while if his values include two of the three cards you need (which he would know to be valuable) he will probably bid again. Both pairs got too high with this hand in the 2004 Vanderbilt when opener held

♠ 10 7 5 4 ♡ K 9 8 3 2 ◇ A K J ♣ 9

and the ♠AQ turned out to be lying over the king. However, since neither pair was playing Flannery, their problems were different from yours.

14. West was at fault for failing to draw a negative inference. If East's hearts were as good as ♡AKQJxx or seven to the ace-king-queen, he would have responded 3NT immediately to show a solid suit.

15. Neither hand justifies a jump shift. The first hand has too many holes in the spade suit. If you bid 1♠ and partner raises (unlikely) or rebids 1NT, my suggestion is to self-splinter in diamonds, but first you need to find out whether partner has any kind of spade support. The second hand is simply missing too many controls.

16. This hand is easily worth a jump shift. If partner has

    ♠ Q x ♡ A x x x x ◇ A J x ♣ Q x x

    (and that hand contains three wasted points!) you belong in a slam.

17. With hand (a) you should rebid 2NT. The difference between a good slam and a poor slam is often the strength of the trump suit. If partner has one loser outside the trump suit and ♠AKJxx, he will need a trump finesse and a 3-2 trump break. If you had four trumps or Qxx, on the other hand, it would be a good slam or at least a fair slam. So you should avoid an immediate raise with three small trumps. With hand (b) you should cuebid either 3♣ or 3♡. My preference is to cuebid 3♣ since partner will probably bid 3◇ and then you can show your heart control cheaply. The 2♡ response tends to deny a five-card suit, unless it is very weak. If you had a suit worth showing (and enough high cards to make a positive response) you would have bid it immediately. While the 3♣ bid is somewhat ambiguous — it could show a hand like

    ♠ x x ♡ x x x x x ◇ Q x ♣ K Q J x

    when it is followed by a heart bid — it must still show a good hand, controls in both bid suits and a fit for partner's suit.

CHAPTER 3

two-over-one

A CHANGE OF HEART

It is human nature to continue to play bridge the way you first learned to play unless someone convinces you that a new way is substantially better. So, for a long time I resisted the concept of two-over-one forcing to game. I could see problems for the responder in deciding whether to commit the hand to game before he knew his partner's distribution, or of being compelled by the system to bid a game he knew wasn't going to make because of a misfit. (I call it committing suicide to avoid losing partner's confidence.) I didn't like the choices between responding 1NT to a major-suit opening with hands like

♠ x ♡ x x ◇ A x x ♣ K Q 10 9 x x x

and perhaps never showing your club suit in some sequences, or of bidding 2♣ and forcing the partnership to game opposite a misfit. For a long time I adopted the Blue Team approach: a two-over-one response was forcing to 2NT and promised a rebid unless opener either jumped to game or bid 2NT. Consequently, after opening 1♠ and getting a 2♣ response from partner, 2◇, 2♡ and 2♠ were all forcing bids because 2NT had not been reached. Likewise 1♠-2♣, 3♡ was a forcing sequence because responder had promised a rebid. Two reasons Blue Team bidders adopted this rule were that they frequently opened a four-card major, even with a longer minor, and an initial 1NT response was not forcing. So after an opening bid of 1♠ with

♠ Q x x x ♡ x ◇ A K x ♣ K x x x x

responder would bid 2♡ with

♠ x ♡ A K J x x ◇ Q J 10 x ♣ x x x

and opener had no reasonable alternative to rebidding a non-forcing 2NT with his misfitting hand. We don't need to feel smug since most players now would get to the same terrible contract by a different sequence: 1♣-1♡, 1♠-2NT or 1♣-1♡, 1♠-2◇, 2NT—and some players would get even higher if they considered the 2◇ bid forcing to game. The most modern trend is to play two-over-one forcing to game, but many experts have adopted a few exceptions which make the system more playable. However, there are still hands that create problems in 'two-over-one.'

I now think that two-over-one forcing to game is better than the old way if you adopt the following exceptions and if you use the forcing to game principle to the fullest extent and play a forcing (not a semi-forcing) 1NT response by an unpassed hand. But I don't think most players use the game-forcing principle to the extent that they should: they try to describe their hands in two rounds of bidding instead of three or four. I shall, of course, explain what I mean. But first, here are the five exceptions to the game-forcing approach, which I recommend.

1) a two-over-one response in competition

Opener	Oppt.	Responder	Oppt.
1♡	2♣	2♢	

is not forcing to game; it does not even guarantee a rebid unless opener cuebids, jumps in his original suit or bids a new suit. Almost everyone agrees that a two-over-one response in competition should not be forcing to game, although there is some disagreement as to whether and when it promises another bid. What I describe and recommend is *Bridge World* Standard. (Of course, the forcing principle is not affected if the opponents compete *after* the two-over-one bid.)

2) A two clubs response to one diamond should not be forcing to game.

3) The auction should not be forcing to game when responder rebids his original suit (unless opener's rebid showed extra values).

4) When opener bids the same suit three times in succession, the auction should no longer be forcing to game. Example:

Opener	Responder
1♠	2♢
2♠	3♣
3♠	

Remember, I recommended opening the bidding with

♠ A J x x x x x ♡ x x ♢ x ♣ A x x

Responder could have a good 14 points and intend to force to game, but if he has no heart stopper and a singleton or void in spades, what game is likely to make? If opener's spades were AQJxxxx or even KJ109xxx with enough high cards on the side to open, he could have jumped to 4♠ over 3♣ since the suit will be playable opposite a singleton or void. I think it is masochistic to bid a game that you know has no chance just to honor an arbitrary rule.

5) When you have tried to get to notrump and discovered that you don't have a suit stopped, you should be able to pass four of a minor.

Exceptions (1) and (5) are recognized by many players; exception (3) is part of *Bridge World* Standard, but (2) and (4) are not generally adopted.

For those of you who are not accustomed to playing exception (3) I had better explain how it affects your bidding. Partner opens 1♠ and you hold

♠ x ♡ K Q x ◇ x x ♣ A K Q J x x x

Even if 3♣ is available as a strong jump shift, you shouldn't use it with this hand. You belong in 3NT (or possibly higher) if partner has a diamond stopper but if the bidding goes

Partner	You
1♠	3♣
3♠	?

you can hardly bid 3NT with two small diamonds. So you start with 2♣ and partner rebids 2♠. Since 3♣ would not be forcing, you should bid 3♡. In the unlikely event that partner bids 4♡ you will bid 5♣, but probably, if he has a diamond stopper, he will bid 3NT. That is the way I would bid, even if 3♣ were forcing, since it clearly indicates to partner what he needs to bid 3NT, your most likely game. Change your hearts to ♡Qxx and I would make what looks like a vast underbid, and merely rebid a non-forcing 3♣. This is an invitational bid, of course, since with a weak hand and long clubs you would have responded 1NT in the first place and followed by bidding 3♣ on the next round. With your actual hand, if partner holds

♠ A K J x x x ♡ J x x ◇ Q J x ♣ x

3NT is the only game you are likely to make. If partner lacks a diamond stopper or has a void in clubs, he will probably hold the ace of hearts, and 5♣ will make. Would the hands be easier to bid if you could bid 2♣ followed by 3♣ and still be in a forcing auction? I don't think so.

SUIT QUALITY CONSIDERATIONS

A two-over-one response should almost always show a five-card or longer suit. I thought that was mostly my own concept but I recently discovered that Mike Lawrence advocated the same thing fifteen years ago. What should you respond with game-forcing strength and no long suit? Bid a forcing notrump! Partner opens 1♠ and you hold

♠ Q x ♡ K J x x ◇ A Q x ♣ Q x x x

How can it hurt to bid 1NT? How can it help to bid 2♣? If you bid 2♣ and partner has

♠ A K x x x ♡ A x ◇ K x ♣ K x x x

can you blame him for taking control and eventually placing the contract in 6♣?

Suppose you hold one of these hands:

♠ Q x　♡ J x x　◇ A K J x　♣ Q x x x

♠ Q x　♡ J x x　◇ A K J　♣ J x x x x

and you bid a forcing 1NT over partner's 1♠ bid. He rebids 2♣. You should now bid 3◇ to show a good hand with a club fit, otherwise partner will probably bid 3NT with a heart stopper or four or five clubs. The jump does not show a splinter after a 1NT response: responder is unlikely to have a singleton unless it is in opener's suit. The jump in a minor (including 1♠-1NT, 2♡-4♣/4◇) shows a feature plus great support for opener's second suit. A jump in the other major (1♠-1NT, 2♣-3♡ or 1♡-1NT, 2◇-3♠) shows a balanced hand with three-card support for opener's major. (If you were playing the Kaplan Interchange, the last sequence would be changed to 1♡-1♠, 2◇-3♠, and it might show

♠ A x x　♡ K Q　◇ K J x x　♣ J x x x

although partner will assume three-card heart support.)

When partner opens 1♠, what would you respond with

♠ J 10 x　♡ Q J x　◇ K J　♣ A 10 x x x

You don't want to stop short of game, but you don't belong in a slam unless partner makes a very strong rebid (like a jump shift or a raise to 2NT or 3NT). So you can bid 1NT followed by 4♠ next round over any minimum or ambiguous rebid. This should discourage any slam tries by partner. If your hand is improved slightly — say to

♠ Q x x　♡ K x x　◇ A x　♣ A J 10 x x

— you would respond 2♣ and, if partner rebids 2♠, raise to 3♠. It is close, but if partner rebids 2♡ I think you should bid 3♠ to show an interest in slam, while if he rebids 2◇ you should bid only 2♠. You are going to get to game at least, no matter what you bid from this point, but the key to accurate slam bidding is to find out about your combined strength and fit — whether your kings and queens are in partner's suit(s) — before you reach the game level.

DELAYED RAISES

I said earlier that two-over-one responses should *almost always* show a five-card or longer suit. When should you make an exception? The answer is, with a good 15 points or more and support for opener's major. Here's an example: partner opens 1♠ and you hold

♠ K x x   ♡ A x   ◊ A x x x   ♣ A 10 9 x

You want the advantage of slow bidding to investigate your slam chances. So you bid 2♣ followed by 3♠ next round whether partner rebids 2♠ or something else. If partner gets ambitious and drives to 6♣, thinking you have a longer club suit, you have to guess whether to return to spades, but usually there will be enough clues from the bidding for you to make the right decision.

When the bidding goes

Opener	Responder
1♠	2♣
2♠	4♠

what kind of hand would you expect responder to have? In the average game, responder would have something like

♠ J 10 x   ♡ Q J x   ◊ K J   ♣ A 10 x x x

the hand I recommended that you respond 1NT with. This is sort of a Fast Arrival bid, saying, 'We belong in 4♠ and no more, so I am bidding it directly.' I may be prejudiced since I don't like Fast Arrival in general, but I think this is lazy bidding. Responder's bidding should show good clubs and spades with no controls in the other two suits, perhaps one of these hands:

♠ Q J x   ♡ J x   ◊ x x   ♣ A K J x x x

♠ Q x x x   ♡ x x   ◊ Q x   ♣ A K Q 10 x

Opener knows that there is no slam unless he has at least a first- and a second-round control in the unbid suits like the ace of one suit and the king or a singleton in the other. If opener holds

♠ Q x x x x x   ♡ A K x   ◊ A x   ♣ x x

he should pass 4♠. He has controls in the unbid suits but he has too much of his strength there and not enough in clubs and spades. He should also pass with

♠ A K x x x x   ♡ K Q   ◊ K Q x   ♣ x x

because, despite his 17 points, the opponents must hold the two red aces. But with

♠ A K x x x x   ♡ x   ◊ A x x   ♣ Q x x

he can bid 6♠ with confidence.

Look at these auctions:

Opener	Responder	Opener	Responder	Opener	Responder
1♠	2♣	1♠	2♣	1♠	2♣
2NT	4♠	3♣	4♠	2♡	4♠

The first two sequences show the same type of hand for responder: good clubs and spades and no controls in the other two suits. The third sequence also shows good clubs and spades and no diamond control, but it does not deny a high honor or singleton in hearts. What would this sequence show?

Opener	Responder
1♠	2♣
2♠	4♣

This is the same type of hand as the first two sequences, with good clubs and spades and no controls in the other two suits, but even a stronger hand, perhaps including ♠Kxx and ♣AKQxxx or ♠KQx and ♣AK10xx, for example. Even with mediocre clubs and spades, opener should at least invite a slam, or probably bid a slam, with a first- and second-round control in the red suits.

What should responder bid when he doesn't have that kind of hand? This

Opener	Responder
1♠	2♣
2♠	3♠

is the catch-all bid. Responder may have no interest in slam or very little interest (but not an exceptionally weak two-over-one since he didn't respond 1NT originally), or he may have a strong interest. He may even be planning to bid again if opener bids 4♠, but this is rare. The ideal approach is to make your slam investigation before getting past the game level. Needless to say, the same pattern would apply with other suits, although for simplicity all my recent examples involved clubs and spades. I was rather proud of this concept and thought it was my own creation, but then I discovered that Mike Lawrence and Marty Bergen had both suggested approximately the same thing fifteen years ago.

FAST ARRIVAL

I've alluded to Fast Arrival several times already, so you already know that I don't like it. The theory of Fast Arrival is that when you have a good hand, you want the bidding to go slowly so that each partner can show his strength, his distribution and the location of his high cards. When you have a bad hand or a minimum for your previous bidding, you want to jump to what you believe will be the best final contract (usually four of a major or 3NT) so as to avoid giving information to the opponents or implying interest in a slam by your slow bidding. That may make sense in a few situations when you know that there is no chance for a slam and when you *know* that partner knows that you know there is no chance for slam. But that situation is unusual. You may know when your hand is not very good, but you don't know whether partner has extra values. And he doesn't know that you know whether he has extra values.

I remember a hand from years ago. My opponents were playing Precision, and the bidding started

Opener	Responder
1♣	1NT
2♡	4♡

Responder, whose first bid had shown a balanced 8-10 points, held something like

♠ x x   ♡ 10 9 x x   ◇ A x x x   ♣ K J x

I thought that the main advantage of a strong club system was that you showed your ranges and created a game force immediately so that there was no need to jump the bidding to avoid being passed or to show your strength (or lack of strength) afterwards. So when the hand was over, I asked responder why she jumped. She said, since her bid showed 8-10 points and she had only 8, she was showing that by her jump. But suppose opener had held something like

♠ A K x   ♡ A K x x x   ◇ x   ♣ A Q x x

Now the location of responder's high cards would be crucial and slam a fine contract opposite her actual hand. If she had held a bunch of queens and jacks, then 20 points opposite 8 would be unlikely to produce a slam, but she didn't hold them. So part of the problem was a matter of hand evaluation: she didn't really have a bad hand. But the main point is that she had no idea how good her partner's hand was or which of her cards would be useful. She and her partner needed all of their rounds of bidding to evaluate their fit and possibly even get to a grand slam if opener had

♠ A K x   ♡ A K x x x x   ◇ x   ♣ A Q x

I go along with the Fast Arrival concept to this extent: if the 1NT response to the forcing club guaranteed 8-10 (and couldn't be stronger) with 4333 distribution, a 4♡ bid *by opener* could show no interest in slam, while a 3♡ bid shows that he probably has, at least, a mild interest. But that would be based on a response that limited the hand opposite. Many players play two or more ranges for the 1NT response, like 9-12 or 15+. They bid cheaply to give opener a chance to describe his hand, and when opener thinks he has made the final bid, and responder has the higher range, he makes a further bid or bids.

In general, unnecessary jumps or jumps when a cheaper bid would be forcing are splinters if they are in a new suit. If the jumps are in a previously-bid suit, they show good values in the jump suit and usually nothing else to cuebid[1]. Thus 1♠-2♡, 4♡ would show good cards in the majors and no control in the minors, e.g. a hand like

♠ A K J x x   ♡ K Q x x   ◇ Q x   ♣ J x

I had a hand similar to that and my partner held

♠ Q x x   ♡ A 10 8 x x x   ◇ A x x x   ♣ —

After I raised 2♡ to 4♡ he used Roman Keycard Blackwood and followed by bidding 7♠ since he could count five top spade tricks, six heart tricks, one diamond and a club ruff for thirteen tricks (while the hands only make twelve tricks in hearts). One doesn't usually use Blackwood with a void, but since I had denied a control in the minors, he knew my controls were in the majors.

Another example: 70 years ago Ely Culbertson said that after an opening 2♠ bid (strong in those days), 4♠ by partner should show good spades (at least four to an honor) and no ace, king, singleton or void elsewhere. I think the modern equivalent (2♣-2◇, 2♠-4♠) should show the same thing. I have seen players jump to 4♠ with three small, even with two small spades, with or without a side value, just to be discouraging. That doesn't make sense to me. Among other reasons, opener may have a two-suiter like

♠ A Q x x x   ♡ A K Q x x   ◇ A K   ♣ x

and if responder has something like these hands

♠ 10 x   ♡ J x x x   ◇ x x x   ♣ J x x x

♠ x x x x   ♡ x x x x x x   ◇ J x   ♣ x x x

I would hate to play the hand in spades. Jumping to 4♠ to show good trumps, as recommended, enables opener either to bid a slam with

♠ A K J x x   ♡ x   ◇ A K Q x x   ♣ A K

---

1. But 1♣-1♡, 1♠-4♣ or 1◇-1♡, 1♠-4◇ are exceptions. Since responder could show a forcing raise of partner's minor suit at the three-level by going through a fourth-suit bid (giving opener the option of bidding 3NT), these sequences show a splinter in opener's first-bid suit. For the first sequence responder might hold ♠ K Q x x   ♡ A K x x x   ◇ K x x   ♣ x

or to bid 5♦, asking about third-round diamond control with a small diamond in place of the queen. How does responder know what he needs for slam? The 5♦ bid must ask about third-round control of diamonds since responder has denied first- or second-round control. The 4♠ bid, denying a control outside of spades, avoids getting too high with bad breaks when opener holds

♠ A K J x x   ♡ Q J 10 x x   ♦ A K Q   ♣ —

since there must be two heart losers. In other words, a jump should not just show a bad hand: it should show something specific to justify losing two rounds of bidding.

Here are a few additional sequences, showing why I don't like Fast Arrival. You open 1♦ with

♠ A 10 x x   ♡ x   ♦ A K Q x x x   ♣ Q x

Partner responds 2♣ and you bid 2♠, which partner raises to 4♠. What do you think partner has for his bid? Since 3♠ would be forcing, why did partner jump? The answer is that he has good spades (and no control in hearts, the unbid suit). His actual hand is

♠ K Q x x   ♡ J x   ♦ J x   ♣ A K 10 9 x

If partner had bid only 3♠ you would be afraid to make a slam try since if he had ♠Qxxx or ♠Jxxx, you might easily lose a couple of trump tricks. Of course, 4♠ wasn't forcing. With a slightly better hand or with the ace or king of hearts, partner would bid 3♠ and bid again if you merely bid 4♠ (or 3NT). But this time 4♠ is just what you wanted to hear since you are no longer worried about your weak trump suit and you can confirm what you believed by using Roman Keycard Blackwood. As it happens, partner does not even need the king of clubs since if spades and diamonds break normally, you can discard four of partner's clubs on your diamonds and ruff the second club.

Suppose you hold

♠ x x   ♡ A K Q J x x   ♦ J 10 x   ♣ J x

Partner opens 1♣ and you respond 1♡. He rebids 2NT. Now what would you bid? I think you should bid 4♡ to show very good hearts and at least a mild interest in slam.

If partner interprets your bid correctly, he will bid 6♡ with

♠ A J x   ♡ x x   ♦ K Q x   ♣ A K Q 10 x

Suppose, instead, that you hold

♠ A x   ♡ A 10 x x x x   ♦ K x   ♣ J x x

With this latter hand you would bid 3♡, not 4♡. Then, if partner has

♠ K x x   ♡ K Q x   ◇ A Q x   ♣ A 10 9 x

he would cuebid 4◇ to show a good hand for hearts and you would get to
6♡. (It is unrealistic to think you could get to seven.) If you had bid 3♡
with the first hand, partner would not show a maximum hand, despite his
19 points, because he would be worried about his poor heart support. It
is only the jump to 4♡, showing really good hearts, which encourages him.
If you had an ace or king along with your solid hearts, you would bid 3♡
since 4♡ isn't forcing (and denies the ability to cuebid). Then whatever
partner did you would continue to bid to the six-level while inviting seven.
With the second hand you simply bid 3♡, figuring that slam is unlikely
unless partner can cuebid to show a very good hand for hearts. What all of
this means is that with

♠ x x   ♡ Q J 10 x x x   ◇ x   ♣ K x x x

when you are almost sure that you belong in 4♡, no more or less, you have
to bid 3♡, and if partner cuebids to show a maximum you just bid 4♡. After
partner has shown a good hand, he has no right to bid past game if you
have not indicated interest (by either jumping to slam directly or making a
return cuebid of some kind).

Here is another example. You hold

♠ Q x   ♡ 10 x x   ◇ A K x x x x   ♣ x x

Partner opens 1♣ and you respond 1◇. He bids 3♠, a splinter bid. How do
you like your hand? The queen of spades is wasted, but ace-king sixth of
your suit is a very good holding. So what should you do? Most players
would bid 4◇, but what can partner do with

♠ —   ♡ A Q J x   ◇ J 10 9 8   ♣ A K J x x

He has first-round controls in three suits, but he doesn't have room to show
all three without forcing the bidding to slam, and he doesn't know how
good your diamond suit is. Since you have good trumps and nothing else
to show, why not bid 5◇? A good diamond suit is all that partner needs to
bid a slam.

Opener had an alternative method of bidding the last hand: he could
have jumped to 2♡ over 1◇. With one fewer diamond and one more club,
responder would have bid 3♣, a mark-time bid. Then, in my opinion, opener should jump again — to 4◇. If he bids 3◇ responder may think he has
something like

♠ x   ♡ A K Q x   ◇ Q 10 x   ♣ A K J x x

a good hand, but with only three-card diamond support. Since responder's
diamonds are so good, he might bid 6◇ anyway, but there are hands, like

$$\spadesuit \, Q \, x \, x \quad \heartsuit \, K \, x \, x \quad \diamond \, A \, x \, x \, x \, x \quad \clubsuit \, J \, x$$

where with a close decision he would be nervous if he didn't know whether opener had three- or four-card diamond support.

I wish I could say that Fast Arrival was never a good idea, but that is not quite true. There are a few sequences where it makes good sense. For example, when you open one of a major and partner raises to the two-level. Since partner has limited his hand, a bid of four of your major must end the auction. Similarly, when the bidding goes 1♠-2NT (Jacoby, showing four trumps, game values and a balanced hand), most people play that 4♠ shows the worst hand — a minimum with no singleton or void. I suspect that there may be better uses for this bid, but I'll admit it isn't totally illogical if it really shows a bad hand. With even a mild interest in slam, opener should try to use the bidding room to find out whether responder had 12 or 18 points, and where his points are. But these sequences are exceptions. In case of doubt, the doubt should be resolved by assuming no fast arrival.

DELAYED SUPPORT

Usually, it is a good idea to show trump support as soon as possible, after which new suits tend to show controls rather than real suits. But sometimes a hand is too strong to raise partner and then subside if he merely bids game. The solution is to make an indirect or delayed raise. This concept will be discussed at length in the final chapter on slam bidding.

The only problem with showing delayed support is that partner may wonder whether you are making a slam try or are making a desperation bid after trying, and failing, to find a better contract. When the bidding goes

Opener	Responder
1♠	2♡
2♠	3♣
3♡	3♠

responder may hold a hand like this:

$$\spadesuit \, J \, x \quad \heartsuit \, A \, x \, x \, x \, x \quad \diamond \, x \, x \quad \clubsuit \, A \, K \, J \, x$$

His hearts are not very good, and opener has probably bid 3♡ on a doubleton. Opener may or may not have a diamond stopper; he certainly hasn't promised one, so the best game contract may be 4♠ if opener holds something like

$$\spadesuit \, A \, K \, Q \, x \, x \quad \heartsuit \, Q \, x \quad \diamond \, x \, x \, x \quad \clubsuit \, Q \, x \, x$$

or

$$\spadesuit \, K \, Q \, 10 \, 9 \, x \quad \heartsuit \, K \, x \quad \diamond \, A \, x \, x \quad \clubsuit \, 10 \, x \, x$$

So, if responder holds this kind of hand:

♠ A J x   ♡ A K J x x   ◇ x x   ♣ A x x

he should jump to 4♠ over 3♡. Note that this action does not guarantee diamond shortage because he had a 4◇ splinter bid available on the previous round. If the bidding goes

Opener	Responder
1♠	2♣
3♣	3◇
3NT	4♠

the 4♠ bid shows a good hand with at least three-card spade support. If responder had been just trying to get to 3NT if opener had a heart stopper, he would have passed when opener bid 3NT.

FOURTH SUIT FORCING IN TWO-OVER-ONE AUCTIONS

When you respond at the one-level, you may have a very weak hand or a very strong hand. Sometimes you need to make a 'fourth suit forcing' bid on the next round to be sure partner will keep the bidding open. When the bidding goes 1♣-1♡, 1♠ and you hold

♠ K x x   ♡ A Q x x x   ◇ 10 9 x   ♣ A J

the only reasonable bid you can make is 2◇. You shouldn't jump in your five-card heart suit, and besides, 3♡ would not be forcing. You cannot logically bid 3NT without a diamond stopper. But 2◇ is not very descriptive: you may or may not have a diamond suit or diamond stopper. However, after a two-over-one response any below-game bid you make, other than rebidding your suit, is forcing. Consequently you should avoid the non-descriptive fourth suit forcing bid whenever possible.

Suppose the bidding has gone

Partner	You
1♠	2♣
2♡	?

and you hold

♠ K x   ♡ Q x x   ◇ x x x   ♣ A K J x x

You shouldn't raise hearts with three-card support or bid notrump without a stopper in the unbid suit. But what is wrong with bidding 2♠? Absolutely nothing! Partner may think you have three-card spade support, and you usually do, but there is plenty of room between 2♠ and 3NT or 4♠ for both you and partner to describe your hands further. If partner has a five-card heart suit, he should rebid it (rather than make the unwarranted assumption that your spades must be better than your hearts). If partner has

♠ A x x x x   ♡ A x x x   ◊ K x   ♣ Q x

he should bid 2NT since with weak spades, a diamond stopper and a club fit, 3NT might be better than 4♠, even if you have three-card spade support. Change your majors to ♠Jxx and ♡KJ and you will see what I mean. However, if partner has

♠ Q J 10 x x   ♡ A K 10 x   ◊ A x   ♣ x x

then 4♠ would be a superior contract. If you had bid 3◊ over 2♡, partner would be practically forced to bid 3NT with a diamond stopper, and you would be in the wrong contract.

Now change your hand to

♠ Q x   ♡ K x x   ◊ A x x   ♣ A J x x x

and I still prefer a 2♠ bid. If you bid 2NT, you will be playing the contract from the wrong side when partner holds ◊Qx. Also, since you hold only a single diamond stopper, a 5-2 spade fit may be a better contract than 3NT. Partner would probably raise a 2NT bid to 3NT with

♠ A J 10 x x   ♡ A Q 10 x   ◊ x x   ♣ x x

since his spades don't look strong enough to rebid without some indication of spade support. (Besides, rebidding spades suggests extra values with 6-4 distribution in the majors. This sequence will be discussed later.) It will be harder to get to 4♠ after you bid 2NT here than it will be to get to 3NT when you bid 2♠ — unless partner decides that you must have three spades and that game in an eight-card major fit is always better than 3NT. As opener I would bid 2NT over 2♠ with

♠ K x x x x   ♡ A J x x   ◊ Q x   ♣ K x

despite holding only the doubleton queen of diamonds: ◊Qx will often provide a second diamond stopper when that hand is declarer and partner has ◊Axx or ◊Kxx When responder has fair three-card spade support and no help in diamonds, he will bid 3♠ now, since he knows you have nine cards in the majors and probably either a singleton club or a tenuous diamond holding. If you happen to hold

♠ J x x x x   ♡ A Q x x   ◊ K Q 10   ♣ Q

you still have a chance to bid 3NT. It is important for neither partner to jump to a game without investigating alternatives.

OPENER'S REBIDS

There are two distinct theories on what opener should rebid after a two-over-one response. Opener's most common distribution for one of a major is 5332. Since his opening bid showed at least a five-card suit, should rebidding it promise six? Many players, including Marty Bergen say that it should. Mike Lawrence says that it shouldn't. A *Bridge World* poll indicated that a majority of experts play the latter way, and that is what seems most logical to me. Why? The simple answer is that requiring a six-card suit to rebid opener's major causes distortions, or the possibility of distortions, in all the other bids. Suppose you open 1♠ with

♠ A K J x x   ♡ x x x   ◇ x x   ♣ A x x

and partner bids 2◇. If you are not allowed to rebid 2♠, you have to bid 2NT. If either of you is going to play a notrump contract, it should be partner, who may have a tenace in hearts. Then again, partner may not have a heart stopper — perhaps he holds

♠ Q x   ♡ J x   ◇ A K Q x x   ♣ K x x x

in which case you belong in 4♠. If you had rebid 2♠, partner would have bid 3♣. You wouldn't like it, but you would take a false preference to 3◇ (the least of evils when you don't have a heart stopper or a six-card spade suit). By now partner will realize that you probably don't have a stopper in hearts and he will bid 3♠, giving you another chance to bid 3NT with a heart stopper while suggesting 4♠ if you don't. Since you don't have a stopper in hearts, and since you have a pretty good spade suit, you will bid 4♠. If your hand were

♠ A 10 x x x   ♡ x x x   ◇ A x   ♣ K J x

then rather than playing in spades with such a weak suit opposite a doubleton, you would bid 3NT, gambling that the opponents could not take enough heart tricks to set you. Partner might hold

♠ J x   ♡ Q x   ◇ K Q J x x   ♣ A 10 x x

You took four and a half rounds of bidding to get to the best game. LHO may not lead a heart from ♡AJx or ♡KJx (and if he does, he has to lead his high honor to avoid blocking the suit). He may lead a low heart from ♡AKxxx, or the hearts may split 4-4. If you and partner could see each other's hands you might choose to play in a partscore, but in this sequence neither of you is allowed to pass before reaching game.

Next case. The bidding starts the same way (1♠-2◇) and this time you hold

♠ A Q x x x   ♡ K x x   ◇ x   ♣ K x x x

If you can't bid 2♠ with a five-card suit, your choices are 2NT and 3♣.

Each has its disadvantages. If you rebid 2NT, partner will raise to 3NT with

♠ x x   ♡ J x   ♢ A Q J x x x   ♣ Q J x

Since he expects you to have at least a doubleton in diamonds, he will think that you can probably take six diamond tricks with the aid of a successful finesse (or you may even have the king). If you rebid 2♠, partner will follow through with his original intentions, and bid 3♢, invitational. With this misfit you would be glad to pass. The alternative is to bid 3♣, but I think bidding a new suit at the three-level (or reversing) should show extra values even after a two-over-one from partner. Players who bid that way say, 'Two-over-one is forcing to game. If we have to get to game anyway, why not show what I have?' I think, in accordance with *Bridge World* Standard, that (a) a two-over-one followed by a rebid of the same suit by responder should not be forcing to game or even to one more round, unless opener shows extra values, but it is forcing to game if opener bids a new suit at the three-level or reverses; (b) if responder has about a king more than he needs for his two-over-one response, he should bid or invite a slam when opener shows extra values.

When opener bids one of a suit, he must bid again over any wide-range response. If he has a minimum with no good alternative, rebidding his original suit should be the 'default' bid. Marty Bergen says 2NT should be the default bid. But 3NT is the most common final contract, and if opener bids 2NT with two or three small in an unbid suit, it will be hard to stay out of 3NT when neither partner has a stopper. As well, when 3NT is the right contact, it will be played from the wrong side. When responder has a long suit, he won't know whether it can run or be easily established, since he won't know whether his partner has a singleton. On the other hand, if rebidding the original major is the default bid, there is a lot of room to find out how good opener's suit is. Responder doesn't have to raise immediately with a doubleton

Naturally, if you can rebid a new, lower-ranking, suit at the two-level, that is an easy solution when you have only five of your first suit. Therefore, if the bidding goes 1♠-2♢, 2♠-2NT, 3♡, you probably have six spades and four hearts with a minimum hand. With extra values you would bid 2♡ followed by 3♠ — another way to show whether or not you have extra values. After a two-over-one response responder should not jump unless he wants to deliver a specific message. With a balanced 16-17 HCP (and stoppers in all unbid suits) he would jump to 3NT. With 29 or 30 combined points there should be no problem in making game, but the jump may be necessary to reach slam when opener has extra values. When each hand has 16 or 17 points, and the hands fit, *someone* has to make a move towards slam. If responder has a balanced 18 or 19 points, he should bid 2NT on the second round, followed by 4NT later. The 4NT bid after an earlier 2NT bid is natural, not Blackwood. (Why? Because 2NT purports to show a balanced hand, and balanced hands seldom take control of the bidding by asking about controls. More about this in the last chapter.)

Another reason why opener should rebid his major as the default bid is that it is the cheapest bid available and gives responder the most room to investigate further. If responder's second bid could be passed, it is important for opener to show whether he has a five- or six-card suit, but responder has at least one more round of bidding before deciding upon the final contract. As bidding 2NT or raising partner's major or taking a preference to partner's major are all forcing, you don't have to find out *immediately* whether you have an eight-card major fit. Nor do you have to play an eight-card major fit when the indications are that a notrump contract will be better. The fact that two-over-one is forcing to game in most sequences (some say 'in all sequences') is what makes the method so popular. The partnership has lots of opportunity to consider all of the alternatives without any risk of being passed before each partner has fully described his hand.

A QUICK QUIZ

Let's look at a few examples to illustrate the problems I have been discussing. You open 1♠ and partner bids 2◊. What would you rebid with each of the following hands?

a) ♠ A K x x x x ♡ x ◊ Q x x ♣ A x x
b) ♠ A x x x x ♡ Q x ◊ K x ♣ A x x x
c) ♠ 9 8 x x x ♡ A ◊ A x ♣ K J x x x
d) ♠ A J x x x ♡ Q x x ◊ x ♣ K Q x x
e) ♠ 9 8 x x x ♡ A K x ◊ A x ♣ x x x
f) ♠ A K Q J x x ♡ J x ◊ Q x x ♣ x x
g) ♠ A K Q J x x ♡ A x ◊ Q x x ♣ J x
h) ♠ A K J x x x ♡ K x ◊ Q x ♣ A x x

a) You should bid 2♠. This bid does not necessarily show a six-card suit, but when you support diamonds next round, partner will realize that with 5-3-3-2 distribution, including three diamonds, you would have supported diamonds immediately. Since you rebid spades first, you must have wanted to show a six-card spade suit.

b) You should bid 2♠. Bidding at the three-level shows extra values. After a two-over-one response, you will usually be forced to game, but it is still important to show your strength below the game level. If you bid 3♣ and partner has 16 or 17 points, he will undoubtedly bid too much. However, a 2NT rebid is a very reasonable alternative. Theoretically you should have stoppers in the unbid suits, but Qx is almost a stopper and may provide a second stopper when partner has the ace or king of hearts.

c) Again you should bid 2♠ — at least, that is what Mike Lawrence and I contend, although not everyone agrees. A better way to bid this hand would have been to open 1♣, treating the spades like a four-card suit.

d) Bid 2♠. You have stoppers (of sorts) in the unbid suits, but you ought to have at least a doubleton diamond to bid 2NT. If partner has ◇AKxxxx, he expects to develop at least five diamond tricks and he will gladly raise 2NT to 3NT.

e) Bid 2♠. You should have stoppers in the unbid suits to bid 3NT. If the final contact is 3NT, partner should be the declarer. When nothing else is good, you rebid your suit, in effect saying, 'I have nothing more to add to the bidding.' Of course, if RHO overcalled, you would gladly pass to say the same thing. If you require opener to have a six-card suit to rebid his major, all the other bids have less well-defined meanings.

f) Bid 4♠. This is a good case for Fast Arrival. A jump to game in a major after a two-over-one response shows a solid suit (at least six-long) with no outside ace or king. Now if responder bids 4NT, since the keycard situation is already known, opener shows any outside singleton or void.

g) & h) Experts' views differ regarding these hands. Most say that when opener jumps in his own suit after a two-over one response, he shows a completely solid suit with at least an ace or king on the side (maybe more). Such an agreement can be very useful when responder has a good hand with a singleton or void in opener's suit. The misfit could make him pessimistic about his slam prospects. I think everyone would agree that 3♠ is the best rebid with (g). But should the jump guarantee a solid suit or could it just show extra values? Most players think it should guarantee a solid suit. But I like to find out whether we are in the probable slam zone by the time we get to game rather than making slam tries that may result in down one when partner rejects with a misfit. I have a solution. *Bid 3♠ with both hands!* This bid shows either (1) a solid suit with at least an ace or king on the side, or (2) a good suit (strong enough to play for no losers if partner has as much as a singleton ace, king or queen) and at least two controls in the unbid suits. If partner raises your major to four or bids 3NT, he is too weak or has too few controls to be interested in a slam. If he has a slam interest and wants to find out whether you have a solid suit, he makes the cheapest suit bid — 4♣ over 3♠, or 3♠ over 3♡. (It doesn't matter whether the cheapest suit bid is the suit he has already bid or a new suit.) Over the cheapest suit bid, if opener has a solid suit and an appropriate hand to assume captaincy, he can use Blackwood and place the contract. Failing that, he describes his hand further in steps: with a suit that might lose two trump tricks opposite a singleton (like AKJxxx or AQ10xxxx or AKxxxxx), he makes the cheapest bid. The next step shows a suit with probably only one loser opposite a singleton (KQJ10xx or AQJxxxx). The third step shows a solid suit but a hand not appropriate for taking control of the bidding, for example

♠ A K Q J x x ♡ A x ◇ x x x ♣ x x

If responder is still interested, he can cuebid or possibly use Blackwood. The hand that might lose two trump tricks opposite a singleton should have no trump losers opposite a top honor (ace, king or queen) in the trump suit or, at most, one opposite Jx, and probably only one trump loser opposite two small. No matter how strong responder is, he will sign off when he has a singleton and receives a first-step response.

HAND PATTERNS AND REVERSES

Opening 1♠ and rebidding 2♠ and then 3♡ shows a weak 6-4, while 1♠ then 2♡ and then 3♠ shows a stronger 6-4. Why is that? Suppose responder has bid 1NT. In the old days before a forcing 1NT was popular, 1NT showed a limited hand. Some authorities said the maximum was 9 points; others said it was 10 points. Even today it could be very weak. If opener held

♠ A Q J x x x ♡ Q x x x ◇ x ♣ Q x

game would be extremely unlikely unless responder intended to bid again over a minimum rebid, and there would be no reason to risk bidding 2♡, which responder might pass with

♠ x ♡ J x x ◇ K J x x ♣ K x x x x.

With

♠ A Q J x x x ♡ K 10 x x ◇ A x ♣ Q

there was still a risk of playing in a dangerous contract by bidding 2♡, but there was a compensating chance for game when responder held

♠ x ♡ A Q x x ◇ K x x ♣ x x x x x

Suppose opener has 6-1-4-2 distribution. Again, with a weak opening bid he would open 1♠ and just bid 2♠ over a 1NT response. With

♠ A Q 9 x x x ♡ x ◇ K J x x ♣ A J

he would rebid 2◇, knowing that responder would be unlikely to pass unless he had a singleton spade. If responder bid 2♡ instead of 2♠ over 2◇, opener would bid 2♠. There would be an inference of extra strength from this sequence and with fitting honors, responder would raise to 3♠ with

♠ J 10   ♡ Q 10 9 x x x   ◇ Q x   ♣ K Q x

After a two-over-one response the partnership is going to get to game most of the time (some people say *all* of the time), but it still helps responder to know, before reaching the game level, whether opener has extra values. After hearing spades, spades and hearts from opener, responder would simply bid 4♠ with

♠ J x   ♡ Q x x   ◇ A x x   ♣ A K x x x

but make a further bid (perhaps cuebidding 5◇) after opener bids spades, hearts and spades. Admittedly the reason that one sequence shows a better hand than the other is not quite the same as after a one-level response, but why not treat similar sequences in similar fashion so as to lessen the mental strain?

Similar reasoning applies to a two-over-one response followed by a reverse. If you are playing Flannery, 1♡-2♣, 2♠ shows 16+ since with a weaker hand, you would have started with Flannery. If you are not playing Flannery, opinions differ. Many players would bid 2♠ to show four spades whether or not they had extra values. Their reasoning is that after a two-over-one response they are going to get to game anyway, so why not show their distribution? I don't accept the 'going to game anyway' argument since if responder rebids his suit, I play his bid as merely invitational (unless opener has shown extra values by reversing or bidding a new suit at the three-level). But even if we are going to get to game anyway, I still like to know whether opener has extra values — just as I think rebidding a new suit at the three-level should show extra values. Besides, if you rebid 2♡, you will get a chance to show spades the next round unless partner jumps to game.

The only other possible 'reverse' is 1◇-2♣, 2♡/2♠. But one of our exceptions to a two-over-one response being forcing to game was after 1◇-2♣. As stated earlier, this only forces the bidding to the 2NT level, and a rebid of 2♡ or 2♠ by opener shows 14+ points and is forcing to game unless the rebid is 2♡ *and* you are playing the Erkoc way where 2♡ suggests a sub-minimum opening bid. If not, you will be forced to rebid 2◇ with

♠ K Q 10 x   ♡ x x   ◇ A K x x   ♣ x x x

DEFAULT BIDS

Suppose you hold

♠ J x x   ♡ K Q x x   ◇ x x   ♣ x x x x

Partner opens 1◇. You respond 1♡ and partner bids 2♠. Partner has forced you to bid, and you really have nothing more to say. You don't want to rebid your four-card heart suit. You don't want to raise partner's second suit with only three-card support. You don't want to bid notrump without a stopper in the unbid suit. So you should bid 3◊, the most non-committal bid. By universal agreement, taking a preference (in this case, a false preference) to partner's first-bid suit is the 'nothing bid.' Earlier I said that when you open 1♠ with

♠ x x x x x ♡ A ◊ K J x x ♣ A x x

and partner responds 2♡, the least misleading rebid is 2♠. It just says, 'I already showed at least five spades. My rebid does not necessarily show extra length or strength. My hand is unsuitable for notrump, for some reason, and, if I have another biddable suit, I am too weak to bid it at the three-level.' After a strong jump shift, you normally make the cheapest bid. It merely says, 'I have nothing unusual — no exceptionally strong suit for my opening bid, no adequate support for your suit, and no strong five-card side suit. So I am just making the cheapest bid to allow *you* to finish describing your hand.

If the bidding goes

Opener	Responder
1♣	1♡
1♠	2◊

and you hold

♠ A Q x x ♡ x x ◊ x x x ♣ A Q 10 x

what should you bid? With ♡Qx or ♡Kx you could bid 2♡ — you don't need three hearts to take a preference — but two small is hardly enough. Taking a false preference to a minor suit is not so dangerous because partner will exhaust all other possibilities before bidding a game in a minor, but if you bid 2♡ there is a strong probability that partner will bid 4♡ with a strong five-card suit. You don't have a stopper in diamonds or any rebiddable suit. Since 2♠ is cheaper than 3♣, you will simply make the cheapest bid without guaranteeing a rebiddable spade suit. (Besides, if you bid 2♠, you can stop in 2NT, which wouldn't be possible if you bid 3♣.) In almost every case, you would be happy if the opponents had bid so that you could pass to say you had nothing more than you have already shown. If you want some guidelines, here they are: taking a preference for partner's first suit, rebidding a suit you have already shown, or generally making the cheapest bid (to allow more room for partner to describe his hand) are the usual 'nothing' bids.

My partner and I had this debacle caused by a confusion as to what the 'nothing' bid was in an undiscussed auction:

Me	Partner
♠ A Q x x x	♠ —
♡ A Q x x	♡ K J x x
◇ x x	◇ A K x x x
♣ x x	♣ A x x x
1♠	2◇
2♡	3♣
3◇	6♡

There was almost no play for 6♡ and it actually went down two. In my opinion, partner should have bid 4♡ over 3◇, as a strong invitation, which I would have rejected. But when this hand was given to a bidding panel, one expert suggested that the 3◇ bid was at fault and that 3♠ would be the 'nothing' bid. Others might choose 3♡. But neither 3♠ nor 3♡ makes good sense to me. Which is more important: to be able to bid 3♡ to show five hearts and 3♠ to show a good 6-4 hand, or to bid either major just to deny a good holding in diamonds? In general, if you have to make a slightly misleading bid (because all available bids have flaws), it is better to misbid in a minor than in a major, since the final contract is much more likely to be a major suit than a minor. The expert's example hand, which he thought would justify the 3◇ bid, was

$$♠ A Q x x x \quad ♡ A Q x x \quad ◇ Q x x \quad ♣ x$$

But with that hand, why wouldn't opener jump to 4◇? That would be the amount of encouragement necessary for get partner to bid 6◇ with

$$♠ x \quad ♡ K x x \quad ◇ A K 10 x x \quad ♣ A J x x$$

There is still another factor to consider in choosing the default bid. Other things being equal, or nearly so, the cheaper the default bid, the more room there is to find the right spot. In this case, if the default bid were 3♠, responder would be unable to *jump* to 4♡. Since he might bid 4♡ over 3♠ with

$$♠ x \quad ♡ K J x \quad ◇ A K Q x x x x \quad ♣ x x$$

for lack of a good alternative, then with

$$♠ — \quad ♡ K J x x \quad ◇ A K x x x \quad ♣ A x x x$$

he would have to bid 5♡ to describe his hand — and with a misfit, that might be one level too high.

THE LAST WORD ON TWO-OVER-ONE

I consider it vital to play some exceptions to two-over-one. If you don't play Bergen responses to a major, it does not make a lot of difference whether you play two-over-one followed by a rebid of the same suit as invitational or a direct jump to the three-level as invitational, but you need to play it one way or the other[1].

I think it is a mistake to play a 1NT response to a major by a non-passed hand as merely semi-forcing, since you no longer have a way to show a three-card limit raise (without risking being passed in 1NT) or of differentiating between an invitational hand with a long suit and a weak hand with a long suit. As a result, you are also sometimes forced to respond at the two-level in a four-card suit.

But if you play the system as I have outlined it, often using three or four rounds of bidding to describe your hand rather than attempting to do it in two rounds, I think the two-over-one forcing to game principle, if not carried to extremes, is well worth while. I could have said this at the beginning of the discussion, but until I showed examples of how it could be used and the inferences that could be drawn, you wouldn't have been able to evaluate my conclusion.

What is your next call with each of these hands?

1. **Partner**　　　**You**

　　　　　　　　pass
　1♠　　　　　　　2♡
　3♡　　　　　　　?

♠ 7　♡ J 9 8 6 5 4　♢ A J 6 5　♣ K 4

2. **Partner**　　　**You**

　　　　　　　　1♠
　2♡　　　　　　　?

♠ 9 7 6 4 2　♡ A J　♢ 6　♣ A Q J 9 5

1.　Actually I think bidding at the two-level and repeating your suit to show an invitational hand is slightly better since opener may rebid 2NT over a two-level response, in which case responder will bid 3NT with ace-queen seventh and a side ace or king, or with ace-king seventh and almost nothing on the side. After the 2NT bid, showing at least a doubleton, responder knows the suit will probably be establishable. If this sequence is not available, responder has to make a decision before hearing opener's rebid. Fearing a singleton or void in his long suit, he can only make an invitational bid on these hands.

3. **Partner**   **You**
Partner	You
1♠	2♣
2♡	2♠
4♠	?

   ♠Q6 ♡Q94 ◇A87 ♣AK1073

4. **Partner**   **You**
Partner	You
1♣	1♠
2NT	?

   ♠KQ10962 ♡7 ◇J954 ♣76

5. **Partner**   **You**
Partner	You
1♠	2◇
2♠	2NT
3◇	?

   ♠Q ♡A653 ◇QJ852 ♣A74

6. **Partner**   **You**
Partner	You
1♠	2♡
3♣	?

   ♠Q98 ♡AK1054 ◇86 ♣K97

7. **Partner**   **You**
Partner	You
1♠	2♡
3♣	?

   ♠Q98 ♡AK105 42 ◇8 ♣K97

8. **Partner**   **You**
Partner	You
1♠	2♣
2♡	2♠
4♠	?

   ♠Q8 ♡K54 ◇A75 ♣AJ742

9. **Partner**   **You**
Partner	You
	1♠
2♣	2♡
4♠	?

   ♠AJ632 ♡K1076 ◇AK6 ♣Q

10. Partner   **You**

Partner	You
	1◇
2♣	2◇
2NT	?

♠ A 8 6   ♡ 9   ◇ A K Q 8 7 3   ♣ Q 5 4

11. Partner   **You**

Partner	You
1♠	2♡
3♣	?

♠ J 6   ♡ A K J 9 5 4   ◇ A 7 6   ♣ Q 8

12. Partner   **You**

Partner	You
1♡	2♣
3♡	?

♠ A 9 6   ♡ 5   ◇ K 8 3   ♣ A K J 9 7 3

(Make a plan for the entire auction on this hand.)

13. Partner   **You**

Partner	You
	1♠
2♡	2♠
3♣	3♡
3♠	?

♠ A 9 6 4 2   ♡ K 6   ◇ A 9 3 2   ♣ Q 8

14. Partner   **You**

Partner	You
	1♠
2◇	2♡
3◇	?

♠ K 8 7 6 3 2   ♡ A J 8 7 6 2   ◇ —   ♣ 2

15. Partner   **You**

Partner	You
	1♠
2♣	2◇
2♠	?

♠ A x x x x   ♡ Q x   ◇ A 10 x x   ♣ K x

16. Partner   **You**

	1♢
2♣	2NT
3♡	3NT
4NT	?

♠ Q J x   ♡ K x x   ♢ A 10 x x x   ♣ K x

---

my answers

1. Pass. If you had the two red tens, you might bid game. Since you are a passed hand, partner should have bid 4♡ if he thought it would make, and you have about as little as you could have for your bidding. Give partner a typical hand for his bidding, e.g.

   ♠ A K J x x   ♡ K x x   ♢ x x   ♣ K x x

   and you are more likely to take eight tricks than ten.

2. It was a mistake to open 1♠ with this hand. It would have been far better to open 1♣ and treat your spades as though they were a four-card suit. Usually you rebid 2♠ as your default bid, but you can anticipate a problem here. Partner may raise to 3♠ with ♠Qxx or ♠Kxx, and your hand is not suitable for a 3NT bid at that stage. If you bid 4♡, partner will think you are showing extra values and may continue to bid. At this stage I think the least of evils is to raise to 3♡. You have a ruffing value for him as partial compensation for raising with a doubleton.

3. Remember, we do not play Fast Arrival! Partner's 4♠ bid shows good spades, almost surely six, and if he bids spades, hearts and spades, he should have a good 6-4 hand. He might hold as much as

   ♠ A K x x x x   ♡ A K J x   ♢ x x   ♣ x

   in which case you belong in seven. It is hard to imagine a hand that won't provide a good play for six, so you should either bid a direct 6♠ or cuebid 5♢, intending to bid at least six if partner shows no interest in a grand slam.

4. Bid 3♠ followed by 4♠ (or pass if partner bids 4♠ himself).

5. Since partner rebid spades before raising diamonds, he must have six spades. He is also likely to have a singleton or a worthless doubleton in either clubs or hearts, in which case 4♠ will be safer than 3NT if there is a spade loser. So you can suggest a spade contract by bidding 3♠.

6. Despite holding only 12 points, you have a good hand for partner when he has spades and clubs, especially since the 3♣ bid shows extra values. For example, partner may have

♠ A K J x x   ♡ x x   ◇ x   ♣ A Q 10 x x

Partner is more likely to hold a singleton heart and a doubleton diamond, so it would be dangerous to bid 3♠ now and then bid again if partner bids 4♠. Instead, you should bid 4♠ now to show good spade support (under the circumstances) since you might have been forced, for lack of something better to do, to bid 3♠ with three small or a doubleton honor. Also, your bidding implies a lack of diamond control.

7. Since you have a singleton diamond, you should bid 4◇. This splinter not only shows a singleton (or void) in diamonds, but also useful cards under the circumstances. This bid will not excite partner unduly if he has ◇Kx or ◇AK(x). Since he doesn't know whether you have spade support or club support, then if he is not interested in slam he should bid 4♠, which you could correct to 5♣ if your splinter was based on good club support.

8. This is quite similar to Problem 3. Partner apparently has six spades and four hearts, and he shows a good hand by his order of bids. But your hand is not quite as good as the responder's hand in Problem 3. I think bidding 5◇, but not driving to slam, is quite reasonable.

9. You know you are missing the ace of hearts. Do you think your trumps are solid? Partner may have bid this way with ♠Kxx and ♣AKJxx, in which case you would need a finesse and a 3-2 trump break to make a slam. Of course he may have ♠Q10x, in which case you would require little more than a finesse. But you can't have a good slam unless partner has the ace-king of clubs and the king-queen of spades, and with that holding he would have bid 4♣ instead of 4♠. So you should pass since even 5♠ is not safe if partner has only ♠Kxx.

10. In this sequence 2NT is non-forcing. Partner could hold something like

♠ K x x   ♡ J x x   ◇ x x   ♣ A K x x x

So you should bid 3♠ (obviously forcing) and if partner does not bid 3NT, you will belong in five or six of a minor.

11. You should bid 3♡, obviously forcing after partner shows extra values with his 3♣ bid. (True, his extra values could be based on distribution, not high cards. If that is the case, this sequence could force you to a hopeless game if you simply had a minimum hand with long hearts. But the odds are that there will be a play for some game after the 3♣ bid. Of course, this is merely a theoretical aside: with the hand in the problem you may easily belong in slam.) If partner raises hearts, you will probably bid 6♡. If he bids 3NT you will raise to 4NT, a natural invitation.

12. You should use your gadget bid of 3♠ to find out what kind of hand partner has. If he bids 3NT, showing two probable losers opposite a singleton, you can take a conservative view and bid either 4♡ or pass 3NT. (However, if partner has a relatively weak heart suit for his 3♡ bid, he will have lots of other high cards, and probably a club fit, so you might be cold for 6♣ or 6NT, so I recommend rebidding 4♣. If partner rebids 4♡, you will give up, but if he raises clubs, you can bid 6♣.)

   If he bids 4♣ over 3♠, showing only one probable loser opposite a singleton, you can cuebid, starting with 4♦. If partner bids 4♦ over 3♠, showing a solid suit, you should bid 4♠, hoping that he will assume control and possibly bid a grand slam; in any event, you won't let the bidding end short of a small slam.

13. Partner is not making a slam try; he is looking for the best game. If partner were too strong for a raise to 3♠, he would have bid 4♠ over 3♡. So you should bid 3NT and hope for the best. Partner holds

   ♠ J x   ♡ A J x x x   ♦ J x   ♣ A K 10 x

   He was hoping you would bid 3NT over his 3♣ bid, but since your diamond stopper is the ace, and you have a doubleton heart honor and a possible ruffing value, you elected to bid 3♡ instead. But you can hardly insist upon a heart contract, and you don't like your spades at all, so you have no reasonable alternative to bidding 3NT now.

14. There are pros and cons to opening this hand, but in the 2004 Vanderbilt final, both teams opened the bidding with it. At this stage, about the best hand partner is likely to hold is something like

♠ Q ♡ J x x ◇ A K J x x x ♣ J x x

and that would give you a very poor play for game. Partner actually held

♠ Q ♡ 4 ◇ A K 10 9 8 6 4 2 ♣ Q 9 7

At one table opener bid 3♡ and passed his partner's 4◇ bid. At the other table opener rebid 4♡ over 4◇. It seems to me that both pairs were lucky not to be doubled on this misfitting hand, and I think opener should pass 3◇. I don't know whether they played 3◇ as forcing to game in this auction, but whether or not it was supposed to be, I would have taken my chances on passing. However, I would be delighted to be playing 3◇ as merely invitational.

15. You should bid 2NT. Your weak spade suit and your club support suggest a notrump contract. The only problem is your lack of a sure stopper in hearts, but if partner has good three-card spade support and no help in hearts, he will bid 3♠. If he has

♠ K x ♡ A x x ◇ J x x ♣ A Q 10 x x

or

♠ x x x ♡ J x x ◇ K Q ♣ A Q J x x

he will gladly raise to 3NT. If partner has the jack of spades instead of the jack of hearts in the latter hand, 3NT will still be the better contract.

16. Bid 6♣! If partner had a balanced hand (either 5332 or 6322 distribution) and enough to invite 6NT when you show 12-14 balanced points, he would have raised to 4NT directly over your 2NT rebid. When he rebid 3♡ before bidding 4NT, he showed a somewhat unbalanced hand. He actually holds

♠ A K x ♡ Q J 10 x ◇ x ♣ A Q J 10 x

With three diamonds and a singleton spade, he probably would have supported diamonds at some stage. If partner's hand is balanced (which it shouldn't be), he can return to 6NT. You accepted partner's invitation because of your three key honors (♡K, ◇A and ♣K). If your diamonds were changed to the king-queen, you should pass 4NT.

CHAPTER 4

notrump bidding

THE RIGHT STUFF

First I will discuss the 15-17 point notrump, which is what most people in North America play.

The usual distributions for opening 1NT are 4333, 4432 and 5332. (Overcalling 1NT is a different matter since you have fewer alternatives.) Occasionally opening 1NT with 6322 or 5422 (the long suit being a minor) is the least of evils, since it will avoid a rebid problem. In a recent bidding panel the vote for a 1NT opening was 6 to 0 with

♠ 9 6   ♡ A J   ◇ K J 8 4   ♣ A Q 9 6 2

Many players would open 1NT with

♠ K x   ♡ J 10 x   ◇ A J 10 x x x   ♣ A Q

since if they opened 1◇ and partner responded 1♡ or 1♠, they would have no satisfactory rebid (the hand is worth about two and half diamonds). Should you open 1NT with a five-card major? I think you should when you have 15-16 points, tenaces and all suits stopped. Most hands with 17 points and *any* five-card suit are probably too strong since partner will usually pass with a balanced 8 points (without good spot cards or a five-card suit of his own).

A hand with a five-card major and a worthless doubleton should usually be opened one of the major, since for notrump it has two strikes against it. But when you have hearts and the worthless doubleton is in spades, 1NT may still be your best choice. If you open 1♡ with

♠ 10 x   ♡ A Q x x x   ◇ K J x   ♣ A J 10

you have a serious rebid problem when partner responds 1♠. Also, when you have a doubleton spade (even Ax or Kx) a 1NT bid may preempt the opponents out of an overcall or a takeout double. That is a factor whether you have three, four or five hearts.

The rebid problem is never quite so serious when you have spades. In fact, when you have *four* spades and a worthless doubleton it is usually better to open your minor suit unless you have exactly 16 points. With a 15-count, say

♠ A J x x   ♡ x x   ◇ A x x   ♣ A Q x x

you can open 1♣ and rebid 1♠ over a red-suit response. Then if partner bids 1NT you can pass. Game is unlikely unless partner has exactly 10 points, and even then it will be no cinch. You will have to make a slight underbid or overbid if partner responds 1♠, by raising him to either 2♠ or 3♠. With a typical 17-point hand you can raise a 1NT rebid to 2NT or a 1♠ response to 3♠. However, with exactly 16 points you may have a rebid problem if you don't open 1NT. After 1♣-1♡, 1♠-1NT if you pass you may miss a good game, and if you raise to 2NT you may get too high; therefore with 16 points you should usually open 1NT.

Most players do not make this distinction. I am the moderator of a bidding panel, and the only panelist I can count on to object to a notrump opening with four or five spades and a worthless doubleton is Fred Hamilton. Most of the others say that if they don't open 1NT with a balanced hand and the right point count, partner will draw the wrong inferences. Incidentally, if you open 1NT with 16 points and a five-card major, you can jump in that suit to the three-level over Stayman. If partner had invited game, you would have accepted with 16 points and a five-card suit, and now he might well choose to bid four of your major when you show five of them. This isn't really dangerous since if partner was planning to pass your bid, whatever it was, he must have both majors, or conceivably he is 4-3 in the majors with a singleton club, so the three-level is probably safe. Partner might even be able to raise to four of your major, despite having intended to pass if you had bid 2♡ or 2♠.

Suppose you hold

♠ K   ♡ K J x   ◇ A Q x x   ♣ K x x x x

If you open 1♣ you have no satisfactory rebid over a 1♠ response. You are too weak to reverse, and opening 1◇ has some disadvantages whether partner bids 1♡, 1♠ or 1NT. Despite rumors to the contrary, I don't go out of my way to open 1NT with a singleton king or queen, but with a hand like this, I think it is your best choice. While the main reason for opening 1NT is to avoid rebid problems, there is another factor favoring that bid: if the final contract is some number of notrump, it is desirable for you to be the declarer. If the opening lead is a low spade from the ace, this holding will give you a double stopper when partner has ♠Qxx. If partner has ♠Jxx, the opponents can't immediately run the whole suit against you after a low spade lead no matter which opponent has the ace. Kit Woolsey sometimes recommends a 1NT bid with 1-4-4-4 distribution including a singleton king (or queen?) of spades. The alternative (1◇ followed by 2♣) appeals to neither him nor me. You have even more reason to make a 2NT opening, or a 2♣ opening followed by a 2NT rebid, with a singleton than you do to open

1NT with a singleton since partner is likely to pass one of a suit when you have 21-24 points. You realize, of course, that these are exceptional situations. Most of the time your notrump openings will show balanced hands.

BIDDING AFTER A 1NT OPENING

There are two popular methods for responding to 1NT. In the Walsh style 2◇ and 2♡ are transfers to the majors; 2♠ is minor-suit Stayman; and 2NT is a transfer to clubs, showing either a weak hand with clubs or a strong three-suiter. Other players prefer four-suit transfers[1] where 2♠ is a transfer to clubs and 2NT is a transfer to diamonds.

Playing Walsh style, the 2♣ response is Stayman, of course. Since in both Walsh and four-suit transfers 2NT is not a natural response to 1NT, in order to invite 3NT you have to bid 2♣, followed by bidding 2NT over a two-level response. Since opener is supposed to bid hearts with four of each major, when opener bids 2♡, he may also have four spades. So 2♠ now by responder is a game invitation with four spades, and (theoretically) 2NT denies four spades.

Not many people play double transfers, but in original Walsh, 2◇ transfers to hearts and if responder next bids 2♠, it cancels any implication of heart length — it shows a minor-suit slam try. Opener is required to bid 2NT: after that, 3♣ by responder shows a weak-suit slam try in clubs (lacking two of the top three honors); 3◇ shows a weak-suit slam try in diamonds; 3♡ shows a strong-suit slam try in clubs and 3♠ shows a strong-suit slam try in diamonds. One way to remember these steps is that when responder has a weak-suit slam try, he has more high cards on the side, and his hand may be almost as strong as opener's, so if a slam is reached it probably won't matter who is declarer. When he has a strong suit he is likely to have fewer high cards on the side, and it is better for opener to be the declarer.

While all this can work well in theory, it has some practical drawbacks. For example, when opener has a super-acceptance in hearts, he is supposed to bid 2♠ over 2◇ in this method. If responder really has hearts he must bid 2NT, transferring opener back to hearts, after which a new suit by responder is natural. If responder bids 3♣, 3◇, 3♡ or 3♠ over the 2♠ super-accept instead of 2NT, it means that he does not have hearts, but is inviting

---

1.   I have seldom played four-suit transfers and cannot make an informed decision whether they are better or worse than Walsh. Usually 2♠ is a transfer to clubs and 2NT is a transfer to diamonds. The reason for bidding two levels lower than the suit you are transferring to is to allow partner to show how well he likes your minor suit. Usually the in-between bid shows the better hand (like 1NT-2♠, 2NT or 1NT-2NT, 3♣. The main advantage of four-suit transfers is that it makes it easier to bid hands with a long minor and a shorter major. You simply transfer to the minor and bid the major next time.

a slam in a minor, just the same as if the bidding had gone 1NT-2◊, 2♡-2♠, 2NT first. But these sequences do not occur very frequently, and many Walsh players don't even know about them. Meanwhile, if the opponents enter the bidding over the 2◊ relay, it can cause confusion if responder may or may not have hearts.

Another issue is that many players like to follow Larry Cohen's advice and bid 3♡ over a 2◊ transfer with four-card trump support, even with a minimum hand, on the grounds that the three-level is 'safe.' The Law says that if you can't make 3♡, the opponents can make something at the three-level, and they may reopen over 2♡. Of course, this strategy interferes with responder's intentions if he has the minor-suit slam-try hand. As a result of all this, not many players use the double transfer.

What *should* opener bid if he has four hearts and responder transfers him to hearts? I don't entirely agree with Larry. With a minimum notrump opener and weak hearts (i.e. with most of my honors outside of hearts), we have fairly good defense, and I don't think the preempt is necessary, especially when I hold 3-4-3-3 distribution. Besides, most opponents do not reopen the bidding automatically when you stop in 2♡. The player holding 11 points and two hearts is not likely to bid over opener's 2♡ rebid since responder's hand is unlimited, and when 2♡ is passed around to the other opponent, he is not likely to reopen with a balanced 8 to 10 points with two hearts. Even if he does, either opener or responder can still bid 3♡. Admittedly in this case there is a stronger chance of a penalty double or further competition than if opener had bid 3♡ immediately, so there is *some* danger in bidding 3♡ belatedly. So with an average hand or a hand with most of his high cards in hearts, it probably does pay opener to bid 3♡ immediately.

With a real super-acceptance (four hearts and either 17 points mostly in aces and kings or a good 16 with a doubleton), I suggest that you bid 2♠ over the transfer to hearts. If responder has no interest in game, he can bid 3◊ to transfer back to hearts at the three-level. (There are many sequences in which a player has rejected a transfer and in which bidding the suit just below the agreed suit forces partner to bid the suit responder transferred to. The purpose is to let the strong hand be declarer.) If responder is interested in game, then he can bid 2NT over 2♠ to ask opener to show a doubleton in a minor or 3♣ to ask him to bid 4♡ if he has a doubleton spade. (Remember, 3◊ asks him to bid 3♡, which responder could pass or raise to game.) In fact, responder, after transferring back to hearts, could bid a new suit to show a two-suiter with an interest in slam. Showing four-card trump support not only makes it more difficult for the opponents to compete when responder has a bad hand, but it solves another problem. Suppose responder holds

♠ x x ♡ K J x x x ◇ x ♣ Q 10 9 x x

If he knows his partner has four hearts, he should gamble on game. If partner merely bids 2♡ (and could have a doubleton), the odds favor a pass.

I am going to make two very controversial suggestions. Some players *always* transfer to a major when they have a five-card major. Others *usually* transfer unless they have a perfect hand with honors in their doubleton suit like

♠ Q J ♡ K x x x x ◇ A Q x ♣ Q 10 x

When you have an unbalanced hand you should transfer, no matter how weak your suit is — even on

♠ x x x x x x ♡ x ◇ Q x x x ♣ J x x

But on a weak balanced hand, with a weak suit, where what little strength you have is mostly outside your suit, e.g.

♠ Q x x ♡ x x x x x ◇ J x ♣ Q x x

I think it is better to pass. Usually partner will do better in 1NT than in 2♡.

When responder transfers to hearts and opener has four hearts, we have just argued that he should usually bid to the three-level for two reasons: when responder has a mediocre two-suiter, he may bid game when he knows about the nine-card fit, and bidding at the three-level makes it more difficult for the opponents to reopen. But when responder transfers to spades, there is slightly less need to preempt. Also partner will open 1NT more often with a worthless doubleton or singleton honor in spades than with weakness in hearts. So when partner bids 2♡ to transfer to spades, my second suggestion is to have all bids other than 2♠ show a good hand of one kind or another. For example, 2NT would show an average-plus hand with four spades or a super hand with three-card spade support — like

♠ K Q x ♡ A x ◇ A x x x ♣ K J x x

With a good hand, four-card support and a doubleton, bid the doubleton. When responder has a close decision whether to stop in a partscore, bid game, or bid slam, knowing whether both hands have the same doubleton or whether there are losers to ruff will be very helpful.

Over 2♠, minor-suit Stayman, opener should bid a four- or five-card minor if he has one and 2NT otherwise. If opener bids 2NT, then 3♣ shows a weak hand with both minors and asks opener to pass or correct. Over either a 2NT or 3♣ rebid, 3◇ is a signoff. Responder may not have a club suit since this is the only way to get to play 3◇. This is the only sequence in which responder does not guarantee both minors with his 2♠ bid. (With a weak hand and a long club suit, responder can bid 2NT to transfer to clubs.) With a good hand responder should splinter in a major at the three-level whether opener bids 2NT or shows a minor suit. This lets opener tell how well the hands fit if he is interested in slam, while if he has a concentration of strength opposite the singleton, he can bid 3NT. This also allows the partnership to avoid 3NT and bid five of a minor instead when opener has Axx or Jxx opposite the singleton but not a particularly good hand. Responder should avoid minor-suit Stayman with 9 or 10 points (or a bad 11): those hands are too strong to sign off in a minor-suit partscore and too weak to look for a slam or five of a minor. If you are going to get to 3NT anyway, there is no point in telling the opponents where you have a singleton or void.

The trouble with Stayman

Continuing that thought, even ordinary Stayman can lose in several ways. An opponent can double 2♣ for a lead. When the bidding goes 1NT-2♣, 2♠-3NT opening leader knows that dummy has four hearts and declarer has four or more spades. So if he has

♠ K 10 x x ♡ Q 10 x x ◇ J 10 ♣ x x x

he will probably lead a diamond rather than a major (while if the bidding had gone 1NT-3NT, he would probably have led a major). Likewise, if the bidding goes 1NT-2♣, 2♡-3NT, opening leader knows that declarer has four (or more) hearts and responder has four spades. Again that will help him on opening lead and help both defenders later in the hand. For that reason I never use Stayman with 4333 distribution unless my hand is worth only an invitation to game (since a direct 2NT response has a conventional meaning). We may not gain a trick by playing in our major fit, if we have one, and if we don't find a major fit, we will have helped the opponents on defense. In fact, with a notrumpish hand and a strong doubleton I often raise partner directly to 3NT instead of looking for a major fit. However, with

♠ x x ♡ K x x x ◇ A x x ♣ K J x x

I would use Stayman because if we have a heart fit, the hand should definitely play better in hearts, but with

♠ K x x ♡ J x x x ◇ Q 10 ♣ A 10 x x

I would raise directly to 3NT. My doubleton is strong and my hearts are weak. If partner has something like

♠ Q J x ♡ K x x x ◇ A J x ♣ K Q x

3NT may have a better chance to make than 4♡, and I won't have given away information to the opponents when we don't find a fit. Strengthen responder's hand to

♠ A Q x   ♡ J x x x   ◇ K J   ♣ A 10 x x

and it is even more likely that the hand will make the same number of tricks (probably eleven) in notrump or hearts, and at matchpoints I would definitely raise to 3NT. With

♠ A Q x   ♡ J x x x x   ◇ K J   ♣ K 10 x

I would probably use Stayman (since if we have nine hearts, hearts may play a trick better) rather than transferring to hearts and bidding notrump — again because when we have very strong balanced hands and a weak suit, it is very likely that we can do just as well (or better) in notrump as in an eight-card major fit. Partner won't know how strong my hand is, and may pick hearts if I give him a choice.

When partner opens 1NT and you hold

♠ x x x x   ♡ J x x x   ◇ Q x x x   ♣ x

you should use Stayman and pass whatever partner bids. About the only time this can lose is when he has 3-3-2-5 distribution and you play in diamonds with a 4-2 fit. When you hold

♠ J x x x   ♡ Q x x x x   ◇ x x   ♣ x x

you can bid 2♣, and if partner bids a major you will pass, while if he bids 2◇, you will bid 2♡. Partner should pass unless he has two hearts and three spades, in which case he can correct to spades. This method is called Garbage Stayman. I would bid the same way with 4-4-1-4 distribution and a weak hand. Some players bid the same way with 4-4-3-2 (or 4-4-2-3) distribution. You have a slightly better than even chance of finding a major-suit fit. If partner has 4333 distribution you have a 50% chance that he has a four-card major, but if he has 4432 distribution you have a better than 50% chance that both of his four-card suits are not minors. The trouble is that if you don't find a major fit, you may get a very bad result for being one trick higher than if you had passed. If your majors are QJ10x and K109x the hand may still play better in a 4-3 major fit, but with

♠ J x x x   ♡ 10 x x x   ◇ Q x   ♣ Q x x

you may wish that you had left partner in 1NT.

Three-level responses

What should it mean if responder bids a suit at the three-level over 1NT? This is simply a matter of partnership agreement. According to Walsh, three of a minor is invitational. Opener needs a fairly good hand, including a high honor in the suit, to bid 3NT. With AKxxxx or AQxxxx, responder would normally bid 3NT himself since with three small opener can probably establish the suit.

The most common meaning of a 3♡ bid is to show an invitational hand with 5-5 in the majors, while 3♠ would show a game-forcing hand with 5-5 in the majors. The next most common treatment, which I prefer, is to show a singleton in the suit bid with three of the other major and 5-4 in the minors (but a weaker hand than you would show with minor-suit Stayman followed by a splinter, a sequence which implies an interest in slam). If partner decides to play in the 4-3 major-suit fit, he will be the declarer.

Smolen

If the bidding starts 1NT-2♣, 2♢, what should three of a major show? Since you usually want the notrump bidder to be declarer, you should adopt the Smolen convention, in which the jump shows four of the suit bid and five or more of the other major. The bid is forcing, and if opener can tell that there is no 5-3 fit, he will normally bid 3NT. If there is a 5-3 fit, he will be the declarer.

Smolen can also be used over a 2NT bid: 2NT-3♣, 3♢-3♡/3♠ would show the same sort of hand — strong enough to be in game and with greater length in the other major. I should caution you that you can't play Smolen after a 2NT opening if you are playing ordinary Puppet Stayman. When using the latter convention, opener bids 3NT over 3♣ when holding neither a four-card nor a five-card major. Obviously responder can't afford to bid 4♠ now with four spades and five hearts. For that matter, even if he abandons Smolen and bids his five-card major, he may wind up in a 5-2 trump fit, which is bad enough, and in addition the weaker hand will be declarer. When playing Puppet Stayman, opener bids a five-card major if he has one.

With one or both four-card majors, he bids 3♢, and responder bids the major that he does not hold; 3NT would show both majors. That way, if there is a 4-4 major fit, opener can bid it and be the declarer. So this can gain over ordinary Stayman when opener has a five-card suit, provided responder has three-card support and a ruffing value, and will lose when responder has 5-4 in the majors. I like ordinary Stayman better since there are few hands where responder would use any kind of Stayman with only a three-card major. Opener has to have a five-card major, in fact the right five-card major, for this sequence to pay off, while *responder's* 5-4 or 6-4 in the majors is a much more frequent holding. A bit later I will suggest a different way to bid after a 2NT opening.

Slam bidding

In the Texas convention, 4♦ or 4♥ over 1NT is a transfer to the next higher suit. The main advantage is that when responder wants to be in game but is not interested in slam, he can make a Texas bid. That way, 1NT-2♦, 2♥-4♥ is a mild slam try, probably without a singleton or void, since responder didn't make a splinter bid on the second round. But there is another advantage, although it seldom occurs. Suppose partner bids 1NT and you hold

$$♠ A Q 10 x x x x \quad ♡ x \quad ♦ K Q x \quad ♣ K x$$

In the unlikely event that partner has three aces and the king of spades, you would like to bid 7NT. If he has three of those four keycards you want to bid 6♠. When partner opens 1NT, either a direct 4NT bid or a delayed 4NT bid (perhaps after Stayman) is natural, not Blackwood. Gerber is available but it won't tell you about the ♠K. There may be other ways to accomplish the same result, but bidding 4♥ to transfer to 4♠ and following up with 4NT is the simplest way to find out what you want to know (4NT is Roman Keycard Blackwood for spades). In other words,

1NT-2♥, 2♠ -4NT is a natural bid, perhaps with

$$♠ K J x x x \quad ♡ A 10 9 \quad ♦ Q 10 \quad ♣ A J x$$

while 1NT-4♥, 4♠-4NT is RKB. What would 1NT-4♥, 4♠-5♣ be? It should be Exclusion Blackwood. Responder might hold

$$♠ K Q J x x x \quad ♡ K x \quad ♦ K Q x x x \quad ♣ —$$

In showing keycards in this sequence, opener disregards any honors in clubs.

Suppose responder holds

$$♠ K Q x x \quad ♡ A x \quad ♦ K J x \quad ♣ Q x x x$$

Opener bids 1NT and responder bids 2♣, Stayman. Opener bids 2♠. If he had bid 2♥ or 2♦ responder would have just bid 3NT (4NT would be a bit optimistic since the maximum combined point-count would be 32). But with a spade fit he would make a slam try. What should it be? The expert bid is 4♦ (safer and better than bidding 5♠ either directly or in a round-about way). The 4♦ bid is a balanced slam try in support of opener's major suit.

Suppose responder holds

$$♠ K Q x x \quad ♡ x \quad ♦ A Q 10 x x \quad ♣ Q x x$$

— two fewer high-card points but better distribution. If opener has

$$♠ A x x x \quad ♡ Q x x \quad ♦ K x x \quad ♣ A K x$$

you would like to be in a slam but if he has more high cards in hearts and fewer elsewhere, even 5♠ could be in danger. The way to make a slam try with a singleton or void is to bid the other major at the three-level: 1NT-2♣, 2♠-3♡ or 1NT-2♣, 2♡-3♠. Opener can make the cheapest bid to ask where the singleton is, and responder will tell him. If opener bids 3NT to ask where the singleton is in the latter sequence, responder will bid 4♡ to show a singleton spade (and avoid getting past the game level).

Unusual sequences

You can't anticipate and discuss every possible sequence, but you can 'invent' solutions to problems which partner can hardly misinterpret. For example, suppose partner opens 1NT and you hold

♠ A x x   ♡ x   ◇ Q x x   ♣ A K J 10 x x

If you are playing four-suit transfers, you could bid 2♠, showing clubs, and jump to 4♡ next round. Unusual jumps to the four-level usually show splinters in support of the agreed suit. When you transfer to clubs, what can the agreed suit be (except clubs)? Your hand is strong enough that, if partner has quite a bit of his strength in hearts, he can bid 4NT, which should be cold. If his hearts are weak, he can probably make 6♣, or at least 5♣. If you are playing Walsh, you can bid 2NT to transfer to clubs. Usually now you either pass with a weak hand and long clubs or bid your short suit at the three-level to show a strong 4441 hand. But following the general procedure about jumps to the four-level showing splinters, you rebid 4♡ to describe this hand. In Walsh 2♠ (minor-suit Stayman) followed by *three* of a major is a splinter with both minors, so 2♠ followed by 4♡ should show a hand like the one above, except with long diamonds instead of clubs. Why? Because you can transfer to clubs immediately and would adopt the suggestion above if your suit were clubs; therefore you must have diamonds for this sequence. And if you had a strong hand with both minors you would splinter at the three-level. Do you trust your partner to figure this out? If not, at least you can use the sequence to show clubs and a splinter.

General principles and point range

Marty Bergen and Larry Cohen have advised players to bid more aggressively over their opponents' strong notrump. Of all the defensive conventions for competing over 1NT, DONT (which they both espouse) is the most active, allowing players to compete with all sorts of distributional hands. Nevertheless, a strong notrump has considerable preemptive value. When the bidding is passed around to you in third or fourth position and you have a solid suit such as

♠ Q x   ♡ A K Q J x x   ◇ Q x x   ♣ x x

I like a 1NT opening. If you have a game, it is probably in notrump — your queens in spades and diamonds are dubious values in a heart contract, and you can hardly expect partner to cover all your losers at the four-level. But against 3NT, LHO may underlead AKxxx of a suit; then your queen will win and partner might have two top winners. The defense is usually not very accurate when you have a long suit the opponents don't know about. However, the main advantage in opening 1NT is that it is preemptive. The opponents might be cold for nine tricks in spades, but you can make seven or eight tricks in notrump — even six will be enough if it is the opponents' hand. Typically, you win the opening lead and cash the next six tricks, and probably get another one somewhere. This bid works particularly well when you have a doubleton spade; when your long suit is spades, there is less reason to preempt.

Why do most players adopt a 15-17 point range for an opening 'strong' notrump? It is so that all hands tempting one to bid notrump can be shown within a three point range at the lower levels, and within a narrower range at higher levels. With 12-14 (although I think it should be a good 12) you open a suit and rebid 1NT. With 15-17 you open 1NT. With 18-19 you open a suit and rebid 2NT over a one-level suit response. (A jump to 3NT over a suit response at the one-level is based on a solid suit of your own.) With 20-21 (or a bad 22) you open 2NT and with a good 22 to 24, open 2♣ and rebid 2NT. The lower ranges, where you open or rebid 1NT, can be slightly wider than at the higher level since once the bidding reaches the 2NT level, there is no room to invite; partner must either pass or raise to game.

So why would anyone choose a different range? One possibility is that he is playing a strong club. A suit opening (other than clubs) followed by a 1NT bid might show 12 to 13+. An opening 1NT might show 14-16 (which is the range I use when playing Precision), and 1♣ followed by 1NT might show 17-19. If you open 1♣ with all hands when holding 16+, the range of a 1NT rebid would be 16-19, which is too wide a range. You may be set when you invite game, or miss a game when you fail to invite. If you open 1NT with 12-15 HCP, that is also too wide a range.

Whether or not they are playing a strong club, some players like to play a weak notrump (12-14) which means that they have to open a suit and rebid a minimum number of notrump with 15-17. There's no doubt that the weak notrump is more exciting. It preempts the opponents who have to double or bid at the two-level if they want to compete. If responder has a good hand, he may be able to penalize the opponents. A weak notrump bid usually results in less accurate bidding for both sides. It will be hard for the notrump bidder's side to find a 4-4 major fit to play in a partscore, and it will be hard for the other side to find its 4-4 major fit at either the partscore or game level.

However, in some ways, making an opening bid of 1NT with 12-14 points seems very dangerous. It can cause a very bad result when someone doubles and opener's partner has 3 or 4 balanced points. There may be no way to escape for less than 500 points, while the opponents haven't quite enough points to bid game, even if they can make it, so it is -500 versus the 120 or 140 the opponents could have made on their own. But there are several problems in penalizing the notrump bidder's side. Most players double a weak notrump with a good 14 HCP or more. However, sometimes the doubler has 20 points and his partner has four. Since the hand with 4 points doesn't know his partner is so strong, he may pull the double, especially when he has a five-card suit. If the partner of the notrump bidder has a long suit, he can bid it (directly or indirectly). Weak notrump bidders usually have a scheme of escape bids, and if they find a fit at the two-level, it is hard to penalize them severely. The notrump bidder's side may steal the pot in an undoubled contract, down three when each opponent has approximately 13 points and neither risks competing — and if an opponent enters the fray with 13 points and finds his partner with 3, his side will be the one that suffers a big set.

If the weak notrump is so destructive, why not lower the range so as to be able to use it more frequently? (The average hand holds 10 HCP, so the closer your defined range is to 10 points, the more frequently you will have a hand within that range.) Many top players play the Kamikaze notrump (10-12 HCP) with certain vulnerabilities — never when their side is vulnerable, but perhaps only when not vulnerable vs. vulnerable, and then only in certain positions (obviously not in fourth position, probably not in third).

Since this book is about uncontested auctions, my concern is not how to defend against a weak or Kamikaze notrump, but how to play it. Surely you will want to play Stayman, no matter what your range is. But some people who play a 12-14 point notrump, and almost everyone who plays a Kamikaze notrump, refuse to play transfer bids. Responder may be as strong as the notrump bidder, or even stronger, so there is no advantage in letting opener play the hand. More importantly, it is easier for the opponents to catch you for a penalty when you are playing transfer bids than when a two-level response in the other three suits is natural and an attempt to play there. That means that responder has to bid 2♣ on almost all strong hands (as well as weak hands) or play two-way Stayman, with a 2◊ response to 1NT being forcing to game.

When partner opens a strong notrump, it is very rare that the next hand has a good penalty double. Because it is so rare, most people play the double of a strong notrump as meaning something other than penalty (like a one-suiter when playing DONT, or showing a major and a longer minor when playing Woolsey). If the opponents are playing penalty doubles, the partner of the doubler won't know when to leave it in (unless he has a balanced six points or more), and if it is left in, the defenders usually mislay at least one trick on defense since they don't know what their combined assets are. Partner of the doubler may hold KQxxx of a suit, but the doubler doesn't find out till Trick 9 that if he had led his doubleton ace they could have run the whole suit, and in the meantime declarer has taken seven tricks. So I think that when 1NT is doubled, both opener and responder should pass unless responder has a weak hand and a long suit.

But while I don't favor runout systems after a strong notrump, it is a good idea to agree upon them when playing a Kamikaze notrump, and perhaps also with an ordinary weak notrump. When a Kamikaze notrump is doubled, the odds are that the notrump bidder is in trouble, and the partners should adopt escape measures. For example, a redouble asks opener to bid 2♣ after which responder can pass or bid his long suit; immediate bids show that suit and the next higher suit; pass asks opener to redouble, and then if responder bids a suit, it shows that suit and a higher ranking non-touching suit. There may be other runout systems that are as good or better.

2NT OPENINGS

After a 2NT opening bid (or 2♣ followed by a 2NT rebid), the same basic system that you play over 1NT can be used — with a few exceptions.

You can't play four-suit transfers. It is impractical to play 3NT as a transfer to either minor.

2NT-3◇, 3♡-4♣ (transfer to a major followed by a minor-suit bid) shows a two-suiter with interest in slam. When opener knows two of responder's suits he can evaluate his hand very well. Opener can show a super, good, average, or poor hand in steps, depending on his distribution and location of honors: 'good' is aces in the unbid suits, honors in responder's suits and length in at least one of them. This is my idea. My original suggestion, years ago, was that you could bid the same way over either 1NT or 2NT, but I now think it should just apply over 2NT. Transferring over 1NT and bidding a new suit could just be looking for the best game, not necessarily for slam, so location of stoppers could be important.

2NT-3♣, 3♡/♠-? Bidding the other major now shows a slam interest, although there isn't room to be specific. It may be either a balanced or unbalanced invitation in partner's major suit.

2NT-3♡, 3♠-4♡ shows a 5-5 hand that hopes to make game: opener must either pass or bid 4♠. In contrast, 2NT-3◇, 3♡-3♠ shows the same distribution, but with some slam interest. With a good fit for one of the majors, opener should bid four of a minor. It is possible to play this way since with 5-4 or 6-4 in the majors, you can bid 3♣ followed by your shorter major (Smolen).

Except for my suggestion to show attitude in steps, the method I have just described is 'standard,' at least among the players I know. While I have found this system adequate over a period of years, I now think there is a better way.

Puppet Stayman — my way

In discussing responses to 1NT I said that ordinary Stayman has disadvantages since declarer describes his distribution, and often responder has, by inference, described *his* distribution. However, except for not using Stayman with 4333 distribution and some 4432 hands with a strong doubleton, I still play ordinary Stayman over 1NT since its advantages outweigh the disadvantages, like being able to play Garbage Stayman or use Stayman and pass whatever opener rebids with

$$\spadesuit A \times x \quad \heartsuit x \times x \times \quad \diamond J \, 10 \times x \times \quad \clubsuit x$$

But I don't like to describe my distribution to the opponents, especially when I don't find a fit despite my efforts.

Many experts like to play Puppet Stayman over a 2NT opener (or 2♣ followed by 2NT). One reason is that with strong hands, like

$$\spadesuit A K Q \times x \quad \heartsuit J \times \quad \diamond K Q \times \quad \clubsuit A Q \times$$

or

$$\spadesuit A J \, 10 \quad \heartsuit A K \times x \times \quad \diamond Q \, 10 \quad \clubsuit A K J$$

there is no reasonable alternative to opening 2NT or 2♣ followed by 2NT. Opening one of the major risks missing game, and even if partner keeps the bidding open by responding 1NT, you don't want these strong hands, with tenaces, to be in the dummy with the weak hand as declarer in 3NT. If there is an eight-card major fit, especially when there is an unstopped suit, four of the major may play better than 3NT. Puppet Stayman allows opener to show his five-card major by bidding it in response to 3♣. However, it loses when responder is 5-4 in the majors and is unable to play Smolen.

One purported advantage of Puppet Stayman is that responder describes his hand and opener places the contract without describing his hand. In practice, it doesn't work out that way. Over 3♣, opener bids 3NT without a four- or five-card major. He bids 3♦ with either major or both four-card majors, and responder either bids 4♣ with both majors or bids the major he does not have (bidding 3♥ to show spades for example). But suppose he bids 3♥ and opener bids 3NT. Obviously opener does not have four spades, but he must have four hearts, or he would have rebid 3NT instead of 3♦. The defenders know just as much about opener's distribution as if he were playing ordinary Stayman — even slightly more, since they know he has four hearts, not five. If you don't mind the complications there are ways to overcome the non-Smolen problem, but only by a further description of each player's distribution.

Before I describe my recommendations, let's consider situations where playing in the eight-card major fit is most likely or least likely to gain a trick. When responder has 4333 distribution, no matter which his four-card suit is, he should just raise to 3NT. Usually 3NT is more likely to make than four of a major, and often you can make the same number of tricks in either contract. In the long run, the gain, when it exists, of possibly making an extra trick in a 4-4 major fit is outweighed by the loss in making it easier for the opponents to defend well when you don't find a fit. The case of 5332 distribution is similar. Responder should use Stayman since he doesn't want to miss a 5-4 major fit, but he shouldn't worry about missing a 5-3 fit. But when responder has 5431 distribution, even 5422 distribution, it is likely that a 5-3 major fit will develop an extra trick, so he should transfer to his suit. When opener has 4333 distribution and responder transfers him to a major followed by bidding 3NT, opener can't tell whether it is better to play 3NT or four of the major. This is because most partnerships don't have any means for responder to show whether he is 5332 or has some other distribution. As a result, opener normally bids four of the major any time he has three-card support.

I have been discussing how to play the standard way (like when 2NT-3NT is a raise of notrump). These are my new recommendations:

Responder should transfer to a five-card major *except* with 5332 distribution. With that distribution he should use Stayman, so a transfer followed by 3NT shows a somewhat unbalanced hand (5422 or 5431).

You can play Texas (or reverse Texas, where the transfer to the four-level is stronger than transferring to the two-level and raising to game, whichever you prefer). Also, bid the same way after a transfer to a major and a new suit (my preference being to show in steps how well you like your hand).

Responder should not bid Stayman with 4333 distribution.

With *one* four-card major (and not 4333 distribution) responder should use Stayman. With *two* four-card majors, responder should bid a direct 3NT (or 4NT or 5NT to invite or insist upon slam while guaranteeing both major suits)!

Over Stayman, opener should bid a five-card major. Otherwise he should bid 3◇ — why should he tell the opponents his distribution unless he has five (which is rather infrequent)? After the 3◇ rebid responder should bid the major he does *not* have. If he bids 3♠, for example, showing hearts, opener bids hearts with four. He makes no effort to find out about a spade fit since responder has denied four spades by bidding 3♠ (with both majors he would have bid 3NT directly over 2NT). However, opener can cuebid 4♣ to show a super-acceptance in hearts. If responder is not interested in slam he can bid 4◊ to transfer the bidding back to opener. Responder could hold 3-5-3-2 distribution, treating his five-card heart suit as though it were four.

If responder has 5-4 in the majors, he has a choice of treatments. When the long suit is weak, e.g.

$$♠ A Q x x \quad ♡ J x x x x \quad J x \quad ♣ x x$$

he normally just bids 3NT, purportedly showing four of each major. He doesn't worry about missing a 5-3 fit. With

$$♠ J x x x \quad ♡ K Q 10 x x \quad ◊ x x \quad ♣ x x$$

where the five-card suit is strong enough to play opposite a doubleton, he bids 4♣ directly over 3◊ to show five hearts and four spades, and he would bid 4◊ to show five spades and four hearts. When the decision is close, he tends to show the 5-4 distribution when he has 3-1 or 4-0 in the minors and just bids 3NT with 2-2 in the minors.

Even when responder does not have a four-card major (or a five-card major with 5332 distribution) he can use Stayman when he has three cards in either major and a singleton or worthless doubleton elsewhere, planning, if opener bids the right five-card major, to raise him; otherwise he will bid 3NT on the second round.

What does responder bid over 2NT when he is strong enough to raise to game but has no interest in a major-suit fit? He bids 3♠ to transfer to 3NT! If he would normally raise to 4NT or 5NT, he bids 3♠ first when he doesn't have both majors. The 3♠ bid can also be the start of a minor-suit slam try. Over the forced 3NT rebid, 4♣ and 4◊ show one-suiters. (Theoretically, it is better to bid the minor one does not have so that opener will be declarer if the minor suit is trumps, although that is just one more thing to remember). Also over 3NT, 4♡ and 4♠ are splinter bids showing both minors. After responder's slam try, opener can show how well he likes his hand in steps.

When responder has a slam try with a four-card major and a longer minor, he checks for a major-suit fit. If he finds it, he doesn't show his minor. If he doesn't find it, he bids the minor, showing four of the other major plus the minor. Note this distinction: 2NT-3♣, 3♡-3NT, 4min shows that a major-suit fit was sought and not found, while 2NT-3♣, 3◊-4min shows a Smolen type of hand.

Among other things, this system enables you to let the strong hand play 3◊ opposite a diamond bust. Of much greater importance, it usually gets you to the right contract while giving the opponents as little useful information as possible.

What is your next bid on each of these hands?

1. **You**   **Partner**
   1NT   2♣[1]
   2NT   3♠[2]
   ?

   1. Minor-suit Stayman
   2. Splinter.

   ♠ A 9 8 5   ♡ A K 7 6   ◇ A 9 2   ♣ Q 6

2. **You**   **Partner**
   1NT   4NT
   ?

   ♠ Q 10 7   ♡ K 5   ◇ A Q 10 7 6   ♣ A 8 6

3. **You**   **Partner**
   1NT   4NT
   ?

   ♠ A Q 10 5   ♡ K 8   ◇ A J 9 4   ♣ Q 9 2

4. **You**   **Partner**
   1NT   2♡
   2♠   3◇
   3NT   4◇
   4♡   4NT
   ?

   ♠ Q 8   ♡ A Q 6 2   ◇ K 7 6   ♣ K Q 10 5

5. **You**   **Partner**
   2NT   3♠
   3NT   4◇
   ?

   ♠ A 7   ♡ A J 5   ◇ K Q 4 2   ♣ A K 6

6. **You**   **Partner**
   1NT   ?

   ♠ A K Q J 8   ♡ Q 7 5   ◇ Q 7 3   ♣ J 3

   What do you bid at matchpoints?

7. You   **Partner**
pass   ?

♠ Q 8   ♡ K 5 3   ◇ A K Q 8 7 4   ♣ 10 3

8. You   **Partner**
1NT   ?

♠ 10   ♡ K J 7   ◇ A J 9 8 6   ♣ 10 8 5 4

9. You   **Partner**
1NT   ?

♠ A K Q J 5 2   ♡ Q J   ◇ Q 10 6.   ♣ Q 10

10. You   **Partner**
1NT   ?

♠ J 7 6 4 3   ♡ Q 10 6   ◇ K J 3   ♣ J 7

11. You   **Partner**
1NT   2◇
2♡   ?

♠ 9   ♡ K Q 10 7 6 3   ◇ K J 7   ♣ K J 5

12. You   **Partner**
1NT   ?

♠ A 7   ♡ K 5 4   ◇ Q 9   ♣ A J 9 6 5 4

13. You   **Partner**
1NT   2♣
2♡   ?

♠ K 8 3   ♡ K Q 9 7   ◇ A J 10 5 3   ♣ 6

For the next two hands, assume you are playing my version of Puppet Stayman.

14. You   **Partner**
2NT   3♠
3NT   4♣
4◇   ?

♠ Q 10 7   ♡ 6   ◇ K J 8   ♣ K J 10 8 7 5

15. | **Partner** | **You** |
2NT	3♣
3◇	3♡
4♣	?

♠ K Q 9 6   ♡ 8 6   ◇ A 5 4   ♣ Q 10 9 8

---

my answers

1. Bid 4◇. Partner probably has 1-2-5-5 distribution and your hand should fit his like a glove. He actually held

    ♠ x   ♡ x x   ◇ K Q J x x   ♣ A J 9 x x

    Your hand could scarcely be better given that you didn't show a minor suit over 2♠. If you bid 4◇, unless partner does something strange, you will bid 6◇ next round. Responder could hold

    ♠ x   ♡ x x   ◇ K Q J x   ♣ A 10 x x x x

    and since he knows you hold only three diamonds, he should correct to 4NT or 5♣ on that hand.

2. First, let us dispose of a side issue. The 4NT bid does not show both majors. Why? Because the new system I suggested only applies after a 2NT opening (or 2♣ followed by 2NT). With good controls and a five-card suit, you may belong in slam with a total of 31 or 32 points; much depends upon partner's diamond fit. So you should bid 5◇ (and pass if partner bids 5NT). This is one of the few sequences where you might stop in 5NT. Usually a 5NT bid lets partner choose a slam since you get no bonus for bidding 5NT — that is cutting it very close. My main point is that you should either pass or show your five-card suit so that partner can evaluate his hand. Some players, if they accept the invitation, respond as though to Blackwood, just in case two aces are missing. To me this seems like a very poor choice.

3. That ten of spades in a four-card suit along with two higher honors would persuade me to accept partner's invitation. I would guess that 6NT has a 50-50 chance of making. But I would bid 5NT, after which both partners show four-card suits up the line. If partner bids 6◇ (or 6♣ and then passes your 6◇ bid with 4-4 in the minors), it may be a superior contract. Or you might even find a 4-4 spade fit — partner wouldn't use Stayman with ♠ K x x x   ♡ A J x   ◇ K Q x   ♣ K x x

4. Pass. Partner did well to sign off in 4NT (rather than 4♠ or 5◊) with

    ♠ A J x x x   ♡ K x   ◊ A J x x x   ♣ x

    when you failed to bid more strongly.

5. Bid 4NT. Partner asked you to show, in three steps, how you liked your hand in support of diamonds; 4NT is the third step (the best).

6. Just bid 3NT. Slam is out of the question, but at least four times out of five you will take as many tricks in notrump as in spades. If you transfer to spades and bid 3NT, partner, not knowing what kind of hand you have, may make the wrong choice. Don't even tempt him to bid spades! At IMPs, I suppose 4♠ would be the safer game since it is just possible that the opponents could run the club suit against you.

7. Bid 1NT. If you have a game, it is probably 3NT. If you play in a partscore, 1NT will probably get you the best result. Since partner has passed, he won't take you to a losing slam and is unlikely to have a six-card major. You don't have much defense, and the 1NT opening has preemptive value (compared to 1◊).

8. Bid 3NT (probably!). However, Stayman is very tempting. Perhaps partner will bid 2♠, which will discourage a spade lead when you bid 3NT next round. This shows four hearts, but since partner bids hearts first with both majors, there is no danger of his bidding 4♡. And if he bids 2♡ in response to Stayman, it is quite possible that 4♡ on a 4-3 fit will work out (but if you then bid 3NT partner may bid 4♠). The bid you *should not make* is 3♠ to show this distribution. Your hand is not strong enough to suggest five of a minor, yet too strong to play in a partscore. If you are going to get to 3NT anyway, there is no purpose in telling the opponents you have a singleton spade.

9. Bid 6NT. I can't even imagine a hand where 6♠ is better, or a way to find out that you are missing the ace-king of a suit. If partner has to guess which of two finesses to take, the opening lead will probably solve his problem unless it is a spade. Another factor in favor of bidding 6NT is that the opponents seldom lead an ace against a notrump slam.

10. Pass. This isn't a case of being greedy: 1NT is more likely to make than 2♠. Where is partner more likely to have a doubleton? In spades or clubs?

11. Bid 3♠, a splinter. If partner doesn't have wasted values in spades, you probably have a slam.

12. If you are playing four-suit transfers, bid 2♠ followed by 4NT. If you are playing Walsh responses, bid 2NT, followed by 4NT. Partner will consider his degree of club fit in deciding whether to bid a slam. I recommended that you drop the Walsh double relay since it is inconsistent with Larry Cohen's advice to bid at the three-level with four-card trump support, but if you are playing the double relay, this would be a good hand for it.

13. Bid 3♠. This shows a good hand for hearts with a singleton somewhere. If he is interested, partner can ask where your singleton is. An immediate jump to 4♣ would be Keycard Gerber.

14. Sign off in 4NT. Partner showed, by using the first step response to 4♣, a poor hand in support of clubs.

15. Bid 4♡. Partner's 4♣ bid shows a super-acceptance of spades. Since spades have not been previously bid, you should transfer to spades so that partner will be the declarer. (You would do the same thing with a much weaker hand.) When partner bids 4♠, you should raise him directly to 6♠. Since a grand slam is out of the question, and you have no intention of stopping short of slam when partner shows a superacceptance, there is no purpose in cuebidding your controls. Your 3♡ bid showed spades and denied hearts, so 4♡ cannot be natural.

CHAPTER 5

precision

In 1988 I published a book entitled *Bridge From The Top, Book 2*. It contained a very long chapter on forcing club systems, and at the end of it I recommended using a combination of Blue Team Club and Precision. My system featured five-card majors and a forcing notrump (from Precision) and control-showing responses to the strong club (from Blue Team). The original Blue Team system used four-card major openings, non-forcing notrump responses and a canapé style (bidding a shorter suit before a longer suit) in certain situations. I think the main reason Precision has become far more popular than Blue Team is that it more closely resembles what most bridge players in North America were taught to play. It is easier to make a few changes than several changes.

THE 1♣ OPENING

In Precision a 1♣ opening is strong, artificial, and forcing. Supposedly it shows 16 or more points and all other suit bids show less than 16; however, you are allowed to use your judgment. With unguarded honors — e.g. a hand like

♠ J x   ♡ K   ◇ K Q J x x   ♣ K Q J x x

— and/or minor suits in a marginal hand, you should open 1◇ and not 1♣. In fact, I would open 1◇ with this hand if my spades were headed by the queen doubleton, which would add up to 17 points. In contrast these hands:

♠ A x   ♡ A K J 10 x x   ◇ K x x x   ♣ x

♠ A K Q x x x x x   ♡ A x x   ◇ x   ♣ x

should both be opened 1♣. In the original Precision system, an opening 1♣ bid followed by a 1NT rebid showed 16-19 points. That was too wide a range, and now many Precision players have changed their range for an opening 1NT to 14-16 HCP from 13-15 or 12-15. With 12-13 HCP, if they have no five-card major they open 1◇ and rebid 1NT.

Many players open 2NT to show 22-24, so that opening 1♣ and jumping to 2NT shows 20-21. I think it is more logical to play an opening 2NT bid as 20-21 and an opening 1♣ followed by 2NT as 22-24. The other way it is hard to distinguish between a 1NT rebid, which may show 19 points, and a 2NT rebid, which may show 20 points. Also, if you open 1♣ and partner responds 2♣ or 2◊, and you then rebid 2NT with either 19 or 20 (and partner raises to 3NT), it is too dangerous for either player to bid again when responder has 12 points and a five-card suit (which might be opposite 17). With 22-24, opener can safely make a further bid to show that he is in the higher range. (But he still rebids only 2NT, planning to make his further bid later, to give responder more room to describe his hand since a 3NT rebid to show extras takes up too much bidding room.)

RESPONDING TO 1♣

Before going further, I should mention that there are two basic ways to bid after a 1♣ opening. Many top players like to play a series of asking bids, starting with the second round of bidding. Suppose the bidding starts:

Opener	**Responder**
1♣	1♠

Now if opener rebids a new suit (2♡, for example), responder shows in steps his degree of support for partner's suit and whether he has a 'good' hand (four or more controls, counting an ace as two and a king as one) or a 'bad' hand. If opener raises responder's suit, it is a different type of asking bid. Responder now shows whether he has a good hand or bad hand and how good his suit is. If opener rebids 1NT it is a third type of asking bid. The three types of asking bids are called alpha, beta and gamma.

Generally I like 'telling' bids better than 'asking' bids, especially at low levels, and I like Standard bidding over a 1NT rebid (with Stayman and transfers). So when opener shows a minimum balanced hand, I think responder rather than opener should be captain. But the players who like asking bids say that asking bids should start as low as possible. If a 1NT rebid is an asking bid, opener can surrender his captaincy by rebidding 2NT rather than 1NT with 17-19 points after a positive response, and there are various ways that players with an unusual or very distributional hand can refuse to make an asking bid or to give the normal response to an asking bid. It is all very complicated, and each pair his its own variations. For example, a 1♡ response might show a positive response in spades; a spade response might show a positive response in another suit; a 2◊ response might show a balanced 8-11 HCP, all with two objectives: (a) to let the strong (1♣ opener) be declarer and (b) to allow the various asking bids to be made at a low bidding level. This method does not appeal to me since it violates the 'telling' rather than 'asking' principle for reasons more fully explained in the next chapter. But the fact that so many good players play this way makes me distrust my own judgment. Rather than attempt to describe how various top pairs play Precision (some play numerous transfers; others play numerous asking bids, and yet others play that a 1♣ bid followed by a 1♡ rebid over a 1♢ response is forcing and artificial, guaranteeing 20+ points), I will discuss a simple version.

In Blue Team, a 1♢ response shows 5 points or less, while in Precision responder could have as many as 7 points or 8 'bad' points. So, in Blue Team, making a game in notrump or a minor is very unlikely after a 1♢ response when opener holds only 18 or 19 points. So opener would now bid a four-card major ahead of a longer minor — with

$$♠ A K x x \quad ♡ x \quad ♢ A Q x x x x \quad ♣ A x$$

for example. If responder holds

$$♠ J x x x \quad ♡ x x \quad ♢ K x \quad ♣ J x x x x$$

he will raise spades when he would have passed a 2♢ rebid by opener. The negative response over a Precision club is not quite so discouraging, but I recommend showing your four-card major anyway. Needless to say, if responder has made a positive response so that opener knows he will be able to bid both of his suits, he should bid his longer suit first.

In original Precision all responses to an opening 1♣ bid from 1♡ through 2♢ are positive, showing 8 or more points, and all positive responses are forcing to game. The 1♠, 2♣ and 2♢ responses all show a five-card or longer suit and are natural as well as positive, and that works well. The only alteration I recommend is to play that the 1♡ and 1NT responses are interchanged, so that 1♡ shows either 8-12 or 15+ HCP without a five-card suit (unless it is a weak five-card minor suit in a balanced hand) and 1NT shows 5+ hearts and 8+ HCP. The reasons for the switch are obvious — to avoid the weak hand being declarer in notrump contracts and to allow the strong hand to rebid 1NT, after which the whole system of Stayman and transfers will be available. (In the early versions of Precision, responder would bid 1NT to show 8-10 points in a balanced hand. Not only did this make the weak hand declarer, but it also caused confusion in another way. Opener would tend to bid 2♣ over 1NT as a type of Stayman bid, looking for a 4-4 major fit, but he would also bid 2♣ with a long club suit, which caused an ambiguity.)

After a positive response to 1♣ responder should avoid raising opener's rebid with three small. Suppose the bidding starts:

Opener	Responder
1♣	1♠
2♡	?

and responder holds

♠ A Q x x x   ♡ x x x   ◇ K x x   ♣ x x

With ♡Qxx or four small hearts, responder would be glad to raise to 3♡ and let opener take over as captain. But after a positive response there is a likelihood that partner will drive to slam with a good hand and what would otherwise be a good slam may turn into a bad slam when the trumps are weak. It is better to bid 2NT now and support hearts on the next round (even if partner raises to 3NT).

A 2NT response to 1♣ shows a balanced 13-14 HCP. Two of a major shows 3-7 HCP with a six-card suit, usually headed by a couple of honors. Frequently opener will pass this response, but if he bids a new suit, it is forcing for one round. I see no need for an 'impossible negative' (a 1◇ response followed by a jump later to show a good hand with 4441 distribution). Simply bid 1♡, which saves about one and a half levels of bidding on average. The only disadvantage is that when opener has a long suit, like AKQxxx, he can't be sure that responder doesn't have a singleton, making the suit less likely to break. Also there is no reason why responder can't show a no-loser suit by bidding 3NT just as he would over a strong 2♣ opening. Opener can also play the Kokish relay by jumping to 2♡ over a 1◇ response.

THE 2♣ AND 2◇ OPENINGS

Since an opening 1♣ bid is artificial, you have to open 2♣ with 11-15 points and a six-card (or longer) club suit. Many Precision players also open 2♣ with a five-card club suit and a four-card major. I dislike bidding 2♣ with a five-card suit. The 2♣ bid is the worst part of the system since it is a limit bid, and if partner has fewer than 9 or 10 points, he can't safely look for a better contract; if he doesn't find one, he is just one trick higher on a misfitting hand. With

♠ Q x x x   ♡ K x x x   ◇ Q x x x   ♣ x

he has to pass over 2♣ and hope for the best (as though his partner had opened a natural club and rebid 2♣). But in Standard bidding, when opener holds one of these hands

♠ K x x x   ♡ A x   ◇ x x   ♣ K Q x x x

♠ x   ♡ A J x x   ◇ J x x   ♣ A Q x x x

there would be room over 1♣ to find a major-suit fit. Even though they are very aggressive bidders, I understand that Meckwell do not open 2♣ with a five-card suit.

What should you open with these two hands in Precision? The nebulous diamond! A 1◇ opening merely shows 11 to 15 points, two or more diamonds, no five-card major and fewer than six clubs. That may seem wild and dangerous, but it works pretty well except occasionally in competitive auctions. Most Precision pairs, including Meckwell, play that way. There is a little ambiguity right away, but if there is a major-suit fit, partner seldom cares whether your raise of a 1♠ response to 2♠ is made with

♠ K x x x　♡ A x x　◇ K x　♣ Q J x x

or

♠ K x x x　♡ K x　◇ Q J x x　♣ A x x

If the bidding goes

Opener	Responder
1◇	1♠
1NT	pass

the opponents don't know which is your better suit, clubs or diamonds (which is an advantage in the play). And if you rebid clubs, that retroactively shows at least four diamonds. If you hold 5-4 in the minors, partner has to guess which is your longer minor, but this can be true in Standard bidding also. Obviously, with 3-3-3-4 or 3-3-2-5 distribution, you either raise partner's major or rebid 1NT, not 2♣.

That leaves 4-4-1-4, 4-3-1-5, 3-4-1-5 and 4-4-0-5 hands. With 11 to 15 HCP most Precision players open 2◇ with three-suiters which include a singleton or void in diamonds. If responder bids 2♡, 2♠ or 3♣, opener passes. If responder has a good hand and wants to know opener's exact distribution he bids 2NT. A 3♣ rebid shows 4-4-1-4 distribution; a 3◇ rebid shows 4-3-1-5; a 3♡ rebid shows 3-4-1-5 and a 3♠ rebid shows 4-4-0-5. The way to remember this is that opener bids below his shorter major. The way I play, if responder has discovered a 4-4 major fit, his bid of a major at the three-level is forcing and may be quite strong. If his suit is opposite a three-card major, his bid of that suit at the three-level is only invitational since there may be only a seven-card major fit. With a strong hand, where responder is interested in slam (despite the disappointing rebid), he can bid 4◇. An immediate jump to the three-level in a major over 2◇ shows at least a five-card suit, but is only invitational. Opener would accept the invitation about 80% of the time when he has four-card support and about 40% of the time with three-card support.

After an opening 2♣ bid, a 2♡, 2♠ or 2NT response is natural and invitational. Opener should not pass any of these responses with a singleton in his partner's suit; instead he should rebid either 3♣ or 2NT. Typically he passes with a doubleton but may raise if it is a strong doubleton with a maximum opening. With three-card support he should raise either to three or four, and with four-card support and good controls he should make a splinter bid. Over a 2NT response he will raise with a maximum balanced hand and pass with a minimum balanced hand. With a singleton, he should rebid clubs with a minimum or bid his singleton with a maximum. A raise to 3♣ is similar to a raise of a weak two-bid, primarily preemptive, although with an unusual hand (perhaps with seven clubs and a singleton or void, or a 6-5 hand) opener may bid again.

Most of the time, if responder makes a bid over 2♣ it will be an artificial 2◊, which is like Stayman, asking for more information. Over opener's rebid, if responder bids three of a major, it is forcing. That's the way responder would bid with

$$♠ A x \quad ♡ A Q x x x \quad ◊ J x x \quad ♣ K x x$$

He is too strong to bid 2♡ (non-forcing), but his suit is too weak for a jump to 4♡. Opener could hold 6-4, so over the 2◊ response, opener should bid 2♡ if he has a four-card major, and if responder is interested, he can bid 2♠ to ask which major his partner has: 2NT shows hearts and 3♣ shows spades. In both cases these rebids show a minimum hand. If no major fit is located, the partnership can stop in 3♣, which will usually be the safest partscore contract. With a maximum, opener would rebid 3◊ to show hearts or 3♡ to show spades. That allows responder, whose distribution is unknown to the opponents, to be declarer. If opener does not have a four-card major, he bids 2♠ (over 2◊) to show a minimum and 2NT or 3♣ to show a maximum — 2NT shows two stoppers outside clubs, and 3♣ shows one outside stopper. If responder is interested in where the stoppers are located, he bids 3◊ to ask. If opener has shown one outside stopper, he bids it (3♡ shows hearts, 3♠ shows spades, and 3NT shows diamonds). If responder can tell that a suit is unstopped, he should not pass 3NT. If opener has shown two outside stoppers, he shows the suit he does not have stopped. This appears to be complicated, but is based on what the Italian Blue Team did over 2♣, which showed the same type of hand as it does in Precision.

Suppose opener has rebid 2♠ to show a minimum with no four-card major. Responder may have plenty of strength to bid game and it is often best just to bid 3NT rather than to ask for a further description (since that may help the defense). But if responder wants to be scientific, he can bid 2NT to find out where opener's stoppers are. Now, again 3♣ says that opener has one outside stopper, and responder can bid 3◊ to find out where it is. Similarly over 2NT, a bid of 3◊, 3♡ or 3♠ says opener has two outside stoppers and the suit he bids is where he does *not* have a stopper.

WHY A STRONG CLUB?

I have given you a lot of detail without much theory. Now it is time to mention some of the advantages of a strong club opening. One is that it helps when you have an 18- or 19-point unbalanced hand. If you hold

♠ A K x x x   ♡ A J x x   ◇ x   ♣ A K x

the hand is too weak for an opening 2♣ bid in Standard bidding. But if you open 1♠, partner will pass with

♠ x x   ♡ K 10 9 x x   ◇ J x x x   ♣ x x

Yet you belong in 4♡. In Precision, you would open 1♣ and rebid 1♠ over a 1◇ response. Having already warned you that his hand is not very good, partner can afford to bid 2♡, which you will raise to 4♡. The reason responder can afford to bid 2♡ is that he now shows only 4-7 HCP and without a heart fit you can pass if you have a balanced minimum for your club opening; you definitely won't jump to game. If responder holds

♠ x x   ♡ K 10 9 x x x   ◇ x x x   ♣ x x

he would pass a 1♠ opening bid if playing Standard, but will respond 2♡ to a 1♣ opening if playing Precision and the partnership should get to a slam! Here is another example:

♠ A K x x x	♠ x
♡ x	♡ A x x
◇ A K x x x	◇ 10 9 x x x
♣ A x	♣ x x x x

Again 1♠ would be passed out in Standard: the odds are that a response on four points and a misfit will get the partnership too high. But when opener shows 16+ and responder has made a negative response, the odds are different. Responder should keep the bidding open any time he has an ace or the equivalent, so the bidding might go

Opener	Responder
1♣	1◇
1♠	1NT
2◇	3♡
6◇	

The 3♡ bid shows either the ace or a singleton, with great support for opener's second suit. (It can't be natural since responder has failed to make a positive response and could have bid 2♡ immediately with 3-7 HCP and a six-card heart suit.) These were both spectacular examples, but the strong club often makes the bidding easier on ordinary hands:

Opener	Responder
♠ A Q 10 x x	♠ K x
♡ A K x	♡ Q J x x
◇ K Q x	◇ J x x
♣ J 10	♣ x x x

Standard bidding might go 1♠-1NT, 3NT. Opener has enough strength to bid game and unless you decide to play 2NT by him as forcing, which creates problems of its own, what can opener do except jump to the most probable game? Precision bidding would be:

Opener	Responder
1♣	1◊
1♠	2♡
3♡	4♡

These are all examples from my earlier book where Blue Team would work out well, but Precision would work also.

In Standard bidding the early rounds of bidding should be descriptive, since neither partner knows whether the other has extra values, enough for a slam. However, in Precision if the opening bid is 1♡ and responder holds

♠ A K x x   ♡ Q 10 x   ◊ J x   ♣ Q J x x

then since a slam is extremely remote, he can jump to 4♡. The next player doesn't know whether responder has

♠ x   ♡ Q x x x x   ◊ x x   ♣ K x x x x

or a strong, balanced hand, so he doesn't know whether he should bid 4♠ or not when he holds

♠ Q 10 x x x   ♡ x   ◊ A K x x x   ♣ A x

Also, the defense will be much more difficult when the bidding goes 1♡-4♡ rather then when the bidding goes 1♡-2♣, 2◊-2♡, 4♡.

Meckwell give the following hand as an example of a raise of an opening 1♡ bid to 4♡:

♠ A x   ♡ J x x   ◊ K Q 10 x x x x   ♣ x

A slam opposite partner's non-club opening is very unlikely as compared to the opponents outbidding you in a black suit if you attempt a slower approach. With

♠ A K x x   ♡ Q 10 x   ◊ J x   ♣ Q J x x

you would welcome a reopening bid over 4♡, but this time you hope to avoid it.

Even at the partscore level limit bids have many advantages. Partner opens 1◊ and you respond 1♡ with

♠ J x x   ♡ A J 10 x   ◊ x   ♣ Q x x x x

Partner rebids 1♠. What would you do? In Standard bridge, you are almost forced to keep the bidding open since you might be cold for game. So you would probably bid 1NT. The danger in raising spades is that partner will assume you have four and may jump to 4♠ when you have a better contract available. Also, a raise to 2♠ is slightly too encouraging. In Precision, game is almost impossible after this start, and at least three times out of four, partner can make more tricks in spades than in notrump, especially at the partscore level. You can safely pass 1♠ playing Precision.

TACTICAL ISSUES

Playing Standard, you often take a false preference to give partner another chance when game is probable. For example, with

$$◇ A J x x x \quad ♡ x x x \quad ◇ Q x \quad ♣ Q x x$$

when the bidding goes 1◇-1♠, 2♣-? you bid 2◇ to keep the bidding alive. Partner might hold

$$♠ Q x x \quad ♡ A \quad ◇ A K x x x \quad ♣ K x x x$$

and be planning to bid 2♠ over a preference bid of 2◇. Or he might be strong enough to bid 2NT over 2◇, which you would gladly raise to 3NT. In Precision, game is remote and partner is just as likely to have longer clubs as to have longer diamonds, so you would pass.

Suppose, with equal vulnerability, partner opens 1♡, playing Precision. RHO passes and you hold

$$♠ x x \quad ♡ K 10 x x x \quad ◇ J x x x \quad ♣ x x$$

This hand was mentioned in the introduction. You are almost certain the opponents have a game (unless partner happens to hold four spades). Give partner a typical hand such as

$$♠ K x x \quad ♡ A Q x x x \quad ◇ K x x \quad ♣ J x$$

Defensively you have at most one spade trick, at most one heart trick, a probable diamond trick and no club trick. The opponents can take ten to eleven tricks in spades. You *could* bid 4♡, but LHO must have a very good hand and will probably bid 4♠ or make a takeout double unless you mislead him. You could try psyching 1♠ or make a two-over-one response; however, the bid that appeals to me is 2NT (Jacoby). If LHO holds 17 points, he will think his partner has a yarborough while you have a balanced 12 points and your partner has opened on 11. So instead of bidding or doubling when his partner is marked with no values, he may simply pass, thinking that it won't occur to declarer to play him for every missing card.

Playing Standard, a Jacoby 2NT bid would be too dangerous on this hand. Partner might drive to slam with 18 or 19 points. But here you know partner can't have a good enough hand to drive to slam. The most he can do is show his hand pattern and perhaps make one cuebid below the game level. (You won't be accepting any slam invitations!) Maybe nothing you do will work, but the 2NT bid is less dangerous than the other alternatives, and if you bid two of a minor, it will be difficult to find credible bids later. If you choose to bid 1♠ (when not vulnerable) and partner rebids a minor, you should pass rather than take partner back to hearts. LHO will be suspicious anyway, with his good hand, but less so if you pass, apparently showing a misfit, than if you return to hearts. Likewise, if partner raises your spades you should pass unless someone doubles.

Suppose you hold

♠ A K Q x   ♡ K x x x x   ◇ x   ♣ x x x

You open 1♡ and partner responds 1♠. What would you rebid? Not knowing any better, I bid 2♠ when I originally held this hand; I know better now. After two passes, RHO bid 3◇. I bid 3♠ and LHO bid 4◇. Partner's hand? Five small spades and an ace. He can make 3♠ and the opponents can make 4◇. Playing Precision, I should have rebid 3♠, not 2♠, and if I had done so, we would have stolen the pot. Since opener cannot have more than 15 points, he should make a jump raise any time he has four-card support for his partner's suit and a singleton. If the contract goes down, the opponents can almost surely make a partscore their way. This kind of 'playing trick' raise gets you to some good games that Standard players miss — for example

♠ A K Q x   ♡ K x x x x   ◇ x   ♣ x x x

opposite

♠ J x x x x   ♡ A x   ◇ Q x x x   ♣ J x

After 1♡-1♠, Standard bidders are afraid to raise to 3♠ for fear responder will bid a hopeless slam, expecting more high cards. What if opener had a better hand — something like

♠ A Q x x   ♡ A K Q x x   ◇ x   ♣ x x x

with which he *would* bid 3♠, playing *Bridge World* Standard? In that case he should rebid 2NT (alerted, of course)! I used to rebid 2NT with a hand like one of these

♠ x x   ♡ A K Q J x x   ◇ Q x   ♣ K 10 x

♠ J x   ♡ K x   ◇ A K Q 10 x x   ♣ Q x x

— a natural bid where the solid suit took the place of more high-card points (which I couldn't have when playing Precision). But based on frequency, one will have many more hands of the former type, with great support for partner's suit. Over the 2NT bid responder could bid 3♣ if he were interested in a slam. With a singleton opener would show it or just bid 3♠ with

♠ K Q x x ♡ x x ◇ A K 10 9 x ♣ K x

So if the bidding goes 1◇-1♡, 2NT-3♣, then 3◇ by opener would show a singleton club.

What is your next call with each of the following hands, playing my version of Precision?

1. **You**   **Partner**
   1◇   1♡
   ?

   ♠ A K 6   ♡ Q 5 4   ◇ Q 8   ♣ Q 9 8 7 5

2. **You**   **Partner**
   1♠   1NT
   ?

   ♠ A K J 7 6 4   ♡ A 8   ◇ Q J 5   ♣ 8 7

3. **You**   **Partner**
   1♠   1NT
   ?

   ♠ A Q J 7 6   ♡ 8   ◇ K Q 10 5 4   ♣ K 2

4. **You**   **Partner**
   1♡   1NT
   ?

   ♠ 9 6   ♡ A Q 10 9 6 3   ◇ A 8   ♣ A 10 9

5. **You**   **Partner**
   2♣   2◇
   2NT   3◇
   3NT   5♣
   ?

   ♠ Q 7 6   ♡ A 5   ◇ J   ♣ A K 9 8 7 5 2

6. **Partner**   **You**
   2♣   ?

   ♠ A K 6 2   ♡ Q 6 3   ◇ Q 9 8 5 4   ♣ 7

7. **Partner**   **You**
   2◇   2NT
   3◇¹   ?

   1. 4-3-1-5.

   ♠ A K 5 2   ♡ A Q 6 5   ◇ Q 8 7 4   ♣ Q

8. **Partner**   **You**
   1◇   1♡
   1♠   ?

   ♠ Q J 6   ♡ A K 7 3   ◇ 6   ♣ Q 7 6 5 4

9. **You**   **Partner**
   1◇   1♡
   ?

   ♠ A Q 10 8 5   ♡ 7   ◇ A K 10 5 4 3   ♣ J

10. **Partner**   **You**
    1◇   1♡
    2NT   3♣
    ?

    ♠ K 7 3   ♡ A Q 5 4   ◇ A Q 9 8 7 5   ♣ —

my answers

1. Bid 1NT. Your ◇Qx is not a terrible holding: opposite ◇Axx, for example, it will provide a double stopper. Besides, even though you can have a doubleton diamond, more often you will have at least three if not more, so your bid may inhibit a diamond lead if LHO has a close decision. The only alternative is to raise hearts, but your queen of diamonds is less likely to be useful in hearts than in notrump. Besides, your heart support is not very good. The bid you must not make is 2♣, since that would retroactively guarantee a real diamond suit — one at least four long.

2. Bid 3♠. Admittedly, you may go down in 3♠, but partner tends to pass over 1♠ with what would be a minimum notrump response in Standard bidding. He won't play you for a better hand for your bid (as he would if you were not playing a strong club system).

3. Bid 3◇. The system is ideal for hands like this. If you were not playing a strong club system partner would expect a somewhat better hand, and you would have to risk bidding 2◇. Yet if partner has as little as jack-fifth of diamonds and the ace of clubs (and many other hands), you belong in game, at least at IMPs. Since you didn't open 1♣ your jump shift is not forcing, and if partner bids only 3♠, you should pass. Partner might hold two small spades and worthless honors in the other two suits.

4. At matchpoints you should probably bid 3♡. If you can't establish the heart suit in time, you could be set several tricks in a notrump contract. However, at IMPs I think you should bid 2NT. You can't have enough high cards to be raising notrump with a balanced hand, so the 2NT bid says that you have a good, long suit. With a fit — something like

   ♠ A x x   ♡ K x   ◇ J x x   ♣ J x x x x

   — you definitely belong in 3NT, and you might make it opposite less. Since partner has not bid a suit, your 2NT bid cannot be misconstrued as showing four-card support with a singleton.

5. You should bid 6♣, and you might do it with a slightly weaker hand. When you showed two stoppers outside the club suit and then told partner that your unstopped suit was diamonds, he bid not 4♣ but 5♣. Obviously he doesn't have a diamond stopper himself and his values are outside the diamond suit. If you could make 5♣ with a worthless doubleton in diamonds, you should be able to make 6♣ with your singleton.

6. Partner *could* have six solid clubs and a red king (preferably in hearts), but the odds are that you will have a very poor play for game, even if partner has 15 points or four spades with this misfit. (If partner has four spades, your red queens are probably worthless.) So I recommend a pass. Even one bid from you may be too many if partner has ♣AJxxxx and gets a bad break in clubs.

7. Since you have found a 4-4 major fit, 3♠ will be forcing. If partner
    cuebids, you probably have a slam. If he bids 4♠, a slam is unlike-
    ly. Opener would bid 4♣ with

    ♠ Q 10 x x   ♡ K x x   ◇ x   ♣ A K J 10 x

    and he really doesn't need the ten of clubs this time. I can't pretend
    that you can tell, for sure, whether you belong in slam or not. As it
    is, you will probably need at least a 3-2 spade break to make a slam;
    if partner's spades are ♠J10xx or his clubs ♣AKxxx, the odds are
    probably against making a slam and even 5♠ may be too high.

8. Bid 2♠. This may seem like a tremendous underbid, but you don't
    have good enough trumps to issue a strong invitation to 4♠ or enough
    high cards for 3NT, facing a probable misfit. Even if partner has

    ♠ A K x x   ♡ Q x   ◇ A x x x x   ♣ x x

    for example, you are unlikely to make any game. Change his dia-
    monds to ◇KJxxx, and it will be a struggle to take eight tricks.

9. Bid 2♠. This is what you would like to bid if playing *Bridge World*
    Standard, but you would be afraid to for fear partner would play you
    for more high cards. The failure to open a strong club protects you —
    this is about the best hand you could have.

10. Bid 4♣. Since 3◇ would show a singleton club, 4♣ should show a
    void. If your hand were weaker you would probably bid 3◇ rather
    than force the bidding to game, but this hand is good enough to make
    game a good gamble, and partner might even get to slam if he held
    something like

    ♠ A x   ♡ K 10 x x x x   ◇ J 10   ♣ J x x

CHAPTER 6

slam bidding

The key to good slam bidding is for both partners to describe their hands accurately in the first two or three rounds of bidding, so that they can still stop safely in game if slam no longer seems likely. Let us review some of the ideas from previous chapters that have a strong influence on slam bidding.

1. *You should avoid bidding bad suits with good hands.*

Opener	Responder
♠ K J x x	♠ A Q x
♡ A Q x x	♡ x x x x
◇ Q J x x x	◇ A K x x
♣ —	♣ A J

If responder bids 1♡ the final contact will probably be 6♡, which requires a finesse plus a 3-2 break, while 6◇ is a greatly superior contract, and even 6NT is a better contract than 6♡. Or perhaps these are the hands:

Opener	Responder
♠ K x	♠ A Q x x
♡ A J x x	♡ 10 x x x
◇ K Q J x x	◇ A x
♣ x	♣ A K J

Again, is there any reason for responding 1♡ to 1◇, rather than 1♠?

2. *Jump bids in forcing auctions should show useful features* — usually a good suit or good support for partner's suits, and in some cases, should deny controls in other suits. For example,

Opener	Responder
1♠	2♡
4♡	

Opener shows good spades and hearts, no controls in the minors.

Opener	Responder
1♡	2◇
3◇	4♡

Responder has good cards in the red suits, but no controls in the black suits.

Opener	Responder
1◇	2♣
2♠	4♠

Responder shows very good spade support, no control in hearts. If responder's second bid is 4♣, he shows the same type of hand, but even stronger.

3. *After a major-suit opening and a two-over-one response, rebidding the major is the default bid.* Consequently, if opener bids 1♠ and rebids 2NT over a 2◇ response, he shows stoppers in the unbid suits and at least a doubleton in responder's suit. Now responder can raise to 3NT with

♠ K x ♡ x x ◇ A Q x x x x x ♣ J x

rather than rebidding 3◇. In the context of slam bidding, responder with AKJxxxx of a minor knows he has a better than even chance of running the suit without loss.

4. *Responder avoids making a two-over-one response to a major-suit opening on a three- or four-card suit (or even a five-card suit with a bad 13- or 14-point hand).* The forcing notrump (followed by a game bid next round) is often used to discourage slam tries by opener.

5. *Slam tries beyond the game level are avoided* because each partner should show extra strength (in either high cards or distribution) if he has it, below the game level. For example, this sequence

Opener	Responder
1♡	2♣
3NT	

shows a balanced hand and 16-17 points.
    This one

Opener	Responder
1♡	2♣
3♡	

shows a good, but not necessarily solid, suit and extra values — or perhaps only slight extra values, but a completely solid suit.
    Finally, this one

Opener	Responder
1♡	2◇
3♣	

shows at least a king better than a minimum opening (plus hearts and clubs, of course).

6. *Some bids show which of partner's high cards are valuable and which are worthless.* Take this auction, for example:

Opener	Responder
1♡	2NT
4◇	

Besides showing at least 5-5 in hearts and diamonds, this sequence shows that opener does not have two quick losers in the black suits. High cards other than aces or honors in the red suits are probably worthless. Likewise, splinter bids tell partner that no honors in the splinter suit are valuable except possibly the ace.

When should you make a slam try? Back in the 1930s the Four Aces suggested a workable test. After finding a fit, if a player had an ace more than he needed to bid game with a balanced hand, he should issue a slam invitation; with an unbalanced hand he needed an extra king. The initial invitation was usually a cuebid.

Let's attack the problem from a different point of view. Instead of concentrating on *methods* of slam investigation, let's consider *when* we want to be in slam. If both hands are balanced and neither has a five-card suit, you usually need at least 33 points to have a good play for slam. If partner opens a 15-17 point notrump and you have 18 points, you can jump straight to 6NT. When you can tell that the combined point-count is, at most, 32 points, you shouldn't even try for slam unless you have a five-card (or longer) suit. When the combined point-count might be 33 points, or 32 points along with your five-card suit, you should invite, usually by showing your suit first, followed by bidding 4NT (which is natural, not Blackwood). Then if partner has a doubleton in your suit he will reject the invitation, even if he has a maximum point-count for his bid. With Ax opposite K10xxx, it is unlikely that you can win four tricks in the suit, while Axx or (better still) QJx from partner will give you very good odds. When either player has a close decision, nines, tens and jacks take on additional value when in four-card suits and in combination with higher honors. For example, K109x opposite AQx has the potential for more tricks than KJx opposite AQx; similarly it is better to have K109x than K9xx with the ten spot elsewhere. Also, for slam purposes, hands consisting of aces and kings are better than hands consisting largely of queens and jacks. The difference is pronounced when either hand has a five-card suit, so remember that while you may not have a five-card suit, it is possible that partner does.

Just as 1NT-2♡, 2♠-4NT is natural, 1NT-2♣, 2♠-4NT is natural. Responder might have bid 6♡ if opener had shown a heart suit; with no heart fit, responder's hand is worth only an invitation to slam. This is just a reminder since sequences such as these were fully discussed in Chapter 4.

When responder has barely enough strength with a balanced hand to insist upon a slam, especially with 4432 distributions, he should usually bid 5NT. In my opinion, this should not invite a grand slam, but suggest bidding four-card suits up the line in the hope of finding a 4-4 trump fit. Frequently a ruffing value makes the difference between a good slam and a poor slam. When responder invites a slam by bidding a natural 4NT, if opener is strong enough to accept he should usually bid 5NT, again asking responder to bid four-card suits up the line. If the four-card suit is weak or if, at matchpoints, you have a surplus (like 35 total points) it is better to just bid 6NT. I recall the following hand.

Opener	Responder
♠ K Q	♠ A J 10
♡ K 10 x x	♡ A x
◇ A x x	◇ K x x x
♣ A x x x	♣ K J x x
1NT	4NT
5NT	6♣

You can see that 6♣ is cold with a 3-2 trump break, while to make 6NT you probably need a winning club finesse, a 3-2 club break and a 3-3 diamond break. If no 4-4 fit is found, you will have to play 6NT.

Jumping to the six-level should show a very good five-card suit (or perhaps even a six-bagger) —something like

♠ x x   ♡ A Q x   ◇ K Q J 10 x   ♣ A x x

Here 6◇ would be safer than 6NT opposite

♠ A J x   ♡ K J x x   ◇ A x x   ♣ Q J x

Some people play that even when 4NT is not Blackwood, they respond as though it were Blackwood if they are going to accept the invitation. Once in a blue moon this avoids a slam missing two aces. I consider this a case of mistaken priorities: it is far better to look for a distributional fit in a suit.

If you are using a different range for a 1NT opening, or if the opening bid is 2NT (or 2♣ followed by 2NT), you follow the same evaluation procedure except that the ranges of the responses will be different. When you are interested in either game or slam, it is customary to count an extra point for a five-card suit. One point is a compromise figure: if you can establish the suit without the opponents taking too many tricks in the meantime, the five-card suit is worth far more than a stray jack. However, the fewer points you have, the more the opponents have. When you have 32 points, they could have two aces or the equivalent. So when you have mostly aces and kings and a five-card suit, you should be optimistic. In fact, mostly aces and kings are always valuable at the slam level since partner may have a five-card minor which he was unable to show conveniently.

Slam bidding is fairly easy when both hands are balanced. It becomes more difficult (and more challenging) when either hand is unbalanced. You need far fewer points to bid slams when each partner has a long suit, especially when the points are mostly in the long suits. Suppose the two hands are

Opener	Responder
♠ A Q J x x	♠ K x x
♡ A x	♡ x x
◇ x x x	◇ A x
♣ K x x	♣ A Q x x x x

Unless either opponent has a void in a black suit, there are thirteen top tricks with only 27 points. But it is very difficult to recognize hands like this with a perfect fit and nothing wasted. Suppose the bidding starts

Opener	Responder
1♠	2♣
3♣	3♠

Now with the right form of six-control Blackwood (which will be explained later) opener can find out about his partner's crucial high cards (♠K, ◇A, ♣AQ), which is all he needs to know to bid a small slam. However, I don't know how he can tell that his partner has six clubs and not five. The more serious problem is that opener isn't strong enough to launch into Blackwood. If he cuebids 4♡ over 3♠, responder might be able to bid a grand slam after asking about controls, although it gets very complicated when there are not only six controls but the queens of both suits to worry about. In most matchpoint events, just getting to 6NT would result in an above average score.

PLASTIC EVALUATION

The key to good slam bidding is visualization. Ely Culbertson coined the term 'plastic evaluation' for the process. What you should do is visualize three hands for partner, consistent with your hand and the bidding, then fit them around your hand like a plastic mold and decide whether they would provide a good or bad play for slam. If your mind worked like a computer, you could visualize 10,000 hands or 100,000 hands, but at the table three is about all you would have time for. Let's consider how that might work. Partner opens 1♡ and you bid 3NT (a splinter in spades) with

♠ x   ♡ x x x x   ◇ A K x x x   ♣ K Q x

Partner bids 4♣, you bid 4◇, and partner bids 4♡. How good do you think your slam prospects are?

Partner was almost compelled to cuebid 4♣ with the ace unless he had something like

♠ K Q J   ♡ J x x x x   ◊ Q x   ♣ A x x

He did not show extra values by doing so, but he needs extra values or a very good fit to bid beyond the game level. Suppose he has

♠ Q J x   ♡ A Q x x x   ◊ x x   ♣ A x x

With a certain spade loser you would need a 2-2 heart break with the king onside — about a 20% overall chance. Change opener's spades to ♠KQx, and you still have a 20% play for slam. Now change his hearts to ♡AKxxx or ♡AKJxx. With the first heart holding you would have a 40% play, and with the ♡AKJ approximately a 50% play for slam. You shouldn't bid a slam if it will be at best 50% and when it may easily be worse (like needing a finesse plus a 3-2 break in a side suit). To have a good play when missing the ace of spades, partner would need ♡AKQxx or ♡AKxxxx. Even if partner has ♡AKQxx, he *might* have 2-5-3-3 distribution, in which case there would be a diamond loser. And partner would probably make a stronger bid than 4♡ if he had such good trumps. So you should pass: even 5♡ might be too high.

This time you open 1♡ with

♠ A x x x   ♡ A J x x x x   ◊ A x x   ♣ —

and partner bids 3♡ (a four-card limit raise). How good are your slam prospects? Not good if partner has a balanced hand. If he has

♠ K x x   ♡ K x x x   ◊ K x   ♣ J 10 x x

you belong in slam. If he has

♠ Q x   ♡ Q x x x   ◊ J x x   ♣ A Q x x

or

♠ J x   ♡ Q x x x   ◊ x x x x   ♣ A K J x

even the five-level is in danger. I suspect that two of the three hands you choose at random will provide no play or a poor play for slam. Fortunately, you have an alternative to cuebidding with this hand: the Mathe Asking bid. This is 3NT over a limit raise to 3♠ (or 3♠ over a limit raise to 3♡) asking partner to show a singleton if he has one. If partner has a singleton diamond or spade, it is quite likely that you have a slam. But if partner does not have a singleton or he shows a singleton club (unlikely), you should simply sign off in 4♡.

Now suppose you open 1♡ with

♠ Q x   ♡ A K J x x   ◊ A x   ♣ Q 10 x x

and partner bids 3NT (a splinter in spades). If partner has

♠ x ♡ Q x x x ◇ Q 10 x x x ♣ A K x

or

♠ x ♡ Q x x x ◇ K Q x x ♣ A x x x

you don't belong in slam, but if he has

♠ x ♡ 10 x x x x ◇ K J x x ♣ A K x

you definitely do. I think you should bid 4♣ and take no further initiative. If partner has the queen of hearts or extra length, the king of diamonds and the ace-king of clubs, he will probably initiate Blackwood. If you and partner play the way I prefer (help-suit slam tries), he knows you don't have a singleton or void in clubs for your 4♣ bid (while many players would conclude exactly the opposite). You may be surprised that I suggested bidding 4♣ — a 'cuebid' with neither first- nor second-round club control. I'll have more to say about that later.

One more example: you hold

♠ A K x x ♡ A x ◇ K 10 x x x x ♣ x

You open 1◇ and partner makes an inverted raise to 2◇. Already your slam prospects look very good. If partner has

♠ x x ♡ K x x ◇ A x x x ♣ Q J x x

(just 7 useful points since his club honors are worthless to you), all you need is a 2-1 trump split to be cold for 6◇. Exchange the queen-jack of clubs for the ace, and you will belong in a grand slam. But partner may have three small spades or no king of hearts with wasted honors in clubs — something like:

♠ x x x ♡ Q x ◇ A J x x x ♣ K J x

or

♠ x x x ♡ J x ◇ A Q J x ♣ K Q x x

I think the best bid now is 2♠. Partner will think you are just showing a spade stopper (and no heart stopper) in an attempt to get to 3NT, but one thing this bid will accomplish is to find out whether partner has a game-forcing or game-invitational hand. If he bids 2NT or 3◇ (either of which could be passed) you will know that a grand slam is very unlikely. When you bid hearts next round, partner will know that you weren't looking for a 3NT contract, but probably a slam instead. Also he will know that three small spades would be a bad holding for his hand. I can't predict how the rest of the bidding will go, but after the third round of bidding you will have a much better idea of your slam prospects than you did after the first round. I wonder why I don't hear more about plastic evaluation (or the same concept by another name) these days, because it is the only way you can consistently bid good slams and stay out of bad slams.

SPLINTER BIDS

Splinter bids have been mentioned from time to time earlier in this book without describing or defining them on the assumption that everyone knows what they are. In case you don't know, they are bids, usually one level higher than necessary to make a forcing bid in the suit, that show a singleton or void. Over an opening bid of one of a major, either an ordinary splinter or a mini-splinter guarantees at least four-card support for partner. On later rounds splinters may show three-card support. For example, with the following two hands, the bidding should be as shown:

Opener	Responder
♠ A x	♠ K Q J x x
♡ A K 10 x x x	♡ Q x x
◊ J x x	◊ x
♣ Q x	♣ A J x x
1♡	1♠
2♡	4◊
4♠	6♡

Responder has a good enough hand to bid 4◊ whether opener rebids 2♡ (showing six) or 1NT, showing only five hearts. The good thing about splinters is that the partner can evaluate his hand, knowing which cards are useful and which are wasted. The player who shows a splinter usually expects his partner to take control of the bidding, but on the rare occasions that the splinter bidder uses Blackwood later, his partner should not show the king of the splinter suit (and in the few cases where the splinter shows a void, not even the ace!). Opener could easily have a good opening bid with the king-queen of diamonds and less strength elsewhere, in which case there would be no play for slam and danger at the five-level.

Opener	Responder
♠ A x	♠ K x x
♡ K Q x	♡ A J x x x
◊ x x x x	◊ x
♣ K J x x	♣ A Q x x
1♣	1♡
2♡	4◊
4♠	5♣
6♣	pass

In my opinion, East made a serious mistake in not responding 2♡ instead of 1♡, but one is not always punished for such mistakes. As it happens, 6♡ is a good contract, but it doesn't pay to be greedy when many pairs won't get to any slam. If opener had held

♠ A x x   ♡ K Q x x   ◇ x x   ♣ K J x x

6♣ would be the only slam that made.

Opener	Responder
♠ A K x x x	♠ Q 10 x x
♡ A Q x x	♡ K J x
◇ —	◇ J x x x
♣ K Q x x	♣ J 10
1♠	3♣¹
4◇	4♡
5◇	6♠

1. Bergen, a sound four-card raise.

Again the splinter makes it easy for responder to evaluate his hand. Since partner must have heart length (he won't be short in all suits), it is proper to cuebid hearts with the king since he has no ace to cuebid. Opener could have a singleton diamond, but since he has a void, he bids diamonds again. Without the splinter, responder could not possibly realize that he had the right hand to bid a slam. Every high card he has, other than the jack of diamonds, figures to be useful.

I said a few paragraphs ago that after a splinter bid partner should not show the king of that suit in response to Blackwood, and when the splinter shows a void, he should not show the ace. When does the splinter show a void? Usually when the splinter bidder bids one more than necessary to show a splinter. In the following uncontested auction:

Opener	Responder
1♣	2♡
2♠	?

bids of 3♣, 3◇ or 3♠ would show a singleton. So 4♣, 4◇ or 4♠ should show a void. That doesn't mean that an ordinary splinter denies a void: for reasons of bidding economy it may be better not to show the void immediately. The last hand (on which responder showed a Bergen raise) is a good example. Opener did not bid 5◇ directly over 3♣ and would not have risked bidding beyond the game level if responder hadn't cuebid 4♡.

According to *Bridge World* Standard (which represents the majority opinion of experts throughout North America), this sequence

Opener	Responder
1♠	2♦
3♡	

shows a two-suiter with both suits being strong, e.g.

♠ A K J x x   ♡ K Q 10 9 x   ♦ x   ♣ Q x

rather than

♠ A K x x x   ♡ K x x x x   ♦ x   ♣ A x

Once he has shown his two strong suits, if responder bids 3NT opener can pass rather than bid 4♡. Playing notrump is the right decision when responder has

♠ x   ♡ x x   ♦ A K Q J x x   ♣ J 10 x x

I don't doubt that this is a useful treatment when you hold a strong two-suiter. But most of my friends and partners play that 3♡ is a splinter bid in support of diamonds, something like

♠ A Q x x x   ♡ x   ♦ K x x x   ♣ A 10 x

I think that, based on frequency, the splinter bid is more useful. Suppose responder has

♠ x   ♡ A x x   ♦ A J 10 x x x x   ♣ J x

Some players, who play two-over-one as unconditionally forcing to game, would consider this hand too weak for a 2♦ response; yet a slam is cold. Nor does opener need an unusual hand for the splinter bid to pay off. If he holds

♠ K x   ♡ J x x   ♦ A Q x x x   ♣ A x x

it might be possible to get to 6♦ without the splinter, but the splinter bid certainly makes it much easier. That is one reason why I am not fond of Redwood, where jumps to the four-level in an unbid suit are keycard inquiries instead of splinter bids. If I had to give up either splinters or Blackwood, I think I would prefer to give up Blackwood.

Finally, I should mention that, with one exception, I never splinter in partner's suit.

Opener	Responder
1♡	2♦
2♡	2♠
2NT	4♡

Here the 4♡ bid is not a splinter: it shows very good heart support, as described in an earlier chapter and later in this chapter. The one exception to this rule is this kind of auction:

Opener	Responder
1m	1M
1NT	4m

Suppose responder holds

♠ K J x x ♡ A K J x x ◇ — ♣ K 10 x x

His partner opens 1◇ and rebids 1♠ over the 1♡ response. This hand could easily make a slam opposite

♠ A Q x x ♡ Q x ◇ Q x x x x ♣ A x

but not opposite

♠ Q x x x ♡ x x ◇ A K Q x x ♣ Q x

With strong diamond support responder could have made a strong jump shift or, if too weak for that, he could have bid fourth suit followed by showing diamond support, so he has no need for a natural 4◇ bid. Obviously, these auctions:

Opener	Responder		Opener	Responder
1♣	1◇		1♣	1♡
1♠	4♣		1♠	4♣

should be treated the same way. Responder could bid the same way with a singleton rather than a void although his minimum in high cards should be slightly higher.

SLAM TRY IDEAS

You and partner have found a fit, and you easily have enough strength to bid a game. When should you cuebid to suggest a slam? The Four Aces criterion that you have an extra ace in a balanced hand or an extra king in an unbalanced hand is still a good rough test, although the degree of fit is important, and so is whether you have good controls. Sometimes you should initiate a slam invitation with less than an extra ace or king, and sometimes you need more, often depending both on controls and on how narrow the range is for partner's bid(s). For example, if partner opens 1NT, showing a range of 15 to 17, you would raise to game with 10 points, or possibly a good nine, but you would not raise to 4NT with 13 or 14 points and no long suit since the partnership total could not exceed 31 points.

Suppose you open 1♠ with

♠ A K x x x x ♡ A ◇ K x ♣ Q 10 9 x

and partner bids 3♠ (limit raise). A slam is probable if partner has the right cards, such as

$$\spadesuit \text{Q x x x} \quad \heartsuit \text{J x x} \quad \diamond \text{A x x x} \quad \clubsuit \text{K x}$$

or

$$\spadesuit \text{x x x x x} \quad \heartsuit \text{x x x} \quad \diamond \text{A x x} \quad \clubsuit \text{A K x}$$

What would you rebid? Some experts cuebid the cheapest ace: they would bid 4♡. Other experts would cuebid their cheapest control (either first- or second-round): they would bid 4◊. By skipping over clubs, they would deny a club control, and if partner had no control in clubs, it would be easy for the partnership to stop in 4♠. This style of cuebidding was made popular by the Italian Blue Team. Despite some advantages of the second style, I recommend a third style, which is to show length or where partner's honors would be most useful — a 'help-suit slam try' similar to a help-suit game try. If I bid 4♣, despite lacking a club control, partner will like his aces, trump honors and club honors. He will consider other honors in hearts or diamonds as dubious values. In the same sequence, suppose opener's hand is

$$\spadesuit \text{A K x x x x} \quad \heartsuit \text{A J x x} \quad \diamond \text{A x} \quad \clubsuit \text{x}$$

With this hand I would cuebid 4♡. If partner has secondary honors I'd rather they be in hearts than in the other two suits. If he has a doubleton, I'd rather it was in hearts than anywhere else. Just as with help-suit game tries, if I had

$$\spadesuit \text{A Q x x x} \quad \heartsuit \text{A K Q x} \quad \diamond \text{K 10 x} \quad \clubsuit \text{x}$$

I would bid diamonds rather than hearts, despite greater length in hearts. I don't care what partner has in hearts, but diamond honors are sure to be useful. After this first 'cuebid,' usually showing length, the subsequent bids by either partner (other than Blackwood) show controls, but the partner of the first cuebidder, in deciding whether to cuebid past game, will be strongly influenced by his holding in the suit of the first cuebid. If the first cuebid was 4♡, responder would not bid past game with

$$\spadesuit \text{Q J x x} \quad \heartsuit \text{x x x} \quad \diamond \text{K J x x} \quad \clubsuit \text{A x}$$

because of his bad holding in hearts, but he would show his ace of clubs if opener bid past game himself. If responder bids 5♣ directly, he should have help in hearts, perhaps

$$\spadesuit \text{J x x x x} \quad \heartsuit \text{Q x x} \quad \diamond \text{K x x} \quad \clubsuit \text{A x}$$

or

$$\spadesuit \text{Q J x x} \quad \heartsuit \text{K x} \quad \diamond \text{x x x} \quad \clubsuit \text{A J x x}$$

This last example illustrates a slight disadvantage of the method. When your suit is spades, if your first cuebid is 4♡ (the help-suit cuebid) partner has no room to show a control in the minors without bidding past game.

Although I think cuebidding length is best, I am somewhat reluctant to recommend it. It is foreign to the way most people play, and you may throw up your hands (or throw out this book) in despair. Cuebidding aces and kings up the line is almost as good — some would say better. That way you can find out whether there are any suits missing two controls, and since aces and kings are treated equally in the cuebidding, you can still bid 4NT to find out whether two aces are missing. Whether you adopt help-suit cuebids or something else, most of my advice still applies. The first cuebid shows extra values. Partner of the cuebidder shows any ace below the game level with no extra values, but he requires a good hand for his previous bidding to bid beyond the game level.

Let's turn to a different kind of slam try. What would you expect opener to hold if the bidding went

Opener	Responder
1♢	1♠
5♠	?

This is an unusual sequence which surely shows a freak hand with no losers in the unbid suits. If opener had a possible heart or club loser, wouldn't he try to find out whether partner had it covered? And since one doesn't like to play 5♠, down one, opener must not have many possible losers in diamonds or spades. An appropriate hand for this bidding would be

♠ J 10 x x x   ♡ A   ♢ A K J 9 x x x   ♣ —

If responder has any four spades, there is a good chance for only two spade losers, and there is not likely to be a diamond loser. (Opposite a singleton or doubleton, declarer can establish the suit by ruffing; if responder has three diamonds, the queen will probably fall.) With nothing but ♠KQxx partner should bid 6♠; with the three top honors or ♠AKxxx, he should bid 7♠. Another possibility is that opener has something like

♠ A x x x x   ♡ —   ♢ K Q J x x x   ♣ A K

In either case the 5♠ bid is a slight gamble, but how else can you describe these hands? Not by cuebidding your voids or singleton aces!

In more normal sequences a bid of five of a major indicates that the bidder wants his partner to go to six if he has a control in the unbid suit (when the bidding indicates that the other suits are well controlled). If the bidding has confirmed that all the side suits are controlled, it asks partner to bid more with good trumps and/or a good holding in the previously bid suits. How can the bidding indicate that all suits are controlled? Either by cuebidding everything or by not cuebidding at all! A failure to cuebid says either, 'I have no controls, or 'I have too many controls to show them all without forcing us to a slam.' Partner should be able to tell which is the case.

The meaning of a bid is often influenced by the bidding level and how much room there is to show one's features. When the bidding goes

Opener	Responder
1♦	1♡
4♡	?

a 5♡ bid should say either, 'I have good hearts (and perhaps a good diamond fit) but no controls in the other two suits,' or, 'I have controls in both unbid suits. If I had just one control, I would bid it. But I am afraid if I cuebid spades you will worry about clubs, and if I cuebid clubs you will worry about spades.' Opener should be able, by looking at his hand, to tell which is the true meaning on this particular hand. With

$$♠A K \quad ♡Q x x x \quad ♦A Q J x x \quad ♣K x$$

he knows partner has no controls in the black suits, but good hearts and diamonds. With

$$♠x x \quad ♡K Q x x \quad ♦A K Q J x \quad ♣K x$$

opener would expect responder to hold something like

$$♠A x x \quad ♡A x x x \quad ♦x x \quad ♣A x x x$$

Likewise, if the bidding goes

Opener	Responder
2♣	2♡¹
2♠	2NT
3♡	3NT
5♡	

1. Artificial positive.

opener is saying, 'Look at your major-suit holdings; I don't care what you have in the minors.' Obviously a failure to cuebid a minor doesn't mean there are no controls in the minors. Opener might have

$$♠A Q x x x x \quad ♡A Q 10 9 x x \quad ♦A \quad ♣—$$

With both major-suit kings responder should bid seven; with one major-suit king he should bid six, and with

$$♠x x \quad ♡x x x \quad ♦K Q x x \quad ♣A J x x$$

he should pass.

THE COURTESY 3NT BID

Suppose you hold

♠ Q x ♡ A J x x x x ◇ A x ♣ K x x

and the bidding goes 1♠ by partner, 2♡ by you, 3♡ by partner. Since a jump to 4♡ by partner would have had a specific meaning (good holdings in the majors and no control in the minors), and since 3♡ is forcing, opener may or may not have extra values. If he has enough extra values, he will bid a slam no matter what you do at this point. But if he holds

♠ A K x x x ♡ K x x ◇ x x ♣ A J x

should he make a slam try or not? If you just bid 4♡, he probably won't. His hand is balanced and, if you take away an ace, he doesn't have an opening bid.

Now that you have found an eight-card major fit (at least), it is unlikely that you will want to play 3NT. Many players bid 3NT with the responding hand to say, 'I don't have a strong enough hand to make a slam try on my own, but I would welcome a slam try by you.' Some players play the 3NT bid as stronger or weaker (usually weaker) than bidding a new suit. I think, instead of stronger or weaker, 3NT should show a balanced hand, while a new suit shows an unbalanced hand. So 1♠-2♡, 3♡-4♣ might show

♠ x ♡ K Q 10 9 x ◇ A x ♣ K J x x x

Opener would like his hand if he held

♠ A J x x x ♡ A x x ◇ x x ♣ A Q x

because of his aces and the club fit but be warned against bidding beyond game with

♠ K Q J x x ♡ A x x x ◇ K Q ♣ x x

When opener has a close decision, he should evaluate a good holding in his first suit (like ♠AKQxx or ♠AKJxx) favorably when responder shows a 'courtesy raise,' but figure this holding is likely to be opposite a singleton or void when responder shows an unbalanced hand. *Caution*! If the bidding has gone

Opener	Oppt.	Responder	Oppt.
1♠	2♣	2♡	pass
?			

the 2♡ bid is not forcing to game, and opener would bid 4♡ any time he has a fit and slightly better than a minimum opening. Also if the 2♡ bid were made by a passed hand, 3♡ would not be forcing. In either case, 4♡ by opener would not deny a control in the minors and 3NT would not be a courtesy bid.

MORE ABOUT DELAYED SUPPORT

After a two-over-one response and a raise, an extra queen in the right spot or good distribution and controls may be enough for a mild slam try. (A mild slam try is a cuebid below the game level, with no intention of making a further effort unless partner shows extra values.) What if responder has such a good hand that he wants to get to slam when opener doesn't have even a mild slam try. What does he do in that case?

Suppose partner opens 1♡ and you hold

♠ A x ♡ K 10 x ◇ A K Q x x x ♣ x x

You respond 2◇ and partner bids 2♡. Partner *could* hold

♠ K Q x ♡ A x x x x ◇ x ♣ Q J x x

in which case you can't make more than ten tricks in hearts and might make fewer with a bad trump break. On the other hand, if partner has

♠ K x x ♡ A Q x x x ◇ x x ♣ A x x

you belong in slam. Yet partner is too close to a minimum opening to cuebid if you just bid 3♡; I also think he is too weak to make a courtesy 3NT bid. So I think you should bid 2♠ over his 2♡ bid. At this point partner will assume that either you are trying to get to 3NT if he has a club stopper or you really have a spade suit. He will bid 2NT with a club holding like ♣Ax, knowing that his failure to bid notrump earlier suggests that he has a flaw somewhere or is not very enthusiastic about notrump. Now if you bid 3♡, partner will think you are giving him a choice between 3NT and 4♡, probably with a doubleton honor in hearts and a weak holding in clubs. You should jump to 4♡ over 2NT so that partner will know you weren't interested in a notrump contract but wanted to play in hearts all along — and were hoping to get to 6♡. He should accept your invitation with the second hand shown above since, among other things, he has a club control. Nor will he think you are showing a singleton club since, if you had a singleton club and a hand strong enough for a slam try, you would have splintered on the second round. This way you make a strong invitation but don't bid past game when partner has the wrong hand. Note that partner's 2NT bid did not guarantee a club *control* (as distinguished from a club *stopper*). He could have held ♣QJx or ♣J9xx.

Suppose your hand is

♠ A x ♡ Q 10 x ◇ A Q x x x ♣ A x x

Again partner opens 1♡; you bid 2◇ and he rebids 2♡. You bid 3♣ and he bids 3◇. You are encouraged by partner's failure to bid 3NT. He probably lacks the king or queen of spades, which makes it very likely that he has the king of diamonds and pretty good hearts. If you now bid 3♡, partner will think you were trying for 3NT, and that when both of you apparently lacked a spade stopper, you bid hearts with a doubleton hoping he has either six hearts or a good five-card suit. If instead you jump to 4♡ rather than bidding 3♡, partner will know you have a good hand with good heart support, but he will think you have no control in spades. You should cue-bid again (3♠), followed by bidding 5♡. Remember, you were encouraged by partner's failure to bid 3NT: if he had bid 3NT, you would have bid only 4♡. Partner would know that you were not trying to get to 3NT (since you didn't pass when *he* bid 3NT), so you must have planned to raise hearts all along, and you must have a very good hand otherwise you would have raised hearts earlier. With either

♠ K x x   ♡ A Q x x x   ◇ x x   ♣ A x x

or

♠ Q J x   ♡ A Q J x x   ◇ J x   ♣ K x x

partner would not cuebid over a 3♡ bid, so you need to take stronger action in the form of a delayed raise.

How do you think the following hands should be bid?

Opener	Responder
♠ A Q J 10 x	♠ K x x
♡ x x x	♡ A K Q J x
◇ —	◇ x x x
♣ K Q 10 x x	♣ J x

The first two bids are easy: 1♠-2♡. Opener's hand is very strong if responder has a good heart suit. If responder has a no-loser trump suit opposite three small, plus the ace of clubs or king of spades, a slam should be cold. So what should opener do? A splinter bid is supposed to guarantee four-card support. Admittedly, I would splinter with good three-card support and a good hand like

♠ A K x x x   ♡ A Q x   ◇ x   ♣ Q 10 x x

since the 2♡ bid guarantees five or more hearts, and if I bid only 3♡ and partner bid 4♡, I would have a left-over feeling. But ♡xxx is not even good three-card support. So I think a 3♣ bid, showing extra values (in this case distributional values) is the best choice, since when followed by heart support it will also imply a shortage in diamonds. Responder will bid 3♠ to show his fit, and opener will bid 4♡. Responder could hold ♡QJxxx with values elsewhere, but instead he has solid trumps, which are great in a potential slam auction. So he should jump to 6♡. This is a good hand for plastic evaluation. Opener could have held a singleton diamond rather than a void, but with

♠ A Q J x x   ♡ x x x   ◇ x   ♣ K Q 10 x

he would have raised to 3♡, knowing there would be no slam unless responder could take the initiative. So if opener had a singleton diamond, his clubs would have to be at least ♣AKxx for this sequence. And it should not be difficult to guess why opener didn't splinter — because his hearts were not good enough.

Here is one more hand with the same general theme. It was mentioned in Chapter 3, under the topic of default bids; for other reasons, it fits in appropriately here. Partner opens 1♠ and you bid 2◇ with

♠ —   ♡ K J x x   ◇ A K x x x   ♣ A x x x

Partner rebids 2♡. You could easily belong in a slam, depending upon whether partner's strength is in spades or elsewhere. It may be tempting to bid 6♡, hoping partner has something like

♠ A J x x x   ♡ A Q x x   ◇ Q x   ♣ x x

But he actually holds

♠ A Q x x x   ♡ A Q x x   ◇ x x   ♣ x x

which gives you a very poor play for slam. In my opinion, the correct bid is 3♣, and over a (false) preference to 3◇, you should jump to 4♡. This series of bids strongly suggests a void in spades (since you can't splinter in partner's suit), four good hearts and a good hand. A 3♡ bid over 3◇ suggests that you are still searching for a playable game, perhaps with

♠ x   ♡ K J x   ◇ A K Q x x x x   ♣ x x

since you apparently lack a club stopper. But the jump to 4♡ means that you had good heart support all along and were too strong to raise to 3♡ and pass if partner just bid 4♡.

REVALUING YOUR HAND

Suppose you open 1NT with

♠ K x   ♡ K Q x x   ◇ A x x   ♣ K J x x

Partner bids 2NT (a Walsh relay to clubs) and you bid 3♣. Partner then bids 3♡, purportedly showing 4-1-4-4 distribution with a good hand. You have a fair amount of duplication in hearts, so you bid 3NT. Partner then bids 4♣. You have already made a discouraging response and partner is still interested in slam. Since he is still interested, you should revalue your hand. You could hold a doubleton club or three small. You could have even more wastage in hearts, perhaps ♡KQJx or ♡AKQ, and the king of diamonds instead of the ace. As it happens, your doubleton spade is of no value to partner, but it could be, if he has ♠Axxx or ♠AJxx. Partner's actual hand, from the Senior Team trials, was

♠ A Q x x   ♡ x   ◇ K 10 x   ♣ A Q x x x

Partner 'violated the system' by showing 4-1-4-4 distribution when he had 4-1-3-5 distribution, but it seemed to him like the least of evils. By bidding 2♣ and then 3♣ he would have implied five or six clubs and a four-card major. Or, playing four-suit transfers, he could have bid 2♠, showing clubs, followed by 3♠. But you weren't playing four-suit transfers, and even if you were, he couldn't have shown the singleton heart, which would help you to evaluate your hand accurately. The only risk in bidding this way with an imperfect distributional pattern was that you would insist upon a 6◇ contract with a weak four-card suit, but this was a small risk; if you showed an interest in a diamond slam (rather than spades or clubs), partner would discourage and probably stop in 4NT. But my main point is that after your 3NT bid (probably showing lots of duplication in hearts, or several queens and jacks rather than aces and kings, or 3-4-3-3 distribution with apparently no eight-card fit) you have as good a hand for clubs as you could have, and should not let the bidding die short of a slam.

ASKING FOR CONTROLS

The same bidding that gets you to the right games and partscores gets you to good slams and helps you to avoid bidding bad slams. I think players tend to place too much emphasis on controls, but of course you don't want to bid a slam missing two cashable aces or two quick tricks in one suit. Blackwood will help you avoid bidding a slam missing two cashable aces, but it won't help you to avoid a slam missing two quick tricks in the same suit, nor will it tell you whether you will have enough tricks.

If I were to tell you that you could get along pretty well without Blackwood of any kind unless you were considering a grand slam, you wouldn't believe me, so let's see how Blackwood works and what the pitfalls are. Most serious players now play Roman Keycard Blackwood (RKB), in which the four aces and the king of the agreed suit all count as 'keycards.' In RKB, assuming the asking bid is 4NT, 5♣ shows 0 or 3 keycards; 5◇ shows 1 or 4 keycards; 5♡ shows 2 or 5 keycards without the queen of the agreed suit and 5♠ shows 2 or 5 keycards with the queen (or that the responder to Blackwood believes the partnership has ten cards in the trump suit, in which case the queen will fall on the first or second round of trumps 78% of the time). This version of RKB is known as 0314, which derives from the first two responses.

The 5♣ and 5◇ responses do not say anything about the trump queen or trump length. So *usually* the 4NT bidder can bid the next suit up (5◇

over a 5♣ response or 5♡ over a 5◊ response) to ask about the queen of trumps. Without the queen or sufficient length the responder returns to the cheapest level of the agreed suit. With the queen or sufficient length, he bids his cheapest outside king if he has one. (The king of the agreed suit is no longer considered a king; it has become an ace.) If he has no king to show, he jumps in the trump suit or bids 5NT, the latter being more encouraging (the basis for the more encouraging bid might be the queen of another crucial suit or extra length in the trump suit). The reason for saying usually the 4NT bidder can find out about the queen of trumps is that if you are trying to get to a small slam, not a grand slam, the cheapest bid may force you to slam, especially when your suit is a minor.

Already you can anticipate problems. Suppose you have a distributional hand (unsuited for play in notrump) and your suit is clubs. Partner responds 5◊ to your 4NT bid, but you needed to find him with two aces to make a slam, and he has only one. What can you do about that? Nothing! You are already too high. Or suppose your suit is hearts and you get a 5◊ response. Should 5♡ ask about the queen of hearts, or should it be a signoff? The answer to the first question (when your suit was clubs) is that 4NT shouldn't have been bid since you can't stand an unfavorable response. A partial answer to the second question is to play 1430 RKB. When playing 1430, 5♣ shows 1 or 4 keycards and 5◊ shows 3 or 0 keycards. When the response shows 0 or 3 keycards, 0 is more frequent; when the response shows 1 or 4 keycards, 1 is more frequent. You are more likely to want to know about the queen of trumps when you receive a one-keycard response than when partner shows no keycards. So when responder shows one (or an unlikely four) keycards by bidding 5♣, 1430 allows you, when your suit is hearts, to ask about the queen of hearts by bidding 5◊. If the response is unfavorable, you can still stop at the five-level.

My recommendation is to play 1430 when the agreed suit is a major and 0314 when it is a minor. When the agreed suit is clubs, you don't want a 5◊ response to show no keycards. Nor do you have the benefit of being able to bid 5◊ to enquire about the queen of trumps (unless you know you are going to bid at least a small slam and need the queen of trumps to bid seven).

According to Eddie Kantar's rule, when the response to 4NT shows 0/3 or 1/4 keycards, the cheapest bid, if it is the trump suit, should be treated as a signoff when responder actually has no keycards or one keycard. Holding the 3- or 4-keycard hand, responder should answer the queen-ask. If opener is going to at least six anyway and the cheapest suit for the queen-ask is the agreed trump suit, it is therefore necessary to bid the next cheapest suit to ask about the queen so that responder will not pass. If the response showed two keycards either with or without the queen, there is no need to ask about the queen, so the next cheapest bid asks about kings. This allows you more room than a 5NT bid to find out everything you want to know. This is an especially important treatment when your suit is a minor and your 'Blackwood' bid was something other than 4NT.

When your agreed suit is a minor

There are still problems when your suit is a minor. Whether you are playing old-fashioned Blackwood or Roman Keycard Blackwood in either variation, the 4NT bid works best when your suit is spades and worst when your suit is clubs. For that reason, many experts make use of asking bids other than 4NT, especially when the agreed suit is a minor. One solution, adopted by several players, is to play that almost any minor-suit bid at the four-level is RKB. However, I don't see how you can logically play all four-level bids of a minor as Blackwood. For example, suppose the bidding goes

Opener	Responder
1♡	2♢
2♡	3♡
?	

and you hold

♠ K x x   ♡ A K x x x x   ♢ A x   ♣ J x

You want to show some interest in slam, and 4♢ is the most descriptive bid. You are showing an additional feature. If 4♢ were asking for keycards, and partner showed two, you would have no idea what to do. As usual, *showing* is more useful than *asking*. However, these sequences, which involve an inverted raise followed by four of the minor

Opener	Responder	Opener	Responder	Opener	Responder
1♣	2♣	1♢	2♢	1♢	2♢
4♣		4♢		3♢	4♢

should all be played as 'Blackwood.' So should these:

Opener	Responder	Opener	Responder
1♠	2♢	1♡	2♣
3♢	4♢	4♣	

There are two tests to determine whether four of a minor is 'Blackwood.' First, the person making the bid must not have limited his hand earlier. Examples of this are:

(a)

Opener	Responder
1♢	2♢
3♢	4♣
4♢	

(b)

Opener	Responder
1♠	2♣
2♠	3♣
3♡	4♣

(c)

Opener	Responder
1♢	1♠
2♣	3♢
3♠	4♢

In sequence (a) opener made a non-forcing 3◇ bid. Responder made a try for 5◇, so opener, who was willing to play 3◇, cannot suddenly assume captaincy and perhaps drive to a slam. In (b) responder made a non-forcing 3♣ bid. He still was unable to bid game, perhaps because he had no diamond stopper, perhaps just because he had a minimum for his previous bidding. In (c) responder's 3◇ bid was only invitational, not forcing. His spades were not good enough to play in 3♠ and his hand was too weak to jump to 5◇.

The second requirement is that the four of a minor bid must be made by the stronger hand. Remember the general rule is that the weaker hand *shows*; if either hand *asks*, it should be the stronger hand.

Opener	Responder	Opener	Responder	Opener	Responder
1♣	1♠	1♣	1♠	1◇	1♠
2◇	4◇	2♡	4♣	2♡	3◇
				3NT	4◇

For the first sequence responder might hold

♠ A K x x x   ♡ x x   ◇ K J x x x   ♣ x

Rather than ask for keycards himself, it makes sense for him to describe his hand: interest in slam with very good diamonds and no control in the unbid suit. Then perhaps opener can take control of the bidding with a Blackwood bid (4NT) himself if he has a control in hearts. After the reverse, 3◇ would be forcing and it would be appropriate with only four diamonds and one more club or heart.

For the second sequence responder might hold

♠ A Q x x   ♡ J x   ◇ x x   ♣ K Q x x x

Again 4♣ is a 'picture bid.'

For the third sequence responder might hold

♠ A 10 x x   ♡ K x   ◇ J 10 x x x   ♣ J x

His hand is not as strong as the two previous hands, so he doesn't strongly invite a Blackwood bid by his partner. When it looks as though his partner probably has a singleton spade, and all of his cards are working, he has to give it another try but is willing to pass if his partner bids only 4NT — perhaps with

♠ J x   ♡ A J x x   ◇ A K x x x   ♣ A Q

Examples where four of a minor is Blackwood are

Opener	Responder	Opener	Responder	Opener	Responder
1♣	2♣	1♠	2◇	1♠	2◇
3♣	4♣	4◇		3◇	4◇

In the first example, opener was willing to stop in a partscore, but responder was unlimited. Usually the minor has to be bid for the third time for it to be Blackwood, but opener's jump raise in the second example is the equivalent of two raises. If he were interested in the location of controls, or whether responder had extra strength, etc., he would have bid 3◊ and perhaps cuebid later. In the third example, if responder were wondering which game to bid or whether to stop short of game, he would bid a new suit, showing where his values were — and perhaps stop at 3NT. With

♠ x ♡ K Q x x ◊ A Q J x x x x ♣ Q

responder couldn't risk a 4NT bid for fear that his partner would bid 5♡ with

♠ A K J x x ♡ x ◊ K x x ♣ K x x x

However, 4◊ as Blackwood is safe.

If four of a minor would not be Blackwood and you still want to ask about controls, you have to bid 4NT even when your suit is a minor. Of course, as with all Blackwood bids, you have to be certain that no response will embarrass you or force you to slam missing two controls. An alternative solution adopted by some is to play 'Redwood': after a minor suit has been agreed upon, a bid of the suit just above it at the four-level asks about key-cards. But this convention is more complicated than it sounds and it leads to many misunderstandings. For example, in both the following sequences

Opener	Responder	Opener	Responder
1♡	2◊	1♡	2◊
4♡		3◊	4♡

the 4♡ bid should be natural. If you choose to play Redwood, perhaps the rule should be that the cheapest *unbid* suit above the agreed minor suit should be Redwood. But I have seen some costly foul-ups where one person thought his bid was natural and his partner thought it asked for keycards, or vice versa. Redwood also conflicts with splinter bids and cuebids. Opener has

♠ A K x x x x ♡ A x x ◊ K x ♣ J x

The bidding has gone

Opener	Responder
1♠	2◊
2♠	3♠
?	

When responder has

♠ Q x x ♡ x x ◊ A Q J x x ♣ K Q x

the hands belong in a slam. When responder has

♠ Q x x ♡ K Q x ◇ A Q J x x ♣ x x

they do not. If 4♡ by opener is a cuebid, a slam should be reached only when the controls are favorably located; if 4♡ is Redwood it won't solve the problem.

Incidentally, I have a rule that a player who has made a *natural* bid in notrump (1♡-2NT, Jacoby, is *not* natural) cannot bid Blackwood. (Maybe there should be an exception to this rule, but I can't think of one.)

Opener	Responder
1♠	2◇
3♣	3NT
4♣	4NT

Here opener has shown a good black two-suiter but responder is not interested. He may hold

♠ x ♡ Q J x x ◇ A K Q x x x ♣ x x

In these auctions, both partners are allowed to suggest a slam and stop in 4NT after an earlier natural notrump bid.

Showing a void

How do you show a void in response to Blackwood? Actually, I suppose the first question should be, '*Should* you show a void in response to Blackwood?' The answer cannot be a simple yes or no. Having a void is not always advantageous. Partner may have the ace anyway, so the void is no more useful than a singleton (or even two small, if you have plenty of tricks and controls are the only problem). So part of the answer should be, 'Do not show a void in a partner's long suit or in any suit unless you are sure that the six-level will be safe.' Partner should be prepared for any response you make at the five-level but may not be prepared for a six-level response. The conservative advice is not to show a void unless partner will know where your void is, but there will usually be enough clues for partner to tell. If the opponents have bid, your void will usually be in their suit. If you have made a splinter bid, your void will be in the splinter suit. Since the void can't be in a suit you have bid naturally, and since you don't show a void in partner's long suit, that only leaves two suits, and partner should be able to tell which one it is.

The most popular procedure is to jump to six of your void when you hold one ace, and bid 5NT with two aces and a void. I have several objections to that procedure. (1) It isn't necessary because partner will almost always know where your void is. (2) This method takes up too much bidding room. You may not be able to jump in the void suit since it is higher-ranking than the agreed trump suit. (However, jumping to six of the trump suit probably shows a void in a higher-ranking suit). (3) Partner may be interested in the queen of trumps and not care about your void. He has asked a question and you have decided to disregard his question and answer a different question. So why not answer his question? Before I give you my solution, let's examine the problem.

I can't imagine jumping to the six-level (or 5NT) with no controls, even with a void. Perhaps your void is useless since partner has the ace, and forcing to slam is too dangerous. A second factor is that there are only four, not five, possible keycards. When you have a void, the most you could have is the ace-king of trumps and aces of the other two suits. In fact, even four keycards is an extremely unlikely response. Usually the stronger hand asks the weaker hand about keycards, and the Blackwood bidder will never have a hand justifying a 4NT bid with no keycards or only a keycard in his partner's void suit. As a practical matter, the responder to Blackwood will usually have a void plus either one or two controls and, on rare occasions, three.

So this is what I recommend: 5NT shows a void plus one keycard or, very rarely, three keycards. With fewer possible keycards the 4NT bidder should be able to tell whether the response shows one or three keycards. Then, unless the agreed suit is clubs, the 4NT bidder can bid 6♣ to ask about the queen or sufficient length. A 6♣ response to 4NT shows 2 (or theoretically 4) keycards without the queen or sufficient length, and 6◇ shows 2 with the queen or length (unless the agreed suit is clubs). These responses will seldom get you too high, and I already warned you not to show your void unless you are pretty sure that you belong in slam. Unfortunately, there won't be room to ask about specific kings. The best the 4NT bidder can do is to bid a new suit over a 6♣ or 6◇ response (if there is room) to say, 'All the keycards are accounted for, and we may belong in seven if you have the right hand.'

An unusual auction came up recently. Responder held

♠ J x x   ♡ A J x x   ◇ x x   ♣ A x x x

The bidding went

Opener	Oppt.	Responder	Oppt.
1◇	pass	1♡	1♠
4♠			

Since 3♠ would show a normal splinter[1] in spades, 4♠ must show a void, especially since it forced the bidding beyond the game level. So responder

---

1. You may have noticed that in some example hands I do not make a jump splinter to show a void. In deciding whether to make a normal splinter bid or 'one-more-than-a-splinter' bid, several factors must be considered. Will the jump splinter take away too much bidding room? Does the splinter-bidder have other controls he wants to show? Will the jump splinter make it very easy for partner to take control and place the contract?

bid 4NT and, upon hearing 5♠ from partner, bid 5NT to show that all the controls were held. Responder did not intend to bid 7♡ himself, no matter which kings opener might show. Once he showed that all the keycards were accounted for, if anyone bid seven, it had to be opener. But since opener held

♠ —   ♡ K Q x x   ◇ A K Q J x x x   ♣ J x

he could bid 7♡ directly over the 5NT bid. The point is that when opener had clearly shown a void already, he didn't have to jump to the six-level over the 4NT bid, which would have left less room for responder to ask for specific kings or to show that all controls were accounted for.

The 5NT extension

If you bid 4NT and partner tells you at the five-level how many keycards he has, a 5NT bid asks for specific kings (not the number of kings). Holding more than one king, the cheapest is shown. If the 5NT bidder now bids another suit, he is asking whether his partner has the king of that suit. But, as usual, I recommend some exceptions.

First, don't show the king of a short suit if it will force you to the seven-level. For example, suppose the bidding starts 1◇-1♡, 4◇. (Remember, this shows a gambling raise to 4♡, based on 4-6 distribution in the red suits.) Responder bids 4NT and opener bids 5♡. Responder holds

♠ A x   ♡ K Q J x x   ◇ x x   ♣ A x x x

and he is willing to bid 7♡ if his partner has the king of diamonds since, at worst, he can probably establish the suit by ruffing. But he doesn't want to hear a 6♠ response to 5NT when opener holds

♠ K x   ♡ A 10 x x   ◇ A Q J x x x   ♣ x

since the grand slam would depend on a finesse. The rule about not showing kings of the wrong suits (above the six-level of the agreed suit) is necessary; otherwise it frequently wouldn't be safe to bid 5NT. However, opener could show the king of clubs if he had it, and his partner could bid 6◇ to ask about the king of diamonds.

The other exception is based on the fact that 5NT should not be bid unless the bidder is interested in a grand slam. If a keycard is missing, he can't be interested, so 5NT says that all the aces and the king and queen of trumps are accounted for, and partner can (and *should*) bid seven directly if that is all he needs to know. So the 4NT bidder can bid 5NT simply to show that no keycards are missing *and* that the previous bidding has not precluded a grand slam. In the sequence shown above, opener should bid 7♡ with:

♠ x   ♡ A x x x   ◇ A K Q J x x   ♣ Q x

or 7NT with

♠ x   ♡ K x x x   ◇ A K Q J x x x   ♣ x

(The first hand may only produce twelve tricks without a ruff.) Sometimes the 4NT bidder bids 5NT with no intention of bidding seven no matter what his partner responds. For example, if the bidding is

Opener	Responder
1◇	1♡
2♡	?

responder should bid 4NT, followed by 5NT over a 2-keycards response, with

♠ A x   ♡ A Q x x x x   ◇ x x   ♣ A J x

There must be a good play for a small slam regardless of what partner has, and partner will be able to bid seven with

♠ x x x   ♡ K x x x   ◇ A K Q J x   ♣ x

Responder must have at least five hearts (since he can't be sure that opener has four) and he needs something extra, probably extra length in trumps, to be interested in seven. Opener can reasonably count on five heart tricks, five diamond tricks, two spade tricks and a club trick. Even if responder has a singleton diamond and the diamonds don't break, a club ruff should produce the thirteenth trick.

When the partner of the 4NT and 5NT bidder can see that the hands belong in a grand slam, he should bid it immediately, rather than showing his king(s) and planning to bid seven the next round. The reason is that his partner may pause to consider bidding the grand slam himself, but decide not to. After obvious thought on his part, if he signs off and the player who should have bid it the last round now bids seven, the director may be called. His first question will be, 'If you thought you belonged in seven, why didn't you bid it on the previous round? Other than partner's hesitation, what changed your mind?' The director will, and should, let the result stand if you are down one, but change the result to six, making seven, if you make your grand.

Usually the 'hesitation Blackwood' occurs on the previous round, over the first response to 4NT. You should *never* use Blackwood unless you have decided, in advance, what action to take over any five-level response partner may make. Then, if you bid it promptly, partner will seldom over-rule you, but on the rare occasions when he does, at least the director won't take your good result away from you (if you get a good result).

I have another high-level exception for you. You will recall that I said, when partner asks for specific kings, not to show the king of a suit that would force you to seven unless you know your king will be crucial — and if you know that, you might as well bid seven yourself rather than force to seven by your response. If the bidding has gone

Opener	Responder
1♠	2♡
4♣	4NT
5♡	5NT
?	

what should opener bid with

♠ A K J x x ♡ K J x x ◇ J 10 x ♣ x

It is possible that responder has

♠ x x ♡ A Q x x x x ◇ A x ♣ A x x

Responder would like to be in 7♡ if opener has the king of spades, since he ought to be able to establish the long spade for a diamond discard. Since the last thing responder cares about is whether the singleton club is the king, opener can bid 6♣ to show that he has a higher-ranking king which might be valuable to partner. Opener can't risk bidding 7♡ himself since responder may actually be looking for the king of diamonds with a hand like

♠ x ♡ A Q x x x x ◇ A Q x x ♣ A x

When two suits are raised

When the bidding starts 1♠-2♡, 3♡ you have a problem when you hold either of these hands:

♠ K Q x ♡ A J 10 x x ◇ A x x x ♣ x

♠ A x x ♡ K Q J x x ◇ A x x x ♣ x

With the first hand you want to bid 7♠ if partner has the ace of spades, the king-queen of hearts and the ace of clubs. With the second hand you want to bid 7♠ if partner has the king-queen of spades, the ace of hearts and the ace of clubs. In either case you want to play in spades so that a club ruff will be your thirteenth trick.

With the first hand, you don't need to show your spade support. You can use Blackwood immediately and partner will tell you what you want to know. With the second hand you should bid 3♠ before using Blackwood so that partner's answer will tell you about the king and queen of spades. Since you have the option of showing support or not showing support for partner's suit before Blackwood, I think that when you show support, the suit last raised should be the agreed suit for Blackwood purposes. The alternative is to play six-keycard Blackwood, when two suits have been bid and supported: the kings of both suits are keycards, giving you a total of six. Then the only problem is locating the two queens. It is seldom that you are missing the queens of both suits, so the response showing two controls and a queen could be made when you hold either queen. Or you could play that the fourth step showed two keycards plus the queen (or great length) in the lower-ranking suit and the fifth step showed two keycards plus the queen (or great length) in the higher-ranking suit. And perhaps the sixth step would show both queens. However this would conflict with the way you show a void.

If one of the agreed suits is a major and the other is a minor, some players bid 4NT to make the major the agreed suit for Blackwood purposes, and make their minor-suit asking bid, whatever it is, ask about the king and queen of trumps in the minor. Frank Lipniski, in a *Bridge World* article, suggested another solution to the problem. If you have the queens of both suits, the two queens constitute one 'key value.' Over 4NT, 5♣ shows 0, 3 or 6 key values; 5◊ shows 1, 4, or 7 key values; 5♡ shows 2 or 5 key values with an even number of key-suit queens; 5♠ shows 2 or 5 key values plus one key-suit queen. If the keycard ask is something other than 4NT, the responses are similar: the cheapest response shows 0, 3 or 6, the next bid shows 1, 4 or 7, etc.

Part of the problem is knowing whether two suits have been actually agreed upon. When the bidding goes

Opener	Responder
1♠	2◊
2♠	3♠
4◊	

are both spades and diamonds agreed upon? Or might opener hold

♠ A K 10 x x x   ♡ x   ◊ A x   ♣ Q 10 x x

in which case 4◊ is just a cuebid, and the queen of diamonds is not crucial (while the queen of spades is). My preference is to have only one 'agreed suit' for keycard-asking purposes with definite rules on how to determine the agreed suit.

INTERFERENCE OVER BLACKWOOD

What should you do when an opponent doubles or overcalls your 4NT bid? The double presents you with fewer problems. Redouble says you would like to play 4NT redoubled and probably plan to double the opponents if they run. If you want to show your controls, you can disregard the double and make your normal response.

An overcall creates a bigger problem. The most popular solution is to play DOPI, an acronym for 'Double shows 0 (or 3), Pass shows 1 (or 4)'; the next bid shows 2 without the queen, etc. The reason I don't like DOPI is that it doesn't let you penalize the opponents unless you show no controls (and even then, partner won't know whether it is better to penalize the opponents or stop at the five-level when too many controls are missing. Often the opponents take a huge risk by bidding at the five-level, just to mess up your Blackwood responses. Suppose you have made a limit raise of spades with

$$♠ J x x x \quad ♡ Q J 10 x \quad ◇ K J x \quad ♣ Q x$$

and an opponent bids 5♡ over partner's 4NT bid. You have a terrible hand for slam purposes since your heart values will probably be useless on offense. If a double merely says 'no controls,' partner won't know to pass your double with

$$♠ A K x x x x \quad ♡ x \quad ◇ A x \quad ♣ K J x x$$

He will just bid 5♠ and you will miss out on an 800 or 1100 point set. So I think a double should be for penalty and pass should show 0 (or 3), etc.

GERBER

Gerber can usually be used whenever a 4NT bid would be natural. Everyone knows that 1NT-4NT, or 2NT-4NT is just a natural invitation to slam; however, some players do not realize that 1NT-2♣, 2♠-4NT and 1NT-2◇, 2♡-4NT are just raises of notrump. For the first sequence responder probably has four hearts and might have bid a slam directly if opener had shown four hearts. For the second sequence opener might hold

$$♠ A x \quad ♡ K J x x x \quad ◇ K x x \quad ♣ A 10 x$$

With such good controls, 31 or 32 points might be enough for a slam provided there is a heart fit. That is why responder showed a heart suit before making an invitational 4NT bid. In the first sequence, responder could have bid 4♣ (Gerber) to ask about keycards. (If he wanted to make a splinter bid, he would have bid 3♡, as you may recall from the fourth chapter.) But in the second sequence Gerber was unavailable since 4♣ would be a self-splinter. If all he wanted to find out about was aces, responder could have bid 4♣ immediately over 1NT. If he wanted to find out about keycards for hearts, he could have bid 4◇ (Texas), followed by 4NT over the puppet to 4♡.

When a trump suit has been agreed upon, Keycard Gerber applies, with responses similar to RKB. The first step shows 1 or 4 (if playing 1430 when the agreed suit is a major), second step 0 or 3, third step 2 without the queen, etc. Again, similar to RKB, if the response does not say anything about the queen of trumps, the next bid asks about the queen and the bid after that asks about kings.

If no suit has been agreed upon, the first step shows 0 or 3, the next 1 or 4, the third 2 without extra values and fourth 2 with extra values. There is no way to sign off in 5♣ since that bid asks for the number or kings. Any other bid after the response to this form of Gerber, including 4NT, is to play.

Perhaps I'd better say that again. When there is an agreed suit, the responder counts the king of that suit as an ace and the two-control responses show whether the queen of trumps is held. If the response shows whether or not the queen of trumps is missing, the next bid asks about specific kings. If the response didn't show or deny the queen of trumps, the next bid asks about it, and the second bid asks about specific kings.

When there is no agreed trump suit, the steps are 0 or 3, 1 or 4, 2 without extra values, 2 with extra values; then 5♣ asks for the number of kings, not specific kings. So there may be an advantage in agreeing upon a suit before using Gerber, depending upon what the Gerber bidder wants to know.

When partner's last bid was 3NT, 4NT is usually a raise, and in many cases 4♣ should be natural. So now a jump to 5♣ is Super Gerber and it asks for the same responses as the usual 4♣, except at a higher level.

EXCLUSION BLACKWOOD

In its simplest form, Exclusion Blackwood is the bid of a new suit at the five-level, usually via a jump. It asks partner to show his keycards in the usual fashion but since you are starting at a higher level, I suggest that you play 0314 rather than 1430. The only exception is that no honor in the ask suit is counted in the response. Suppose you open 1♠ with

♠ A J x x x x   ♡ —   ◇ K Q J x x   ♣ A Q

Partner bids 3♠ (a 4+ card limit raise). If partner has the king of spades and the ace of diamonds you are willing to bid seven. Partner may also hold the ♣K or ♡A. If not, you can probably get rid of dummy's clubs on your diamonds and ruff the ♣Q. At worst you will need a club finesse and conceivably a spade finesse, if the spades are 3-0. But I like the odds for seven if partner has the right two keycards. So you bid 5♡, Exclusion Blackwood. A response of 6♣, the third step, would show you the missing honors, but if partner only shows one you will stop in 6♠.

Whenever the Blackwood bid is something other than 4NT (like four of a minor when the minor has been agreed upon, or Exclusion Blackwood), after partner shows his controls, the cheapest bid other than the trump suit asks about the queen of trumps (unless the response either showed or denied it). The next bid, other than the agreed trump suit, asks about specific kings. If the response showed or denied the queen of trumps, the next (cheapest) bid asks for specific kings. However, after an Exclusion Blackwood bid and response, there probably won't be room to ask about kings.

Just to be complete, I have given a lot of detail to RKB, Exclusion Blackwood, Gerber where there is an agreed suit and Gerber when there is no agreed suit. But unless your memory is better than mine, there is a high probability of a mix-up on the rare occasions when you use some of these unusual sequences. Learning to use plastic evaluation will do you much more good because you can (and should) use it in every potential slam auction.

DOING WITHOUT BLACKWOOD

There is nothing disgraceful about bidding a slam without using Blackwood. Indeed, using Blackwood often helps the opponents, both on opening lead and later in the hand. Suppose you bid 4NT and partner responds 5◇. This gives RHO (who will probably be the partner of the opening leader) a chance to double for the lead. Even if he doesn't double, opening leader can draw a negative inference from that failure. Occasionally the 4NT bidder will not be the declarer. Isn't the defense still easier when you know whether declarer is missing an ace? But the main reason why bidding 4NT (perhaps followed by 5NT) costs is a lack of discipline. Perhaps you know that you lack the playing strength for a grand slam; perhaps you can't find out everything you need to know. But you bid 4NT anyway. Partner's response shows that no controls are missing. You figure, 'How can it hurt to bid 5NT?' and partner figures, 'We have all the controls so since I like my hand, I'll bid seven.' Why place temptation in each other's way?

Suppose partner opens a 15-17 point notrump and you hold

♠ K x x   ♡ Q x   ◇ x   ♣ A K Q 10 x x x

Two aces could be missing, and one approach would be to use Gerber. If partner has only one ace, you could sign off at 4NT. (Remember, you can't sign off in 5♣, and even if you could, you wouldn't want to play 5♣ at matchpoints despite the fact that 4NT is not 100% safe.) Playing Walsh responses with a sophisticated partner I could bid 2NT to transfer to clubs and hope that he would interpret a 4◇ bid as a splinter. (I really think he should, but some partners don't like to be put to the test by a previously undiscussed sequence.) Any other bid I make is a gamble of sorts. Bidding 5♣ directly over 1NT should be safe, but it probably won't score well at matchpoints, and it could lose a slam swing if partner has the right sort of hand. So I think the percentage action is to transfer to clubs and raise directly to six. With partner playing the hand, there is a very good chance that the opening lead will be favorable, and since whatever you do is a gamble you may as well get as good odds as you can. On the actual hand, partner could make his contract if he guessed which of two finesses to take and the opening lead was destined either to give him the contract immediately or to suggest which finesse was more likely to work.

Frequently, even when Blackwood would be helpful, the wrong player uses it. Unless you are sure that you can place the contract, it may be better to describe your hand to partner and hope that he can make the right decision, either with or without Blackwood. When one hand has mostly aces and the other has king-queens and singletons, it is the holder of the latter hand, if anyone, who should be using Blackwood. It is very bad to use Blackwood with two quick losers in an unbid suit. If an ace is missing, the Blackwood bidder still doesn't know whether there are two quick losers. There has to be a better way to bid the hand.

THE GRAND SLAM FORCE

In the chapter on notrump bidding I mentioned that after

Opener	Responder
1NT	4♡¹
4♠	?

1. Texas.

a 4NT bid by responder is RKB and 5◊ is Exclusion Blackwood, both with spades being the designated trump suit. It is hard to imagine a hand that would be suitable for the next suggestion (I've never had one yet), but logically 5NT should be the Grand Slam Force, perhaps with

♠ A   ♡ K 10 9 x x x   ◊ —   ♣ A K J x x x

as distinguished from 1NT-2◊, 2♡-5NT, which would ask opener to bid either 6♡ or 6NT. But don't hold your breath till you get an opportunity to use the grand slam force in this sequence.

Everyone knows that the Grand Slam Force asks one's partner to bid a grand slam with two of the top three honors. But experts disagree on the best responses with weaker holdings. A *Bridge World* poll showed a slight preference for 'the more you bid, the more you have,' and that's what I play. Over 5NT, 6♣ denies the ace or king of trumps. (If the 5NT bidder has the ace and king of trumps himself, he can bid 6◊ to ask about the queen, assuming, of course, that the agreed suit is a major.) A 6◊ response to 5NT shows either the ace or king of trumps. A 6♡ response shows the ace or king and that there are at least ten trumps in the two hands. That enables you to bid a grand slam when opener bids one of a major with AJxxx and responder holds Kxxxx. If one hand may hold a four-card suit, his partner needs six to show the queen when he doesn't have it.

Responder can't bid beyond six of the agreed suit over a Grand Slam Force without two of the top three honors. However, some players suggest that when holding two of the top three honors one should jump to 7♣, just in case (for example) partner asked in hearts, but intends to play in clubs or diamonds. Theoretically this is a good idea, but it is hard to visualize hands where it might be appropriate. Perhaps, at matchpoints, one might bid 7◇ over 7♣, when the agreed suit was a major, to give partner a choice between bidding seven of the major and 7NT.

Most 5NT bids are *not* the Grand Slam force. Obviously that is not the case when 5NT is bid after 4NT as part of Blackwood. Many players play that 1NT-5NT or 2NT-5NT forces to 6NT and invites 7NT, but I don't play that way. I think 5NT in these auctions should still be forcing, but should ask partner to bid four-card suits up the line. After all, if you find a 4-4 fit, a slam in that suit may be better than 6NT. The ruff is often the twelfth trick.

I mentioned that for me the sequence

You	Partner
1NT	2◇
2♡	5NT

asks partner to choose between 6♡ and 6NT. Often 5NT asks partner to pick a slam. For example, in these auctions

You	Partner	You	Partner
1♡	1♠	1NT	2◇
3◇	3♠	2♡	3◇
4◇	5NT	3NT	5NT

5NT asks partner to choose between 6◇, 6♠ and 6NT in the first sequence, and between 6◇, 6♡ and 6NT in the second sequence. How often is it that responder knows there is no loser outside the trump suit while missing one or two top honors in the trump suit? When trying to decide whether 5NT is the grand slam force, that is what you should think about — whether partner could know there is no loser outside of his trump suit.

WHO IS THE CAPTAIN?

With a strong hand, you should plan ahead to find out what you want to know. Sometimes the captaincy switches back and forth. For a change, I am not going to give you a hand where my recommended solution is bound to work. Anything you do could turn out wrong in this example, but the discussion will illustrate the way you should attack the problem.

Partner opens 1♠ and the opponents are silent. You hold

♠ K Q x x   ♡ —   ♢ A K Q J 10   ♣ Q J 10 x

You belong in 7♠ if partner has the two black aces: you can count five spades, five diamonds, the ace of clubs and two heart ruffs. The ace of spades plus the king of clubs would be enough for six. There would be other possibilities opposite a singleton or void in clubs. Since you already know about partner's five-card spade suit and can place the contract if you find out about the two black aces (or the spade ace and a second-round club control) *you* should be the captain — the player who attempts to get information from his partner and make the final decision. How can you find out? I can think of four approaches, all of which have defects.

First, you could bid 4NT directly. If partner shows three aces, you can bid 7♠. If he shows one or two, you will bid 6♠. With no natural bids except spades, how will an opponent know what to lead? This is the best sequence to 'steal' a slam when missing a club control since it gives the opponents the least information. Even if partner has the right two aces for a grand slam, it will be difficult for most pairs to bid it unless opener also has the third ace.

If responder wants to bid more scientifically, he has several choices. One is to bid 2♢; then over a 2♠ or 2NT rebid, he can bid 4♡. He is planning to bid 5♠, putting the spotlight on clubs, even if opener signs off in 4♠. Over 5♠, opener will bid 6♠ with second-round club control or 6♣ with first-round control unless he has something like five spades to the jack or ten. With such a bad trump holding I would be tempted not to bid a slam with second-round club control or even to show first-round club control if I had it (but I could easily be wrong).

The biggest danger is that opener may rebid 2♡, and he would bid 2♡ with his actual hand:

♠ A J x x x   ♡ A Q x x x   ♢ x   ♣ K x

That interferes with responder's plan to splinter in hearts. His best bid now would be 3♠ to show good spade support and slam interest, hoping to follow up with a cuebid in hearts next round. (If he bids only 2♠ to save a round of bidding, his later heart bids could be interpreted as natural and opener will have no idea that responder's hand or his spade support was so strong.)   Unfortunately, over 3♠ opener would probably bid 4NT, and responder would not have a chance to find out about the ace of clubs or to show his void in hearts. Although the right contract (6♠) would be reached, I wouldn't call this a success story since the partnership could have missed a grand slam if opener had weaker hearts and the ace of clubs. But at least responder gave himself a chance to find out what he wanted to know. When opener assumes control (captaincy) of the bidding, responder knows that a small slam should be safe since opener would not use Blackwood without a club control of some kind (ace, king or singleton).

Another choice is for responder to splinter by bidding 4♡ immediately over 1♠. Then if opener just bids 4♠, responder can bid 5◇, which would, since his hand is unlimited after the unexpected bid over a signoff, force opener to bid a slam with second-round club control or to bid 6♣ with first-round control. But the odds are that opener would assume control (captaincy) over a 4♡ bid since a 4♠ bid would usually be passed. He is less likely to assume control over our second sequence.

Still another approach is to bid 2NT (Jacoby — to make it clear spades are trumps, despite having a very unbalanced hand), followed by 5♡ (Exclusion Blackwood). This might result in a small slam, down one, but there are two chances: opener may have second-round control in clubs or the opponents may not lead a club, although this bidding sequence is much more likely to induce a club lead than a less scientific sequence. But this gives you the best chance to get to seven with both black aces and no king of hearts.

Mark Bartusek read this book in manuscript for me and made several very helpful suggestions. I am embarrassed that I didn't think of his solution to this problem (perhaps because I play Bergen raises with most of my partners). Here it is: 1♠-3◇(strong jump shift); 3♡-4♡ (showing shortness), after which a cuebid in clubs would be almost mandatory with the ace (*possibly* with the king or a singleton, although, with second-round control, he would be more likely to take control by bidding Blackwood himself).

There are other hands where you can't find out for sure whether you belong in a small slam, but you plan to bid it because you have a very strong hand with lots of controls. However, while *you* can't tell whether you belong in a small slam, you can bid in such a way that partner, with the right hand, can bid a grand slam! Earlier I mentioned

♠ A x ♡ A Q x x x x ◇ x x ♣ A J x

If partner opens 1◇ and raises your 1♡ response to 2♡, how will partner know (or be able to tell you) that these hands

♠ x x ♡ J 10 x x ◇ A Q x x x ♣ K Q

♠ K x x ♡ K 10 x x ◇ A J x x x ♣ x

are enough for a good small slam? So you must bid 6♡ yourself. But you should bid 4NT and 5NT on the way to six so that partner can bid 7♡ with a hand like

♠ x x x ♡ K x x x ◇ A K Q J x ♣ x

The following hand is an ideal illustration of a hand on which it is a gamble to a small slam but where you can give yourself a chance to bid a grand slam with assurance. Partner opens the bidding with 1♠ and you hold

♠ A 10 x x x ♡ A x x x ◇ A x x ♣ A

With an aceless hand, partner won't be very cooperative in any slam suggestions you may make, but there are more hands that will make slam than not. (Don't forget to use 'plastic evaluation.') Partner doesn't even need an opening bid if he holds either of these hands

♠ K J x x x ♡ J x ◇ J x x ♣ K Q x

♠ K 10 x x x ♡ K x ◇ x x ♣ K 10 x x

(which in my opinion, are not even close to opening bids). And no matter how strongly you invite him, partner won't like

♠ K Q x x x ♡ Q J ◇ Q J x ♣ Q x x

which requires only one of two finesses for slam. So you should not let the bidding stop short of 6♠. But it can't hurt to tell partner what he needs to bid seven. My suggestion is to bid 4♣. Partner, with his aceless hand, will almost surely bid 4♠. Then you use RKB and he will show one keycard, the king of spades. Then when you bid 5NT, what does partner know about your hand? There will be no trump losers since you didn't ask about the queen of trumps. There are no club losers, as indicated by your splinter. You have to have the aces of hearts and diamonds to be interested in a grand slam. So if he has Kx and Kx if the red suits, there will be no losers! The same applies if he has KQ doubleton of one red suit and two small of the other, or stiff king of a red suit and Kxx of the other.

Incidentally, many players refuse to splinter with a singleton ace, as I suggested here. It is true that you would like your hand better if you had a singleton small with your ace somewhere else, so as to support partner's secondary honors. But in general, I don't have any objections to splintering with a singleton ace since it tells partner that his secondary honors in the suit are less valuable than they would be if located elsewhere. Usually when you splinter it transfers captaincy to partner, but in this case, it was part of a planned sequence. You had no intention of passing if partner bid 4♠ (which he was almost certain to do with his aceless hand).

MORE ABOUT CUEBIDDING

As a general rule, when one player cuebids, his partner should cuebid an ace if he can do so *below* the game level — even with no extra values. Cuebidding *above* the game level requires extra strength. Remember, we hate to bid above the game level and risk going down in five of a major. If the cuebidder has a strong slam try, he can cuebid again even though it is above the game level.

When the opponents have bid, and someone plans to make a slam try, he should plan to cuebid the opponents' suit at some stage provided he has a control in their suit. If he has room, he can cuebid his length or whatever he would normally bid first and cuebid the opponents' suit later. But if there is only room to make one cuebid below the slam level, the first obligation is to cuebid the opponents' suit. If the bidding goes

You	Oppt.	Partner	Oppt.
1♠	3♡	4♠	pass

and you hold

♠ A Q x x x x   ♡ x   ◇ A J 10 x   ♣ A x

you should bid 5♡, not 5♣ or 5◇. Partner may hold

♠ K x x x x   ♡ J x   ◇ x   ♣ K Q x x x

which is all you need for a slam, but he is stymied by a lack of heart control if you don't bid hearts, and all he can do over a cuebid in a minor is sign off in 5♠. He knows you need a strong hand for your slam interest, probably including controls in both minors. You would not risk bidding to the five-level voluntarily without a good hand but, unless you cuebid hearts, you might have

♠ A Q J x x x   ♡ x x   ◇ A K x x   ♣ A

Actually, with the latter hand, I would bid 5♠, which demands that partner bid a slam with heart control.

I have heard people say that bidding five of your agreed major asks partner to bid six with good trumps. That could be true in some sequences, but it depends upon the previous bidding. Suppose the bidding starts 1♠-3♠ (limit raise) and you hold

♠ J x x x x   K x   ◇ A K J x x   ♣ A

You cuebid 4◇, and if partner bids 4♡, you should bid 5♣. Now all suits have been cuebid, and if partner has good trumps, he will realize that he has what you need, especially if he also has the queen or doubleton in diamonds, but if he has

♠ Q x x x   ♡ A Q x   ◇ x x x   ♣ K x x

he will know that honors in your short suits are not what he needs, and he can only hope that 5♠ won't be too high. You could have bid 5♠ directly over 3♠ to ask partner about his trump holding, but you don't want to bid even to the five-level, let alone six, if partner doesn't cuebid 4♡. He might hold

♠ Q x x x   ♡ Q J x   ◇ Q x   ♣ K J x x

CUEBIDDING KINGS

As suggested earlier, the first cuebid normally shows length. There was an example where, spades having been agreed on as a trump suit, I recommended that opener 'cuebid' clubs with ♣Q109x so that responder could tell where his honor strength would be valuable. Usually, however, a cuebid shows either an ace or a king in the suit.

After the cuebidding has started, you should not cuebid a king when it is likely that partner is short in the suit. (It is quite normal to cuebid a king in a suit partner has bid, either naturally or as a cuebid.) Sometimes you cuebid a king as a last resort when there isn't much room left. Partner is going to have to make a decision to bid a slam or not bid a slam depending upon whether you have a control in a suit. For example, the bidding goes

You	Partner
1♠	3♠
4♡	5♣
?	

You have

$$♠ A Q x x x x \quad ♡ A Q x \quad ◇ K x \quad ♣ K x$$

Partner has shown extra values by cuebidding past game. You hope he has the perfect hand:

$$♠ K x x x \quad ♡ K x x x \quad ◇ x x \quad ♣ A x x$$

but if he does, he will be worried about a diamond control if you don't bid 5◇. Incidentally, a king is considered a control; the ace will be on side half the time unless the suit has been bid on your left, and partner may have the queen or he may hold the jack and guess right when the suit is played.

DON'T SHOW WHAT YOU HAVE ALREADY SHOWN

In Chapter 3 I suggested that after an auction such as

Opener	Responder
1♠	2♣
3♠	

responder could make use of a gadget bid to find out whether opener has a good suit or an absolutely solid suit. Normally when Blackwood is used responder shows all of his keycards since, as we have seen, a cuebid does not always guarantee an ace. But if one player has definitely shown AKQJxx or better, he does not show any of these honors in response to Blackwood. That would also apply to Blackwood after a 3NT response to 2♣, showing a solid suit (or four of a suit, showing AQJ10xx(xx) or

KQJ10xx of the next higher suit). You would just show controls that you haven't already shown.

Here's a subtle example of this principle. You hold

♠ K J x x   ♡ K x   ◇ —   ♣ A K Q x x x x

You	Partner
1♣	1♠
4◇	4♡
?	

Since 3◇ by you would have shown a singleton diamond, 4◇ shows a void. So you can bid 4NT (rather than 5◇) as Exclusion Blackwood. That way you will be able to find out about the ♠Q if partner shows only one key-card (outside of diamonds, of course).

1. Partner opens 1♡ with both sides vulnerable. What would you respond, using Bergen raises, with

   a) ♠ J 10 5 4   ♡ J 5 4 3   ◇ 7 2   ♣ 9 7 4

   b) ♠ Q 7 5 3 2   ♡ 8 7   ◇ J 7 5 4   ♣ Q 7

2. Partner opens 1♣ with neither side vulnerable. What would you respond with

   a) ♠ 8 6 5 4   ♡ Q 8   ◇ A J 10 6 4 3   ♣ J

   b) ♠ K 6   ♡ J 8 7 6   ◇ K Q 4   ♣ 8 5 4 2

3. You open 1♣ and partner responds 1♡. What would you rebid with

   a) ♠ J 5 4 3   ♡ K 7 5   ◇ K J 6   ♣ A Q 8

   b) ♠ J 5 4 3   ♡ K 7   ◇ K J 6   ♣ A Q 8 7

4. You open 1♠ with

   ♠ A K 7 5 3 2   ♡ A 8   ◇ K Q 7 5 3   ♣ —

   Partner raises to 2♠, you rebid 3◇ and partner bids 3♠. What would you bid next?

5. The bidding has begun as follows:

You	Partner
1♣	1♠
2♦	2♡

What call would you make with

♠ A   ♡ J 7   ♦ A K   ♣ A K 10 9 8 6 5 3

6. You hold

♠ A 10 5 4   ♡ A 7 5   ♦ Q 6   ♣ K 10 8 4

Partner	You
1♣	1♠
2♦	?

What call would you make?

7. Who is at fault in the following bidding sequence?

Opener	Responder
♠ K Q J 6 2	♠ A 9
♡ K Q 7 4	♡ J 10
♦ 5 4	♦ A 8 7
♣ Q 5	♣ K J 8 7 4 2
1♠	2♣
2♡	2NT
3NT	

How should the bidding have gone?

8. With neither side vulnerable, you open 1♡ with

♠ 10   ♡ A K 9 8 5 4   ♦ Q J 8 6   ♣ J 5

Partner raises to 2♡. What is your next call?

9. You open 1♣ with

♠ A K J 6   ♡ 8   ♦ K Q   ♣ K 10 9 6 4 2

Partner raises to 2♣ (inverted). What is your next call?

10. Partner opens 1♡ and RHO passes. How do you plan to bid the following hand?

♠ A K Q 9 8 5 4   ♡ K 9 4 3   ♦ —   ♣ J 4

11. You hold

    ♠ A J 7 6 5 ♡ K 9 6 5 4 ◊ Q 7 ♣ 8

Partner opens 1◊ and your respond 1♠. He rebids 2♣.

a) What is your next call?

b) If you bid 2♡ and he bids 2♠, what is your next call? What if he bids 2NT over your 2♡ bid?

12. Who is at fault in the following bidding sequence?

Opener	Responder
♠ A Q 6	♠ K J 5 4 2
♡ 9 5 4	♡ A K Q
◊ A K 5	◊ Q 10 7 2
♣ 10 7 6 4	♣ 8
1♣	1♠
1NT	2♣
3♠	4♠
pass	

How should the bidding have gone?

13. You hold

    ♠ J 8 4 ♡ A 10 9 7 5 2 ◊ A J 7 3 ♣ —

Partner opens 1♠ and you bid 2♡. He bids 4♡. How do you plan to continue the auction?

14. Apportion the blame for the following auction:

Opener	Responder
♠ A Q 6	♠ K J 5 4 2
♡ 10 9 5	♡ 8
◊ A J 6	◊ K 8 3
♣ Q 10 8 4	♣ A K J 5
1♣	1♠
1NT	2♣
2NT	3♣
3◊	4♡
6♠	pass

How should the bidding have gone?

15. Apportion the blame for the following auction:

Opener	Responder
♠ A Q 7	♠ K 8 2
♡ K Q 10 8 5 4	♡ A 7 6 2
◇ 7	◇ A 10 6 4 3
♣ A 8 7	♣ 5
1♡	4♣
4NT	5♡
5NT	6♡
pass	

16. You open 2♣ with

♠ x ♡ A K x x x ◇ A K x x ♣ A K x

Partner responds 2♡. You bid 3♡ and partner bids 3♠. What call do you make now?

17. Partner opens a Gambling 3NT and you hold

♠ A K 5 3 ♡ A K J 8 5 4 ◇ 6 ♣ 9 7

RHO passes. What call do you make at IMPs? Would you make a different call at matchpoints?

18.
Opener	Responder
1♠	2♡
3♣	4♡
?	

What call would you make with

♠ A J 10 9 4 2 ♡ — ◇ A Q x ♣ A Q x x

19.
Opener	LHO	Responder	RHO
1♠	3♣	5♠	pass
?			

What call would you make with

♠ K J 9 x x ♡ K x x x ◇ A J x x ♣ —

Opener   **Responder**

Opener	Responder
1♡	1♠
2◇	2NT
4◇	?

What call would you make with

♠ Q 10 9 x x ♡ x ◇ Q ♣ A K x x x x?

my solutions

1a) I think you are too weak for a preempt of 3♡. Perhaps you would bid it with a fifth heart or a singleton, but even a preempt should have some playing strength. Also your spade holding makes a preempt less necessary or desirable. My recommendation is to respond 1NT, since there is slightly less chance of getting too high, whereas bidding 3♡ might encourage partner to take an unnecessary sacrifice.

b) Pass. The chances of making game with this hand are very slim, and you are already in a seven-card fit. Is it worth bidding with this weak hand in hope of finding an eight-card fit? If you do find a fit, partner will almost surely bid too much.

2a) Bid 1◇. You don't want to play in spades unless partner has four and bids them himself. If partner rebids 1NT, missing an eight-card spade fit, you will probably do as well or better in notrump, where partner can use your diamonds. Suppose you bid 1♠, over which LHO bids 2♡, and partner makes a support double. What then? (Remember 3◇ would be forcing.)

b) Bid 1NT. It is more important to shut out a 1♠ overcall than to look for a heart fit.

3a) It is clear-cut to bid 1NT. You don't want to bid 1♠ on this balanced hand and risk a 2♣ bid by partner.

b) It is not quite so clear-cut as 3(a), but I think you should bid 1NT anyway. If the final contract is some number of notrump, which is quite probable with your balanced hand and weak spades, you would like to be the declarer.

4. Bid 4◊. If partner has as little as the queen of spades and the ace of diamonds, you belong in slam; even four small spades and the ace of diamonds may be enough. It will distract partner from what is important if you start bidding your controls in the other two suits. An alternative is to bid 5♣; partner will almost surely bid 5◊ over that if he has the ace (and you will bid 5♡). The trouble is that if partner has three small diamonds, even 5♠ could be too high.

5. Bid 5♣. The odds are that you won't have a trump loser, but you are pretty sure to have two heart losers. Partner's 2♡ bid is the most discouraging bid he could make; if he had a heart stopper, he probably would have rebid 2NT.

6. Bid 4♣. It will be hard for you to place the final contract (although you will not let the bidding die short of a small slam). This is the ideal hand to show your strength (although you could be weaker for this bid); 3♣ would be forcing, but partner wouldn't know that he should take control of the bidding. The odds are that over 4♣ partner can bid 4NT and then 5NT, and place the contract in 7♣, gambling on third-round diamond control.

7. No game contract is a cinch, but 4♠ is far better than 3NT. Responder should have bid 2♠ rather than 2NT over 2♡. If you had bid 3♠ over 2NT, you would be showing a strong 6-4 hand. If you bid 3♠ over 2♠, partner can bid 3NT showing a single stopper in diamonds, but you would bid 4♠ anyway with your aceless hand and no help in diamonds.

8. You should bid 3♡, purportedly asking partner to bid game with good trumps (and with ♡QJxx and an ace, he might bid it). But your main objective is to keep the opponents out of the bidding with your weak defensive hand.

9. Bid 4♣, asking for keycards. If partner has two you will bid 6♣, which should, at worst, require a spade finesse but will probably be cold.

10. There are two distinct ways to bid this hand: the gambling way and the scientific way. The gambling way is to bid 5NT. Partner will bid 7♡ with the ace and queen of hearts and 6♡ with the ace to six, in which case you will bid seven. It is quite likely this is a five or seven hand, depending on the opening lead or partner's club holding, and with no clues to your distribution, the lead could be any of four suits. If the opening leader has the ace of clubs he may not lead it, either

because he doesn't think you would force the bidding to a grand slam without a void in the suit, or because he has two aces and guesses to lead the wrong one. So your legitimate chance (partner may have the ace of clubs), plus the chances that the opponent will make the wrong lead, gives you pretty good odds. The scientific way is to bid 2♠. Over partner's probable 2NT bid you will bid 4◇. Since 3◇ would show a singleton with heart support, 4◇ must show a void. If partner has the ace or king of clubs, he may use Blackwood himself. If he simply bids 4♡ you can use Blackwood, knowing he won't show his diamond honor(s) in response. Having decided in advance what you will do, if partner shows one control you will promptly bid 5♡. Visualizing your problem, partner may still bid 6♡ if he has the king of clubs. Incidentally, if partner bids 4NT and 5NT, do you remember what you should bid? Partner's 5NT shows that he has either the queen of hearts himself or great length with the ace. With your actual hand you should bid 7♡. If your spades were headed by the ace-king instead of AKQ, you would bid 6◇ to show the king of spades.

11. The right bid for part (a) depends upon whether you play fourth suit as forcing to game. If so, you should just bid 2◇. If 2♡ does not force to game, you should bid it (and pass when partner bids 2♠ or 2NT).

12. Here 6♠ would be a very marginal slam, but often you will get a clue to the distribution and be able to tell whether to play for a 3-3 diamond split (if the jack hasn't dropped doubleton) or to finesse. But West should have bid 2NT to show a maximum with three-card spade support (maximum because his high cards are located favorably). That would allow East to splinter into 4♣, and West, with nothing wasted in clubs, would drive to slam.

13. It is unusual to bid Blackwood with a void, but you can do it with this hand since partner has denied controls in the unbid suits. If you bid 4NT and 5NT, surely partner, with ♡KQ and ♠AKQ, will bid 7♡, which you will correct to 7♠. You need a club ruff for your thirteenth trick.

14. I think responder should have bid 2♠ as his first response, followed by 3♡ to show four-card (or longer) club support and a splinter in hearts. Opener would bid 3♠ and responder should jump to 5♣ to show very good clubs. Opener would have no reason not to bid 6♣. Here 6♠ is not a bad contract since it depends upon little more than a diamond finesse, but since many pairs will not get to any slam, it is better to bid 6♣.

15. With a minimum for his bidding, responder was afraid to bid 6♠ since that would force the bidding to the seven-level. However, he could have bid 6♣ to show a higher-ranking king than the agreed trump suit.

16. Bid 4◇. After partner's positive response it is quite likely that you have a slam somewhere. Perhaps partner has

   ♠ A J 10 x   ♡ Q x   ◇ Q x x x   ♣ x x x

   If 2◇ was merely a waiting bid, you would not want to bid past 3NT, but you can afford to bid out your hand after the 2♡ response — just as you would bid 3◇ rather than 2NT with

   ♠ A Q x   ♡ A x   ◇ A K J x x   ♣ K Q x

   in case partner held

   ♠ x x   ♡ K J x   ◇ 10 x x x   ♣ A x x x

   Partner actually held

   ♠ A Q J x   ♡ Q 10 x x   ◇ Q x   ♣ x x x

   and he thought he was too strong to bid just 4♡. Over the actual 3NT rebid, he bid 5♡, but over a 4◇ rebid he would have bid 6♡, knowing that the ◇Q was a useful card. This might have led to a pretty good grand slam since the 3♠ bid retroactively showed the ace (or why bid spades at all with good heart support, as indicated by the subsequent bidding?). Incidentally, the 3♠ bid showed strength, not length, in spades. With a five-card spade suit and enough for a positive response, responder would have bid 2♠ rather than 2♡. This is especially true when his suit is headed by the ace or king (or both). A positive response requires at least one ace or king, which opener knew had to be in spades.

17. I think at either matchpoints or IMPs you should bid 5◇. Except for 4◇, which asks partner to show a singleton if he has one (4NT would show a singleton in the other minor), all minor suit bids over a Gambling 3NT mean 'pass or correct.'

   If partner's suit is clubs he should have seven club tricks, four tricks in a major and a diamond ruff unless the opening lead is a trump; in that case, he should be able to establish the heart suit and make seven (not to mention the possibly that partner has a queen in a major). If partner's suit is diamonds and he has a singleton club, something like

♠ Q x   ♡ x x x   ◇ A K Q J x x x   ♣ x

or an eight-card diamond suit, partner may visualize your hand and bid 6◇. At matchpoints, it may be tempting to bid 4♡, but when partner's suit is clubs you will probably lose to the slam bidders, and when it is diamonds there is a good chance of losing two club tricks and two heart tricks.

18. Bid 6♡! A 3♡ bid from partner would have been forcing after your 3♣ bid, showing extra values. As usual, a jump in a forcing situation should show a strong suit and at least an interest in slam. In this sequence I think 'strong suit' means so strong that partner doesn't have to worry about his lack of support, since you are likely to have a singleton or void in hearts. Responder's actual hand was

♠ K x   ♡ K Q J 10 9 x x   ◇ x x   ♣ K x

I'll admit that I don't know how responder could show the difference between this hand and one with a suit headed by the AKQJ with less strength on the side. I think that opener has a very close decision. Diamonds split 5-1, so the nine of hearts was crucial. With a diamond lead, declarer had to refuse the finesse and play three rounds of clubs before pulling trumps.

19. You should bid 6◇. Partner's bid showed two or more losing clubs and asked you to bid 6♠ with second-round club control. Of course, partner could be gambling slightly, so it would be a bit aggressive to bid 7♠ just because you have first-round control, but you should, at least, invite a grand slam. The thoughtless way to invite is to bid 6♣ — but the correct way is to bid 6◇! You wouldn't invite seven without first-round club control, and while you are at it, you might as well show first-round diamond control also. Partner had

♠ A Q x   ♡ A Q J x x   ◇ K Q   ♣ J x x

and a grand slam looks like a good gamble to him. It is doubtful that partner would have invited a grand slam with weaker spades or with the ace of clubs instead of the king of hearts.

20. Pass! Perhaps the problem should have been what to bid on the first two rounds of the auction. Many players would have bid 2♣ followed by spades and more spades. I am not that optimistic. If partner can raise spades, I will bid 4♠. If he had rebid 1NT over my 1♠, I would have checked to see if he had three spades and, if not, bid 3NT, hoping the clubs would run. But the 2◇ rebid was not unexpected, and

now with an apparent misfit it seems right to make a non-forcing bid. When partner bids 4◇, I can't conceive of making another bid — whether 4◇ is supposed to be forcing or not. Remember, he didn't bid 3◇ over 1♠, so it is unrealistic to expect him to take ten or eleven tricks opposite this misfitting hand. Even a return to 4♡ is dangerous, and no one has doubled 4◇ yet. Players are more reluctant to double a strongly bid partscore contract than to double a game contract. Besides, you have got past one opponent, undoubled: why give your opponents another chance?